ULTIMATE DOG CARE

A Complete Veterinary Guide
Over 300 illustrations

Sue Guthrie BA, BVetMed, PhD, MRCVS, Dick Lane BSc, FRAgS, FRCVS
& Professor Geoffrey Sumner-Smith BVSc, MSc, DVSc (Liv), FRCVS

Sue Guthrie BA, BVetMed, PhD, MRCVS,
Dick Lane BSc, FRAgS, FRCVS,
Prof Geoffrey Sumner-Smith BVSc, MSc, DVSc (Liv), FRCVS

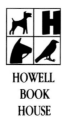

HOWELL
BOOK
HOUSE

ACKNOWLEDGEMENTS

Many thanks to Hill's Pet Nutrition for use of their *Atlas of Veterinary Clinical Anatomy* for some of the illustrations, as credited. All other line drawings by Viv Rainsbury.

A QUESTION OF GENDER

The 'he' pronoun is used throughout *Ultimate Dog Care*, in favour of the more impersonal 'it'. Of course, we recognise that female dogs exist too, and no gender bias is intended.

Copyright © 2001
Ringpress Books, PO Box 8, Lydney,
Gloucestershire GL15 4YN, United Kingdom.

All rights reserved including the right of reproduction in whole or in part in any form.

HOWELL BOOK HOUSE
IDG Books Worldwide, Inc.
An International Data Group Company
Foster City, CA • Chicago, IL • Indianapolis, IN • New York, NY • Southlake, TX

ISBN 0-76456-340-8

Library of Congress Cataloging-in-Publication Data
available on request

Manufactured in China through Printworks Int. Ltd

10 9 8 7 6 5 4 3 2 1

CONTENTS

CONTRIBUTORS

EDITORS

SUE GUTHRIE BA, BVetMed, PhD, MRCVS, Dip Mgmt (Open) qualified from the Royal Veterinary College in 1986. She received the first Guide Dogs for the Blind Association Fellowship, to study osteochondrosis of the dog's elbow, for which she was awarded a PhD. Sue held a Lectureship in Small Animal Orthopaedics at the RVC, and established a radiographic screening service for dogs' elbows in the UK. Sue was also Chief Examiner for the National Veterinary Nursing Examinations. Sue is currently working for Voluntary Services Overseas in a remote area of Nepal. She dedicates this book to Caleb, the Ultimate Dog. *Chapter 4: Canine Structure (Locomotive Disorders)*.

DICK LANE BSc, FRCVS, FRAgS has been in small-animal practice for the last 45 years. Dick has been awarded the Fellowship of the RCVS and the Fellowship of the Royal Agricultural Societies. Other successes include the British Small Animal Veterinary Association's Dunkin Award and Melton Award, and the first-ever J.A. Wright Memorial Award. *Chapter 5: Life Support Systems (Cardiovascular system; Urinary system); Chapter 6: The Respiratory System; Chapter 7: The Dog's World (The senses; The brain and nerve control)*.

PROFESSOR GEOFFREY SUMNER-SMITH BVSc, MSc, DVSc (Liv), FRCVS is *Ultimate Dog Care's* North American editor. He has lived in Canada since 1967 and specialises in orthopaedics and osteology at the Ontario Veterinary College, University of Guelph. He is a past president of the Association for Osteosynthesis, and an Honorary Member of both the British Veterinary Orthopaedics Association and the European Society of Veterinary Orthopaedics and Traumatology. He is Editor-in-Chief of the international journal *Veterinary Orthopaedics and Traumatology*, and University Professor Emeritus (the University of Guelph). *Chapter 4: Canine Structure (part one)*.

CONTRIBUTORS

PROFESSOR PETER BEDFORD BVetMed, PhD, FRCVS, DVOphthal, DipECVO is a graduate of the Royal Veterinary College, and is the Guide Dog for the Blind Association Professor of Canine Medicine and Surgery at the Royal Veterinary College. He is Head of Small Animal Medicine and Surgery. Professor Bedford is a world authority in ophthalmology and has received many awards for his contribution to veterinary work. He is a RCVS Foundation Diplomate in Veterinary Ophthalmology, and a Diplomate of the European College of Veterinary Ophthalmology. He has been appointed Visiting Professor in Veterinary Ophthalmology at the University of Illinois. *Chapter 7: The Dog's World (Disorders of the Eye)*.

DR HARRIET W. BROOKS BVetMed, PHD, MRCVS qualified at the Royal Veterinary College in 1985. She worked in general practice before returning and gaining her doctorate. Harriet worked in Veterinary Pathology at the University of Liverpool before moving to the Department of Pathology and Infectious Diseases at the Royal Veterinary College. *Chapter 6: The Respiratory System (Canine respiratory disease)*.

LISA CLARK qualified as a veterinary nurse in 1996. She is currently studying for her Diploma in Medical Nursing, and is responsible for the training of future veterinary nurses within her practice. *Chapter 2: The Healthy Dog (Bandaging; First-aid kit; Temperature; Vaccination guidelines; Ectoparasites; Endoparasites; Fleas; Giving medication; Nursing the sick dog); Chapter 4: Canine Structure (Care of the amputee)*.

TIM COUZENS BVetMed, MRCVS, VetMFHom, CertVetAc graduated from the Royal Veterinary College in 1980. Tim is a member of the Faculty of Homoeopathy, The Royal London Homoeopathic Hospital, and is one of the first vets in the UK to gain the VetMFHom qualification. Tim now specialises in complementary medicine, and has run his own practice for 10 years. He is a member of the British Association of Homoeopathic Veterinary Surgeons, and the British Holistic Veterinary Medicine Association. *Chapter 12: Alternative Approaches (Acupuncture and acupressure; Homoeopathy; Herbal medicine; Bach flower remedies; Nutraceutical medicine)*.

CELIA COX BVetMed, CertVR, FRCVS graduated from the Royal Veterinary College in 1981. She gained her Diploma of Fellowship in ear, nose and throat (ENT) surgery, and the Royal College of Veterinary Surgeons has awarded her specialist status in this subject. Celia runs a referral clinic for dogs and cats with ENT disorders and also The Hearing Assesment Clinic, one of few centres in the UK that regularly assess canine hearing. *Chapter 7: The Dog's World: The Senses (Deafness in dogs; BAER testing)*.

HOWARD DOBSON BVM&S, DIP. SURGERY, CERT. EO, DVSc is a faculty member in the Radiology Section of Ontario Veterinary College, and is currently an associate professor. He is the Chief Radiologist at the Veterinary Teaching Hospital, and is responsible for the Ontario Veterinary College Hip Dysplasia Certification scheme. He is also a Diplomate of the American College of Veterinary Radiology. *Chapter 4: Canine Structure (Panels: Hip dysplasia; Elbow dysplasia)*.

LAURIE EDGE-HUGHES BScPT qualified as a physiotherapist from the University of Alberta. She was a founding member, and Secretary, of the Canadian Horse and Animal Physical Therapists Association, and was one of the first physiotherapists to treat dogs. Laurie has her own physiotherapy clinic, and teaches, lectures and writes. *Chapter 12: Alternative Approaches (Physiotherapy).*

MARK ELLIOTT BVSc VetMFHom, MRCVS, MIPsiMed qualified in 1989 from Bristol University. In 1994, he established the Kingley Veterinary Centre, one of the first practices to integrate alternative medicine into routine day-to-day animal therapy. Mark has written books and edited journals on homoeopathy. *Chapter 12: Alternative Approaches (Radionics).*

NEIL EWART is breeding manager for the Guide Dogs for the Blind Association, and has helped to produce more than 1,000 guide dogs each year. Neil regularly presents lectures throughout the UK, and was recently made a Fellow of The British Institute of Dog Trainers. *Chapter 9: The Next Generation (part one).*

MAGGIE FISHER BVetMed, MRCVS graduated from the Royal Veterinary College in 1986. Having spent some time in practice, she returned to the RVC, where she became a lecturer in parasitology. Today, Maggie runs a veterinary parasitology consultancy, and she continues to teach and lecture for various groups, including veterinary nurses. *Chapter 2: The Healthy Dog.*

ALISON JONES BVetMed, MRCVS qualified from the Royal Veterinary College in 1987. After spending seven years in mixed practice, she joined Hill's Pet Nutrition to become Veterinary Affairs Manager. In January 2001, Alison opened her own small-animal practice. She has a keen interest in the nutritional management of disease. *Chapter 3: Feeding and Nutrition.*

GRAHAM KENSETT qualified as a Guide Dog Mobility Instructor in 1988 and is currently employed as an Area Team Manager for the Guide Dogs for the Blind Association. In 1997 he gained a post-graduate diploma in Companion Animal Behaviour Counselling from Southampton University. Graham gives regular presentations and works on referral as a Canine Behavioural Counsellor. *Chapter 7: The Dog's World (Learning and Memory).*

SORREL LANGLEY-HOBBS BVetMed, DSAS(O), DipECVS, MRCVS graduated from the Royal Veterinary College in 1990. After working as an intern and in general practice, she trained as an orthopaedic surgeon, gaining her RCVS diploma in Small Animal Surgery (Orthopaedics) and her ECVS diploma in Surgery. She is currently the University Surgeon in Small Animal Orthopaedics at Cambridge University. *Chapter 11: The Canine Athlete.*

SUSAN LONG BVMS, PhD, MRCVS qualified at the University of Glasgow. She gained a Diploma at the European College of Animal Reproduction and works as Senior Lecturer at the School of Veterinary Science, University of Bristol. She has gained recognition from the Royal College of Veterinary Surgeons as a specialist in reproduction. *Chapter 9: The Next Generation (part two).*

MIKE MARTIN MVB, DVC, MRCVS qualified from Dublin Vet School in 1986. He worked in mixed practice, before moving on to Edinburgh Vet School as a house physician and as Resident in Cardiology. Mike runs his own referral-only practice, specialising solely in respiratory and cardiac diseases. He has been Honorary Secretary and Chairman of the Veterinary Cardiovascular Society, and has won numerous awards, including the British Small Animal Veterinary Association's Dunkin Award, and the Melton Award. *Chapter 5: Life Support Systems (Disorders of the cardiovascular system).*

TIM NUTTALL BSc, BVSc, CertVD, Cbiol, MIBiol, MRCVS graduated with degrees in Zoology and Veterinary Science from the University of Bristol in 1992, and has since passed the RCVS Certificate in Veterinary Dermatology. Tim has written and edited numerous articles on skin disease. He is a founder member of the Pet Allergy Association, and is currently studying dust-mite allergies in dogs for his PhD. *Chapter 8: The Skin.*

MELANIE O'REILLY BSc qualified as a Veterinary Nurse in 1990, progressing to a position at the Royal Veterinary College as a Veterinary Nurse and research technician. In 1996, she graduated, with honours, from University College London with a Zoology degree, specialising in the interactive behaviour of captive wolves. Melanie currently teaches student veterinary nurses at the Royal Veterinary College. *Chapter 1: The Wolf's Descent.*

EMMA WEIGHELL BVetMed, MRCVS graduated from the Royal Veterinary College in London in 2000. Since qualifying, she has worked as a small animal assistant, and plans to study for a surgical certificate. *Chapter 7: The Dog's World (The endocrine system).*

MALCOLM WILLIS BSc, PhD, Hon Assoc RCVS recently retired as Senior Lecturer in Animal Breeding and Genetics at the University of Newcastle-upon-Tyne. He has written several award-winning books on dogs and canine genetics, and lectures all around the world. He has been involved in dogs since 1953, and judges around the world. *Chapter 10: The Question of Inheritance.*

1 THE WOLF'S DESCENT

When we look at our much-loved pet dog, lying contentedly at our feet, it is difficult to imagine that this canine companion has descended from one of man's most feared predators. The wolf, throughout history, has had a much-maligned reputation and has therefore suffered greatly at the hands of human beings. It has become apparent through the ages that what man fears, man destroys.

The wolf has featured as the wicked demon of many a myth in cultures all over the world. The image of the evil 'big bad wolf' has indoctrinated many societies, and in some cultures it is believed that the wolf represents the devil himself. Due to the inborn fear and hatred surrounding the wolf, it has been relentlessly persecuted. It has been hunted and killed to extinction in many parts of the world and this once-ubiquitous carnivore is now found only in a relatively small number of places.

It is only recently that we have come to understand the wolf and we now know that, instead of fearing this magnificent animal, we should perhaps be learning from its remarkable social organisation. It is now recognised, by most people, that the wolf is, in fact, wary of humans. It is therefore elusive and in no way poses a threat to mankind – though we are a very significant threat to its future survival. This skilled predator is, of course, a killer, but it also lives in a highly structured social organisation, which prevents true violence occurring between pack members. It kills only to eat, as the process of hunting involves a skilful and gruelling team effort by the adult members of the wolf pack.

EVOLUTION

To better understand the story of our pet dog's progenitor, we must start at the dawn of time, when life first appeared. The journey the wolf has taken through its evolutionary history obviously started with the development of all forms of organic life. From single cells to multicellular organisms, and from invertebrate to vertebrate forms, the story has been long and arduous. The process of evolution in all life forms has taken place over many millions of years, and, although the complete picture is still little understood, we know that many of the primitive lines that developed ended in extinction. The reasons for these extinctions are not fully understood and perhaps we will never really know all the facts.

Due to the modern understanding of genetics and natural selection, we are now able to get a better picture of the process of evolution than that first proposed by Darwin. From his work, we came to understand that some individuals are better suited to their environment – or, in his terms, 'fitter' – and are therefore more likely to survive. These successful individuals will then breed and pass on these qualities to their young. Of course, we now know that the 'blueprints' for these 'improvements' are carried in the genes.

Every animal inherits a set of genes from both parents, which are reshuffled in a random way. Therefore, successive generations are slightly different, which is what gives each animal its individuality – though they will share a number of characteristics with their parents. This mechanism, which enables the offspring to acquire new characteristics, is the means by which evolution has occurred. Of course, not all these new traits are desirable and some of them will, in fact, be disadvantageous to the animal.

This, to some extent, explains why many of the early prototypes of animals died out. It is further complicated by the fact that nothing in nature is static. In other words, the environment is constantly changing and a species that was successful for millions of years may begin to find itself less adapted to the prevailing conditions and therefore less likely to survive. This has certainly been the case for many animals, and it is evident from fossil records that there was huge species diversity in comparison to those which have survived to the present day.

This fossil record is the evidence that has survived through time, which has provided us with the facts that we know today about evolution. The soft parts of animals cannot as yet be traced from fossilised remains, as only the skeleton is preserved in the majority of cases. Therefore, scientists must speculate on the anatomy and physiology of these species, from the evidence provided by fossilised bones found on archaeological sites. Hence, the evolution of the wolf is still subject to some debate, but its general ancestry is reasonably well understood.

MAMMALIAN DEVELOPMENT

We will pick up the 'story' from when the first mammal-like reptiles appeared about 290 million years ago, during the Carboniferous period. The most probable ancestors for the mammals were an extinct group of synapsid reptiles that began to show mammalian features during this time. By the Late Permian period (258-245 million years ago), this mammal-like lineage was more discernible in a group called the therapsids. This group contained varieties of forms, both carnivorous and herbivorous, which were well adapted to a more terrestrial existence.

During the Triassic period (245-208 million years ago), a group of therapsids called cynodonts became established. The cynodonts showed changes in their teeth and jaw structure, and their stance became better adapted to running. Their hearing and sense of smell became more acute, which enabled them to exploit a nocturnal lifestyle. This meant they were not in direct competition with or being preyed upon by the dinosaurs, which were ruling the environment at this time.

It is the peculiar jaw structure of the mammals that has enabled them to be traced through the fossil record, and the first 'true' mammals appeared in the Late Triassic/Early Jurassic period. This has been discovered from fossils such as those of *Morganucodon*, a small, weasel-like animal. Palaeontologists have concluded that this animal was nocturnal and had mammalian characteristics, such as a covering of hair. There was also evidence that these animals were endothermic, which meant that, unlike the dinosaurs, they were able to regulate their body temperature.

For over 100 million years, these early mammals walked in the shadows of the dinosaurs, which were dominant during this period. Mammals were evolving and becoming more diverse, and the main branches of our modern mammals were evident long before the dinosaurs disappeared. However, while dinosaurs walked the earth, none of these mammals was bigger than a polecat and they scuttled about at the feet of the giant reptiles, mainly under the cover of darkness. However, by the end of the Cretaceous period (65 million years ago), the dinosaurs had become extinct, opening up a whole new world of opportunities for the mammals.

It is during the Cenozoic period that the mammals came into their own and radiated to fill many of the niches that had been left vacant by the dinosaurs. Mammals developed rapidly in most parts of the world, and within 10 million years a vast array of mammalian forms had developed.

EARLY CARNIVOROUS MAMMALS

By the Mid-Palaeocene epoch, a small, shrew-like creature, called *Cimolestes*, had given rise to two mammalian orders that were dedicated to carnivory. These were the creodonta and the carnivora. The key aspect of their adaptation to a carnivorous diet was the presence of cheek teeth, which had been modified into specialised carnassial teeth. These teeth are scissor-like blades that can shear through skin and flesh. Initially, the creodonts dominated, but, by the Late Miocene period, they had entirely disappeared. It is the other group that concerns us here as they gave rise to the modern carnivores.

These early carnivores were known as miacids and they resembled the pine marten of today. They were lithe hunters that dwelled in the trees of the lush tropical forests of the time, around 60 million years ago. There were two forms of miacids – the vulparines and the viverravines, which gave rise to the dog branch (Canoidea) and the cat branch (Feloidea). These branches of carnivores then diversified and evolved separately. In the New World (North America), the Canoidea gave rise to four caniform families: dogs (canidae), bears, raccoons and weasels. In the Old World (Asia and Europe), the Feloidea gave rise to four feliform families: cats, civets, hyaenas and mongooses. When the Bering land-bridge emerged 30 million years ago, due to changes in the sea levels, the two landmasses of North America and Asia (Eurasia at the time) were no longer separated. This allowed the exchange of species from one continent to another. Thus, these two separate branches of carnivores interchanged between North America and Eurasia. However, the canids did not enter Eurasia until the Miocene period (around 6 million years ago). Let us go back, however, and look at how these canids evolved.

THE FIRST CANIDS

When the carnivores began to diversify and assumed a variety of different lifestyles, the dog branch adopted a mobile, generalist one. One of the dog family's ancestors came down from the trees and took up an omnivorous lifestyle on the floor of the forests that covered the northern hemisphere. These creatures, called *Hesperocyon* (or dawn dogs), appeared in North America 35 million years ago, and had low-slung bodies that enabled them to move easily through the forest undergrowth.

About 5-7 million years ago, some of these 'true' dogs crossed the Bering land-bridge and entered Eurasia. It was one of these early dogs, called *Canis davisii*, which probably gave rise to the two main canid lines – the wolf-like lupine dogs and the fox-like vulpine dogs. These two groups began to diversify, and, at the same time, many of their main competitors, such as the amphicyonids (bear-dogs), died out.

As the climate changed, so too did the vegetation, and forest gave way to grasslands. Immense herds of ungulates (hoofed animals) grazed these grassy plains, and these fast, powerful creatures had soft underbellies that could be torn by the long-muzzled jaws of dogs. It is thought that it was when faced with the opportunity of exploiting this abundant source of food that the dog altered its hunting style and began to co-operate with members of its own species. This meant that the hunter could bring down a prey animal much larger than itself and would allow several animals to share a kill. The ungulates were fast, but the dogs had stamina, and together they could outmanoeuvre and eventually wear down the fleeing prey. This style of co-operative pack hunting requires intelligence and a strict social structure with a clearly defined hierarchy. Living in a pack has other benefits too, such as the collaborative rearing of young. Many members of the dog family today have adopted this lifestyle, but none quite as successfully as the wolf.

An early member of the lupine lineage, called *Canis arnensis*, gave rise to the Etruscan Wolf found during the Pleistocene period (2.5 million years ago). The Etruscan Wolf later gave rise to the Grey

Morganucodon: 250-100 million years ago

Cimolestes: 100-50 million years ago

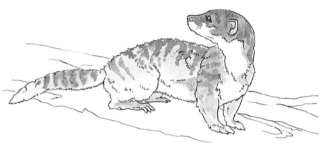

Miacis: 54-38 million years ago

Hesperocyon: 38-26 million years ago

Early wolf: 2 million years ago

Wolf, which became the most widespread wild mammal in the world. The species *Canis arnensis* was, in fact, a common ancestor of those members of the dog family that are most closely related to the domestic dog, namely the wolf, coyote and the golden jackal.

The Dire Wolf (*Canis dirus*) was also found during the Pleistocene. This creature was much larger than the Grey Wolf, and had strong shoulders, a deep chest and powerful legs. A pack of Dire Wolves could bring down a Mammoth or Giant Sloth, or, if these were unavailable, they would scavenge from the kills of the mega predators, such as Smilodon (sabretooths). For half a million years, up until 7,500 years ago, the Dire Wolf was more common than the Grey Wolf in North America. It is thought to be the disappearance of the mega herbivores of this time that led to the eventual extinction of the Dire Wolf. With the mega herbivores gone, there was more grazing for other ungulates. The Grey Wolf was able to exploit this and take over the Dire Wolf's territory in North America.

Wolves and men evolved alongside one another during the harsh conditions of the last Ice Age, both hunting in social groups and for the same prey. It is here that one of the most remarkable relationships between two species began.

HUMAN HUNTERS

The Palaeolithic hunters of the northern hemisphere had a similar lifestyle to that of the wolf during the Pleistocene period. Both lived in social groups and used co-operative hunting skills, and both species hunted the same prey. This meant that they were in competition with each other, and, despite the fact that wolves had been established members of the ecosystem for nearly a million years, the humans were causing a significant impact. Wolves kill old, sick, weak or young animals, but the Palaeolithic hunters were far less discerning. Obviously, wolves make these choices because these animals are easier to hunt – not because this is better for the population. Humans hunted randomly but efficiently, due to their use of weapons. They were probably wasteful, and killed more animals than were needed, as they were able to hunt these animals relatively easily. Also, humans were now using fire. The combination of these factors started to have devastating effects on the environment, and the numbers and diversity of large mammal species were greatly reduced. Towards the end of the last Ice Age, many species of these large mammals became extinct, such as the Cave Bear and the Mammoth in

Europe, and the Mastodon and the Giant Sloth in the Americas.

DOMESTICATION

It is not known when human hunters first tamed wolves, because this cannot be traced in the fossil record. Any wolf bones found in association with a human settlement could be there because they had been killed for food, or because they were a threat. Thus, it is only when the association between wolves and humans became common, and the physical characteristics of the wolf bones began to differ from those of wild wolves, that they could be considered as a significant presence in archaeological sites.

One can imagine how the wolf and human hunters might have developed a relationship, albeit distant at first. It is highly probable that wolves would have scavenged from the kills of Palaeolithic hunters, and it is possible that they began to follow these humans in anticipation of an easy feast. It has been suggested that these wolves may have eventually joined in the hunt and aided the humans by heading off the fleeing prey – a behaviour seen in livestock-herding breeds of dog today. These animals would then have been rewarded with a share of the kill. This could have been the start of the association between wolves and humans.

Dogs were the first species to be domesticated by humans, and it is believed that this occurred about 14,000 years ago (though this is subject to some debate). The earliest evidence of a domesticated dog is a mandible found at a Late Palaeolithic site (14,000 years ago), at Oberkassel in Germany.

During the Neolithic period, the nomadic hunter-gatherer lifestyle of the early humans shifted towards one of human settlements, with the eventual development of agriculture. It is believed that people brought wolf pups into these settlements, perhaps to eat or to keep as pets. Some of these young wolf pups would have become 'tame' as they grew up in the human community. This may have been the case with other species, but something developed further with regard to the wolf. The young of many wild animals can be tamed and kept as pets, for example bears and raccoons, but these species have not become domesticated like the dog. This is because there are certain factors that are necessary for the domestication of a species to be successful.

During the process of taming, an animal is removed from its natural environment where it would have learned from birth either to hunt or to flee from prey. When it is brought into a human culture, it is, in effect, being brought into a

Selective breeding is responsible for breed diversity. The Chihuahua (above) and the Great Dane (below) are genetically very similar, despite huge differences in their appearance and size.

protected place, where its food is provided and its reproductive activities are controlled. A tamed animal must learn a whole new set of rules, such as a reduction in fear of unfamiliar things and a corresponding reduction in its natural tendency to react aggressively or defensively.

The traits that an animal must have to favour domestication are, therefore, a placid temperament with the ability to be submissive but not overly fearful. One of the factors that gave the wolf such potential for domestication was its highly structured social group. The wolf pack has a distinct hierarchy, which is maintained by dominance-submission relationships between the individual members of the pack. This behaviour is communicated by means of clear body language: posture, position of ears, facial expression, etc. These signs are obvious and can be recognised by humans. To the same extent, visual signs of human dominance (such as voice and posture) can be understood by dogs. Therefore, wolves that had been tamed from a young age, or that had been bred in captivity, would have accepted the humans as dominant pack members.

During the early stages of a young animal's life there is the development of an attachment to another individual (or group of individuals), and learned reactions to an object or another animal – this is known as 'imprinting'. Therefore, early socialisation with humans will lead to the animal being unafraid and less reactive to people and unfamiliar objects. Over successive generations, this becomes more pronounced in the offspring and the animal becomes more tame and easier to train. In other words, the 'wild' temperament is bred out of them.

SELECTIVE BREEDING

A domesticated animal is the product of a breeding population that is isolated from the wild population of its species. Domestication is the result of the combination of two processes, one biological and one cultural. The biological process involves a number of factors; for example, domesticated animals are not free to breed with their 'choice' of individual, as they are in the wild. Also, they are not subjected to the same forces of nature that influence their survival in the wild (e.g. finding food, finding a mate, etc.), which governs the natural selection process for a species.

The cultural process would have begun when the animals were incorporated into the social structure of a human community. There would have been changes in their behavioural and physical characteristics due to the effects of both natural and artificial selection processes. They would naturally be adapting to their new environment, and humans would be artificially selecting traits that they desired their animals to possess. An example of a 'useful' trait, which has been selected for in dogs, is the ability to bark. Wolves in the wild do not bark – they use other methods of vocal communication, such as whining and howling. Therefore, barking is a behaviour that is characteristic of the domestic dog.

The change from tamed wolf to domesticated dog would have been, in relative terms, fairly rapid, because the rate of evolution is speeded up when a small population is 'isolated', due to the degree of inbreeding. In the early stages of domestication of a species, there is a characteristic reduction in the size of the animal. This is evident in the fossil remains of early domesticated dogs. A shortening of the facial region and consequent crowding of the teeth is apparent. Of course, this alters as different traits are selected for by humans, and the range of sizes that can be seen in breeds of domestic dogs, such as from the Great Dane to the Chihuahua, is an example of this artificial selection process at its most extreme.

NEOTENY

A significant factor, that has linked evolution and domestication, is something called neoteny, which is the retention of juvenile characteristics by an adult. The domestic dog has retained certain characteristics that are present in the young of its wild progenitor,

Many domestic dog breeds have puppy-like features (such as large eyes and a high-domed forehead), which make them more appealing to humans.

the wolf. Examples of these juvenile traits are shorter muzzles, high-domed heads, large, round eyes, curly tails and soft coats – all found in many of our domestic dogs.

Neoteny has an effect on the behaviour of the animal as well. Dependence and a need for care and attention, playfulness, submissiveness to other members of the pack; are all behavioural traits that are seen in wolf pups. However, these traits are also seen in domestic dogs. As a wolf pup gets older, these behavioural traits will lessen and eventually disappear. Submission is still shown to the dominant members of a pack, but is not as excessive as that shown by a wolf pup. When a pet dog licks your hand, we see this as a demonstration of affection. However, this actually stems from a care-soliciting behaviour shown by wolf pups, which will lick the corners of an adult wolf's mouth to stimulate it to regurgitate food.

SEVERAL ANCESTORS

It is believed that the domestic dog is most probably the result of a number of independent domestications, in many parts of the world, and therefore several subspecies of wolf have contributed to the ancestry of the domestic dog. These different races of Grey Wolf arose because they had to adapt to the particular environment that they lived in. In Western and Southern Asia these subspecies would have been the Arabian (Desert) Wolf (*Canis lupus arabs*), which is a very small wolf that is adapted to survive in arid conditions, and the Indian (Asian) Wolf (*Canis lupus pallipes*). In Europe and North America it would have been the much larger Grey Wolf (*Canis lupus lupus*), which is adapted to living in a cold climate.

MAN'S BEST FRIEND

During the Late Mesolithic and Early Neolithic periods, it is probable that people were experimenting with the breeding of the early domestic dog. Of course, these people would have had no concept of traits being passed on to offspring, as they had absolutely no knowledge of the science of inheritance. Therefore, they would not have been consciously selecting for traits in their animals because they would not have understood that these could be passed on to the young of the animals they were breeding from.

However, those animals that were easier to train and to handle and those that were distinctive in some way (such as a difference in their coat colour, ears and tail) would have been favoured. There were likely advantages in being distinguishable from wild wolves because humans could easily identify these domestic animals when they accompanied them on hunts. These distinctive features may also have increased their 'value' to these early people, as their owners would perhaps have been seen as more prestigious. Therefore, human preference would have started to 'shape' these early types of dog, and, when combined with the factors that are involved in the process of domestication (reduction in size, retention of juvenile characteristics), the variation in both physical appearance and behaviour would have increased rapidly. This is evident from the variable remains of dogs found from the Iron Age.

EARLY DOG BREEDS

From about 3000-4000 years ago, distinctive breeds of domestic dog are apparent, and dogs that look like Greyhounds are depicted on paintings and pottery from Egypt and Western Asia from these dates. The Greyhound appears to have been one of the most ancient breeds of dog, along with the Mastiff which has been used for thousands of years as a hunting and guard dog.

During the Roman period, there were definitive breeds of dog, and it is possible that some of these were 'pure lines'. Dogs were bred for a multitude of purposes such as hunting, guarding property, livestock herding and guarding, and even for companionship (Romans had small dogs the size of spaniels). We know of these different breeds of dog because their qualities and uses are recorded in Roman literature and art. In the 1st century AD, a Roman called Columella, who was an authority on agriculture, described the three founder breeds of dog – the hunting dog, the shepherding dog and the guarding dog. In his writing, he gave the following advice:

"The shepherd prefers a white dog because it is unlike a wild beast, and sometimes a plain means of distinction is required in the dogs when one is driving off wolves in the obscurity of early morning or even at dusk, lest one strike a dog instead of a wild beast. The farmyard dog, which is pitted against the wicked wiles of men, if the thief approaches in the clear light of day, has a more alarming appearance if it is black."

In China, there was a parallel development of dog breeds taking place, and these dogs became important elements in the societies and economics

Egyptian mural, showing Greyhound-type dogs, from the tomb of Beni-Hassan, 2200 BC.

The Mastiff's ancient roots date back many centuries to when it was used as a hunting, guarding and war dog. Courtesy: Mike Homan.

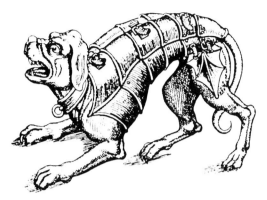

Above: War armour (Albert du Hamel, 1449-1509). Courtesy: Mike Homan.

Hunting became an important symbol of power in the Middle Ages. Pictured: Gaston Phebus surrounded by huntsmen and dogs, from his Treatise on Hunting, written in the 14th century.

of the Orient. There were also valuable small breeds of dog that were bred for other reasons. The Pekingese, Pug and Lhasa Apso have been bred since before the time of Confucius (551-479 BC).

The diversity of dog breeds continued to increase, and, during the Middle Ages in Europe, there was great proliferation of dog breeds. There was the establishment of the aristocracy and a period of feudalism at this time, and hunting was an important symbol of power, wealth and status because it was forbidden to the peasant classes. The rituals of hunting became complicated, and particular breeds were used for certain types of hunting. There were various kinds of hounds, such as Greyhounds, Bloodhounds and Wolfhounds, as well as terriers and spaniels. These breeds have been depicted on tapestries and paintings, and in books from this period.

There were several main groups of dog breeds that were commonly found, and they had particular uses. These included Greyhounds, which were swift sighthounds for hunting; scenthounds, which are bred to have stamina and a good sense of smell to follow their prey over long distances (examples are the Foxhound, Beagle and Otterhound); the Mastiffs, which were guard dogs; and the herding dogs, which were bred for restraint in attack, instant obedience and the ability to round up domestic herd animals (such as sheep).

Some breeds were used to protect the herds or flocks from predation by wild carnivores, and each country, and in some cases different regions, developed their own breed for this purpose. Examples of livestock-herding and guarding dogs are the Belgian Shepherd, Maremma Sheepdog and Old English Sheepdog (for sheep), and the Rottweiler

and Corgi (for cattle).

There were also terriers or 'earth dogs' – tenacious little killers that were bred to pursue their prey below ground – and companion or 'lapdogs', such as the Pug and Bichon Frisé. Spitz breeds were distributed worldwide, and these stockily built dogs were used for many forms of work, such as pulling sleds and carts, hunting, and even for food. Examples of the Spitz type of dogs are the Samoyed, Alaskan Malamute and Chow Chow.

LATER DEVELOPMENTS

With the adaptation of firearms for food hunting, breeds of dogs were developed to assist this different kind of hunting. There is variation among the gundogs as to what their function is. Some of them are bred to 'point', which means that, on finding the prey, they freeze and will often raise and bend one leg. Setters are similar in function, but they will freeze and crouch. Other breeds were bred to flush out prey, or to retrieve the prey once it was shot by the hunter. There were also dogs that were bred to work in water when assisting the hunter.

As the uses and functions of dogs increased, so did the number of breeds, and today there are about 400 breeds of dog. As the use of working dogs has diminished, the dog has adapted to its new role as that of companion. Some breeds have changed to meet this need successfully, and are therefore popular breeds to keep as pets, while others are still better suited to the purpose for which they were bred, so, sadly, some of these breeds have disappeared or become rare.

Of course, there are still many uses for dogs today other than companionship, and they are still to be found herding and guarding livestock, guarding

The adaptable dog will soon settle into a home environment, but close supervision is the key to keeping your dog safe, and ensuring that your home is not wrecked – particularly if you have a puppy. The best way of puppy-proofing your home is to go down on your hands and knees to get a canine perspective on the world.

- Trailing electrical flexes are probably the biggest hazard – make sure they are out of the puppy's reach.
- Houseplants can be very tempting to a young puppy, and should also be moved.
- Household cleaners and bleaches should be stored securely.
- Breakable ornaments should be removed from low surfaces. Try to keep things tidy – a book or a magazine left on the coffee table is an open invitation to a curious puppy that wants to chew, and no pup can resist shoes or slippers.

◀ *Puppies are naturally inquisitive, investigating everything they encounter.*

GARDEN DELIGHTS

The garden is a wonderful environment for a growing puppy, but, again, you must guard against potential trouble. No dog should be left alone in the garden for long periods.

- Make sure your garden is properly fenced. Some dogs are accomplished escape artists and will tunnel their way out, or perform amazing athletic feats to leap the fence in pursuit of the neighbour's cat.
- Some dogs just love to dig, and there is very little you can do to stop them. The best solution for the confirmed digger is to provide a special 'digging pit' (a small ungrassed area, or a tub with earth in it) where your dog can dig to his heart's content.
- There are a number of plants that are poisonous to dogs (ask your garden centre for advice).
- Be very careful if you are using any form of insecticide or rodent killer – most of these are lethal to dogs. Make sure that all garden materials are stored securely.
- The garden pond or swimming pool could well prove irresistible, and so precautions must be taken to keep your dog well away.

Watch out for the escape artist.

The garden pond or swimming pool is a potential hazard.

Some garden plants are poisonous to puppies.

A special digging pit will save your plant's demise.

property or hunting. They are also used for other purposes, such as guide dogs for the blind, hearing dogs for the deaf, and as sniffer dogs and other 'service' dogs used by the police and military. They are used for sporting purposes such as racing, field trials, Agility and sled racing. There are even a few famous film stars! But, whatever its purpose, the domestic dog is a successful and adaptive mammal that has found its way into all parts of the world, and, in many cases, into our hearts too.

PRIMITIVE DOGS

There are some types of dog, which are found today, that are said to be 'primitive'. These dogs are believed to have descended from the Indian Plains Wolf (*Canis lupus pallipes*), and are still in an early stage of domestication. Examples of these primitive dogs are the Dingo, the New Guinea Singing Dog, the Basenji, and the Pariah dogs. Some of these dogs now live in the wild and are said to be 'feral'. Many of these feral dogs survive on the outskirts of human habitations by scavenging from refuse. However, the Dingo can survive as a hunter in a wild population.

The Dingo has lived wild in Australia for thousands of years, but is thought to be the descendant of dogs taken to Australia by people migrating to the continent. The Dingo is possibly the oldest dog in the world, being a relic from the early domesticated dogs. The New Guinea Singing Dog, from Papua New Guinea, is also of ancient origin.

The domestic dog differs from its wild progenitor the wolf in that it has two breeding cycles a year. The wolf has only one breeding cycle a year, and this trait is shared by some of these primitive dogs, such as the Dingo and Basenji.

THE WOLF TODAY

Although the wolf was once the most ubiquitous mammal in the world, it is now an endangered species clinging to existence. It lives, in dwindling numbers, in a few restricted areas where it can survive without threat from humans. The range of the wolf now consists of a few large forests in Eastern Europe, some isolated mountain regions in the Mediterranean, wilderness areas in Asia and North America, and some semi-desert and mountainous areas in the Middle East.

Wolves have been exterminated from the British Isles and throughout most of Europe, but populations can still be found in places such as Poland, Slovakia, Portugal, and Italy. There is a

Dogs have adapted with society and now have new roles, including assistance (service) dog (left) and drug and explosive detection dog (right).

campaign to save a subspecies of wolf that is unique to the Iberian Peninsula, called the Iberian Wolf, because there are only about 1,500 individuals remaining. Wolves can also be found in the former Soviet Union, and in the Middle East in countries such as Iran, Israel, Jordan, Syria, Lebanon and the United Arab Emirates. They may also be found in parts of India, China, Mongolia and Tibet.

The most endangered canid in the world is the Ethiopian Wolf (previously known as the Simian Jackal), and there is a conservation programme to save the last remaining individuals of this subspecies. There are currently only about 400 Ethiopian Wolves left and these are to be found in the Bale Mountains.

WOLVES IN THE AMERICAS

In Alaska and parts of Canada, there are large populations of wolves, but the status of the species is more precarious in North America where it is mainly found in wilderness areas. Alaska has about 5,000-8,000 wolves, and visitors to the Denali National Park are often treated to glimpses of these elusive animals. However, the hunting and trapping of wolves is still legal in much of Alaska – a topic that has caused outrage in organisations that are dedicated to protecting the wolf.

There are reasonable numbers of wolves in Minnesota and there is a 'famous' population of wolves on Isle Royale, Michigan, that has been the

Many owners prefer their dogs to live in their home. However, it is not necessarily unkind to expect your dog to sleep in 'outside' quarters, provided due consideration is shown.

For many dogs, it can be beneficial for them to spend a good part of their lives outside. Humans have created a rather unnatural environment for dogs, as our homes have been sealed up with double glazing, are expensively carpeted, and are often warm because of central heating. Some dogs (especially the thick-coated breeds, such as the Alaskan Malamute) do not benefit from this lifestyle.

HUMAN COMPANY

Dogs need human company to enjoy a good quality of life and to integrate successfully with people. Therefore, a puppy should, initially, be home-reared for at least six months to learn social skills. Your dog should only sleep in the kennel. Under no circumstances should he be left day in and day out. His normal life should be with people, and adequate exercise and stimulation should be organised.

CANINE COMPANY

Being social animals, kennelled dogs require canine company. If the dogs are not entirely

A kennel set-up is essential for breeders who keep a large number of dogs.

compatible yet, put them in a couple of kennels and runs alongside each other so that they can interact.

PROS OF KENNELLING
- Kennels offer a healthier environment, particularly in hotter climates.
- A kennel allows you to keep a dog, even if a family member is allergic.
- A correctly-designed kennel and run can afford the dog more freedom when he is left for lengthy periods.

CONS OF KENNELLING
- Dogs can miss out on human company if left alone for too long.
- Not suitable for very young or elderly dogs.
- House-training may break down.
- Not ideal for all breeds, particularly short-coated ones (e.g. Whippet), or in colder climates.

Visit major dog shows to view various kennel designs and materials. These can be wooden, metal or fibreglass. Kennels vary in cost, but it does not pay to skimp; quality is paramount.

MAIN CONSIDERATIONS
The kennel should be:
- Large enough for your dogs to stretch out fully, and be able to turn around in comfort.
- Dry, draught-free and acceptably warm. Some kennels include built-in heating systems.
- Easy to clean.

The kennel should have:
- A run area attached, where the dog can relieve himself, obtain a drink of water at all times, and play with suitable toys.
- A raised bed that allows enough room for the dog to spread out.

Every kennel should have its own run.

- Plenty of light so the dog is not left in darkness.
- Adequate, clean bedding (thick wads of newspaper, blankets, etc.). Straw can harbour mites.
- A door between the kennel and the run that can be closed easily, in cold or wet weather.
- Padlocked exits to the outside world.

WARNING: Do not leave a 'choke' or 'slip' chain, or 'Halti™' on your dog when he is left in a kennel. It can easily get caught up on something and strangle him.

subject of detailed predator/prey studies for more than 40 years. There are several reintroduction programmes taking place in the United States, such as the high-profile release of wolves into Yellowstone National Park, and the Mexican Wolf has been reintroduced in Arizona and New Mexico.

The Red Wolf was once considered to be a separate species to the Grey Wolf, and was called *Canis rufus*, but it is now believed to be another subspecies of the Grey Wolf. There are very few Red Wolves left (about 240-317 total population), and this particular subspecies has interbred with the Coyote, so its lineage is now uncertain.

However, there is a conservation programme running, and populations are closely monitored in restricted areas in which they are present, namely eastern North Carolina and the Great Smoky Mountains National Park in eastern Tennessee. Recently, new information, the result of a genetical survey, has shown that the so-called 'Grey Wolf' in Algonquin Park, Ontario, is in fact a Red Wolf. This has caused considerable excitement among zoologists, who had believed it to be extinct in Canada.

THE WOLF'S FUTURE

Even in areas where the wolf is protected, it is never really welcomed by all. Humans constantly threaten this species, contributing to its endangered status through persecution by hunting and the destruction of suitable habitats. Wolves are shy, elusive animals that rarely venture near humans (though in Italy it has been reported that wolves scavenge rubbish tips at night).

Therefore, as human populations are ever increasing, the wolf's natural habitats are vanishing, and although this remarkable animal is adaptive and resourceful, it is becoming increasingly difficult for it to survive.

WOLF IN SHEEP'S CLOTHING

The wolf today is better understood than it was, and we are generally more aware of what is fact and what is fiction. The wolf is a highly social animal, with strong family ties, and demonstrates extraordinary care-giving behaviour.

The pack consists of a dominant male and female – the 'Alpha' pair – the only animals that breed in the pack. Usually, the rest of the pack consists of their current offspring and a few yearlings or other wolves. The subordinate wolves in the pack will show submission to the dominant animals. This is evident in the body posture of these animals. The dominant animals will carry their head and tail high, while the lower-ranking animals of the pack will lower their tails, often tucking them between their legs, and they will lay their ears back and crouch.

These postures are all familiar to us as pet-dog owners – and when your dog thinks you (the dominant member of the pack) are displeased with him, he will show submissive behaviour, such as creeping towards you with his tail between his legs, and trying to avoid eye contact. In contrast to this behaviour, a dog showing dominant behaviour will stand tall and erect, holding his head up with his ears pricked, and he may stare directly at the person or other dog. Occasionally, this behaviour may escalate to true aggression, and the dog will raise his lips to bare his teeth and growl a warning that is best heeded (see Chapter Seven for more information on dog behaviour).

An investigation showed that, of the 90 different behaviour patterns exhibited by domestic dogs, the wolf shares 71 of them. Thousands of years of domestication have created some behaviour patterns in the dog that would have no place in a wild wolf, but many characteristics are still shared. So, it could be said that your pet dog really is a 'wolf in sheep's clothing' and what is often seen as a behavioural problem in our pet dog may be a normal behaviour in his ancestor, the wolf.

A domestic dog shares other characteristics with the wolf (and with the coyote and jackal), such as the number of chromosomes and the same method of copulation with a 'tie'. The domestic dog, wolf, coyote and jackal can breed with each other and produce fertile offspring.

However, there are significant differences between domestic dogs and wolves, due to the artificial selection processes that have been used by people over the thousands of years that the dog has been domesticated. These differences include the number of breeding cycles a year (the wolf has only one, the dog has two), a curly tail, a single-coloured coat, lop ears and the ability to bark.

The story of the wolf and our pet dog is intricately interwoven, and we should, therefore, ensure that the wolf continues to have a place in our hearts, and in the wild.

2 THE HEALTHY DOG

Good health is related to maintaining the body in as good a condition as possible. A dog in top condition is able to fend off opportunist disease, is in the best state to enjoy the demands of the life that he leads, and has the best opportunity to recover from a major illness, should that occur.

SIGNS OF GOOD HEALTH

Although dogs come in many shapes, sizes and ages, there are some attributes that indicate good health regardless of the breed or age.

EARS
- Held normally for the breed.
- Head and ears move towards sound.
- No discharge or smell from the ear canal (normal ear wax is brown, and present in small quantities).
- No matted hair down the ear canal.

EYES
- Clear, with no cloudiness on the surface or within the eye.
- Third eyelid showing slightly.
- The third eyelid and the conjunctiva around the eye should be pink not red.
- No excess tears or signs of tear-overflow on to the face (brown staining on the face).
- No mucus on the surface of the eye.
- Eyelids should lie on the surface of the eye, eyelashes pointing away from the surface.

NOSE
- Normally slightly moist, though it may be more dry and crusty in older dogs.
- No excessive discharge from the nostrils.

MOUTH
- Should contain pink gums (though some dogs may have dark pigment in their gums).
- The two rows of teeth should meet (they should not be overshot or undershot except in the Boxer).
- The teeth should be white to off-white, and regularly arranged.
- Breath should not smell.

RESPIRATION
- Most dogs breathe through their noses at rest, but some may pant with an open mouth.
- Chest movement and breathing rate increase with exercise. Normally, we see panting after exercise, which is associated with dissipation of heat and an increased demand for oxygen.

HEAD
- Features on the head should be symmetrical.

SKIN AND COAT
- Should be characteristic for the breed.
- No areas abnormally without hair (alopecia).
- No matted coat.
- No areas of abrasion or dermatitis (particularly in the skin folds or between the toes).
- No bad smells.

LEGS
- Normal length and appearance for the breed and age of the dog.
- No staining between the toes (the presence of which indicates licking).

- Nails not overgrown.
- Even weight taken on each leg, with no limping or reluctance to place any paw on the ground.

ABDOMEN
- Not distended.

TAIL
- May be entire or docked (the end removed leaving a stump), according to the breed, and your preference.
- Should be held as is typical for the breed.

BODY CONDITION
- Dogs should be symmetrically muscled across the body.
- Good condition – not too fat and not too thin.

Assess condition by comparing your dog's weight to typical, adult breed weight (males are typically heavier than females). Also assess condition by feeling the bones through the skin. The amount of cover over the ribs, for example, indicates whether the dog is thin, in normal or good condition, or overweight.

In normal condition, it should be possible to just feel the individual ribs, but they should have a covering of flesh over them.

The assessment of body condition is less applicable, and less easy to define, in pups and growing dogs. For example, normally growing dogs of some breeds may look thin and gangly at stages during their growth.

ROUTINE HEALTH CARE

EXERCISE
- Prevents boredom and the destruction that may ensue because of it.
- You need to increase a level of exercise gradually as the pup grows or before any major increase in performance – be it racing or accompanying you on a long-distance walk or cycle ride.
- Do not overexercise – especially true for larger or giant breeds, and particularly not early in life – as there is a risk of damaging bone and cartilage in the limb. This can lead to long-term lameness and reduced exercise capacity (see Chapter Four).

FEEDING
Providing the correct amount and balance of nutrients is one of the most important routine health care measures.

The amount of food, in terms of calorific intake, should be appropriate for the dog's stage of life. Puppies and growing dogs need food for life, growth, and exercise. Adult dogs need food for life and exercise. Neutered dogs need rather less food than entire dogs so the total amount should be cut back appropriately. Food requirements increase during pregnancy and particularly during lactation.

It is important to provide not just the correct amount of food and calorific or energy value, but also the correct amounts of essential nutrients. You have a choice of feeding home-prepared or commercial dog food, but, whichever you choose, you need to ensure that it provides the variety of nutrients in the correct proportions to meet your dog's needs (see Chapter Three).

Whatever you decide to feed, always ensure that there is always fresh water available. The amount of water drunk will be greater if exercise increases or if a moist food is replaced with dry food.

TOOTH CARE
The dental formula for a pup's milk teeth is:
- I3 C1 P3 (upper row)
- I3 C1 P3 (lower row).

I = incisors used for grasping and nibbling
C = canines used for tearing
P = premolars used for shearing and grinding
M = molars used for shearing and grinding.

Pups begin to lose their milk (deciduous) teeth by four to five months of age. They should have lost all of their milk teeth by seven months of age.

◀ *Gingivitis and receding gums, with a heavy build-up of tartar.*

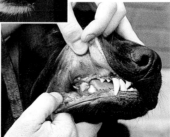

An ulcer can be ▶ caused by tartar on the teeth rubbing against the gums.

CANINE DENTITION

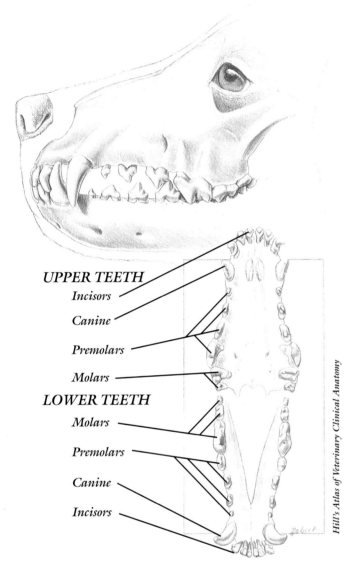

UPPER TEETH
Incisors
Canine
Premolars
Molars

LOWER TEETH
Molars
Premolars
Canine
Incisors

Hill's Atlas of Veterinary Clinical Anatomy

Occasionally, particularly in small breeds, milk teeth fail to fall out and have to be extracted. With teeth that do not fall out, there is a risk that food will gather between the old and new teeth and cause the new teeth to rot.

The adult dog's teeth has the following formula:
• I3 C1 P4 M3 (upper row)
• I3 C1 P4 M3 (lower row).

An adult dog's teeth need to be kept clean, or else plaque will gather close to the gum margin. Unless removed, this will develop into tartar, a hard substance. This results in bad breath (halitosis), receding gums, and tooth decay. Build-up of plaque can be prevented by regular cleaning of your dog's teeth with a toothbrush (see panel, opposite), or by

providing some hard food that cleans the teeth as he eats. There are now some proprietary foods that do this.

Take your dog to the veterinarian and get his mouth checked if you notice:
• Blood coming from your dog's mouth.
• Your dog eating in an unusual manner.
• Smelly breath.
• Your dog avoiding hard foods or avoiding eating altogether.

GROOMING
The need for grooming obviously depends enormously on the breed of dog. It may be daily for some longhaired breeds or much less frequently for some shorthaired breeds. Regular grooming of dogs with longer coats will help prevent mats from forming and provides an opportunity for a close scrutiny of the skin and coat (see Chapter Eight). This will help to detect ticks and early signs of flea infestation.

Grooming and clipping will also prevent odours from building up in the coat that might attract blowflies in the summer. It is particularly important to keep the area under the tail clean, for example, when your dog has diarrhoea.

PARASITE CONTROL
Control of many of the parasites that may infect dogs has become part of routine health care, both for the wellbeing of the dog and of the humans around him. Details of parasites and parasite control can be found from page 24.

REGULAR HEALTH CHECKS
Regular health checks are a good way of ensuring that:
• Your dog is keeping healthy.
• Any developing disease is caught early when treatments can be put in place to remedy or to control the problem.

It is suggested that dogs should have a routine health check once annually. It may be convenient to get a thorough check-up each time the dog has his booster vaccinations. It is more important to get your dog checked regularly as he gets older.

NEUTERING
If you intend to breed from your dog or bitch, then there is no question that he or she must remain entire. If, however, you do not wish to breed, then you should consider having your dog neutered: castrated in the case of a male and spayed in that of

There are a number of canine products specifically designed to clean teeth, ranging from special meaty-tasting toothpaste to dental chews.

- Accustom your puppy to having his mouth inspected from an early age. It is essential that he learns to accept this routine handling.
- Check the gums daily. Redness or inflammation is the first sign of gum disease, caused by the build-up of tartar.
- Clean the teeth on a regular basis (at least once a week), making sure you gently rub away all traces of plaque.
- Some dogs prefer a human type of toothbrush, while others prefer the smaller, 'finger glove' types.
- Provide dental chews or rawhide chews for your dog. A raw marrow-bone to gnaw on is excellent for cleaning teeth, but it should only be given when the dog is under supervision. Never feed cooked bones or poultry bones, as these can splinter and cause considerable damage.
- Pay particular attention to teeth and gums when a puppy is teething (between four and six months) and in veteran dogs.

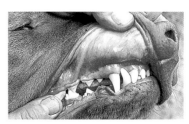

Accustom your puppy to having his mouth examined.

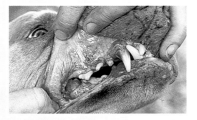

Plaque may accumulate on the teeth.

Regular brushing prevents the build up of plaque and the development of tartar.

The teeth after brushing.

a female. In a castration, both testicles are removed. This is usually carried out once the dog is about six months of age. It is normally a routine operation but may be more complicated if the dog has only one testicle in the scrotum (see Cryptorchidism, Chapter Nine).

There are several potential advantages of spaying a bitch. She will not come into season once or twice yearly, so spaying obviates the need to ensure that she does not mate during that time. If spaying is carried out early, before the age of two years, there is a reduced risk of her developing mammary tumours in later life. Normally during the operation, both the ovaries and uterus are removed, so a spayed bitch cannot develop a life-threatening pyometra (pus in the uterus) later in life.

Once neutered, a dog's food requirement decreases, so it is essential that a dog's weight is monitored and the amount of food cut back accordingly. It may be advisable to reduce food by 10 per cent immediately after the operation and to monitor weight thereafter. If food consumption is not monitored and reduced as necessary, your dog is in danger of becoming overweight.

For more information on neutering, see Chapter Nine.

EUROPEAN TRAVEL

There are a number of requirements for taking a dog to and from mainland Europe from the UK. The requirements for entry into the UK are detailed in the Pet Travel Scheme (PETS). Current requirements can be found on the MAFF website http://www.maff.gov.uk/animalh/quarantine. Your veterinary surgeon can advise on how to ensure that you comply with the requirements, not just for your destination, but also for any country that you will travel through *en route* and for return to the UK.

There are a number of diseases that are present in mainland Europe that are not present in the UK. The most notable of these are: Ehrlichia, Babesia, Leishmania, heartworm and *Echinococcus multilocularis*. The first two infections are tick-transmitted, so tick control is important during your stay, in addition to requirements designed to ensure that you do not bring ticks back on your return to the UK. Leishmania is transmitted by sand flies in the Mediterranean area. *Echinococcus multilocularis* occurs throughout central Europe, particularly in Switzerland, but also in other areas, including parts of France and Germany. Heartworm is transmitted by mosquitoes in southern Europe. Obtain specific advice about how to prevent your dog acquiring any

A microchip is often required for dogs entering other countries.

of these infections by discussing with your veterinarian the part(s) of Europe that you intend to travel through and to.

NORTH AMERICAN TRAVEL

All of the certificates described in the next section must be signed by a veterinarian who is licensed by the Ministry of Agriculture (or the equivalent) in the country exporting the animal. Please note: it is not sufficient that the veterinarian be 'licensed to practice' in the country of origin (e.g. an MRCVS).

Exporters are recommended to get in touch with the Canadian or American legations in their own country to ensure that the regulations regarding that country have not changed. Most veterinarians in practice do not do many certifications for export and the owner should ensure that they have the up-to-date information before going to their veterinarian.

CANADA

If the imported dog is from a country that is not free from rabies, he must be accompanied by a Certificate of Health (a statement of general health that also describes the animal) and a rabies vaccination certificate. The vaccine must have been administered within the last three years, and the certificate must show the name, make and lot number of the vaccine.

If the imported dog is from a country that is free from rabies, he must be accompanied by a Certificate of Health and a certified statement that there has not been a case of rabies in that country over the last six months and that, as far as the veterinarian is aware, the dog has been in that country for all of the last six months.

UNITED STATES

If the imported animal is from a country that is not free from rabies, he must have a rabies vaccination certificate. The certificate should be in English or accompanied by a translation. It should identify the animal, and specify the date of vaccination and the expiry date of the vaccination. The certificate should be signed by a licensed veterinarian. If no date of expiry is present on the certificate, the dog will only be accepted if the date of vaccination was less than 12 months prior to arrival.

Unvaccinated dogs from countries that are not free from rabies may still be admitted if the dog is immediately placed in confinement (at a place of the owner's choice) and vaccinated within four days of being quarantined or up to ten days after arrival at the port of entry. Confinement must continue for 30 days after vaccination.

If the dog has been vaccinated prior to arrival, but the vaccination was received less than 30 days before arrival, the animal must be confined (at a place of the owner's choice) until 30 days have passed since the vaccine was administered.

If the dog originates from a country that is free from rabies, he must be accompanied by documentary proof that he has not been anywhere other than a US-Public-Health-Service-certified rabies-free country during the previous six months. He will also be subjected to a veterinary examination at the port of entry.

PUPPIES

Puppies less than three months of age are subject to separate rules of entry in the US. On arrival, the puppies must be immediately confined (at a place of the owner's choice) until they reach three months of age, at which point they should be vaccinated. Confinement must continue for a further three months following vaccination.

CAUSES OF DISEASE

The causes of disease may be conveniently split into two: infectious and non-infectious.

NON-INFECTIOUS DISEASE

Non-infectious disease occurs when some part(s) of the dog's body malfunctions. For example, if the pancreas fails to produce the normal amount of digestive enzymes, food is not adequately digested. This leaves large amounts of undigested food in the faeces, causing the faeces to be loose and evil-smelling.

Normal function of a dog's body is maintained by a system of regulation that includes components from the brain, nearby organs, and local tissue. In the case of the pancreas, normal production of digestive enzymes relies on local information from the stomach that food is present. The pancreas then

A vaccination is designed to provoke the body into developing an immune response against an infectious organism. By producing antibodies, it can subsequently protect your dog against that organism if he becomes exposed to it at a later date.

Maternal antibodies provide adequate cover to most puppies until they reach six to eight weeks of age, assuming that they have received colostrum at birth. At this point, they will need a vaccine to stimulate the body to create its own defences. It is essential that vaccinations start as soon as possible and are continued throughout your dog's life. There are six organisms against which dogs can be vaccinated.

Potential Guide Dogs in the UK are vaccinated at six weeks of age, earlier than most pet dogs.

VACCINE SCHEDULE
To give your puppy full immunisation against these often-fatal diseases, your veterinarian can begin with two primary vaccinations (starting as early as 6 weeks of age), giving immunity for the first year of life. It will then be necessary to boost your dog's immunity every 12 months.

NORTH AMERICAN AND UK SYSTEMS
In North America, vaccines are divided into two groups:
- Core vaccines: Diseases that are determined to be widespread, cause serious illness and/or are highly contagious.
- Non-core vaccines: Those recommended on an individual basis.

Distemper, infectious hepatitis, parvovirus and parainfluenza are all a necessary part of the primary vaccination regime, with rabies, bordetellosis (second strain of kennel cough) and leptospirosis given when an individual case warrants it. In the UK, primary vaccinations include all core elements, plus Leptospirosis.

DISTEMPER
This can cause lasting neurological symptoms, and severe gastrointestinal and respiratory problems. It is found in areas of dense population, and is spread by direct contact. It is seen most commonly in three- to nine-month-old animals, and can be fatal. The fox, ferret, badger and mink can be carriers.

INFECTIOUS HEPATITIS
This causes damage to the liver, the respiratory system and the eyes. It is spread in urine, faeces and saliva. Often fatal in dogs of any age, infectious hepatitis frequently presents as sudden-death syndrome in puppies.

PARVOVIRUS
A widespread and often fatal disease that is spread through direct or indirect contact, usually via faeces. It causes either severe gastrointestinal or cardiac disease.

LEPTOSPIROSIS
This bacterium is zoonotic (can cause disease in humans via animals) and causes severe liver and kidney disease, sometimes proving fatal. Leptospirosis is spread through direct contact with urine, and rats are thought to play an important part in the disease's transmission.

PARAINFLUENZA
This virus can combine with bacteria to cause respiratory disease. It is spread via direct contact from air droplets, and is, therefore, prevalent in kennels and rescue establishments. It produces a highly-contagious hacking cough – hence the name 'kennel cough' (Chapter Six).

BORDETELLA
This is thought to be a primary instigator of 'kennel cough' when combined with Parainfluenza virus. There is a nasal vaccine that has to be given every six months, as opposed to twelve months for other vaccinations.

RABIES
Rabies is a viral disease that affects the nervous system and is deadly to man and beast. It is spread via direct contact, usually through a bite (this disease causes severe aggression and behavioural changes). Rabies is a notifiable disease (i.e. it has to be reported to the government).

Dogs travelling to and from the UK under the PETS scheme (page 21) must be rabies-vaccinated. In North America, rabies is often a non-core vaccine. When vaccinated, revaccination is advised every three years.

responds by producing the digestive enzymes.

Most of the time this system of regulation functions very well, controlling not only the function of organs but their size and number of cells as well. Occasionally, one or more cells begin to divide, regardless of the regulation, and this results in cancer. The exact signs that are seen depend on the type of cell that has begun this uncontrolled type of replication.

Sometimes, the lumps formed are benign or harmless, like the fatty lumps (lipomas) that can sometimes be felt under the skin of older dogs. Others are more dangerous because of their characteristics to spread locally, or metastasize (to spread in the blood to other organs). Examples of locally spreading tumours are the bone tumours, osteosarcomas. Tumours that may metastasize include mammary tumours. Typically, in this case, small pieces of the cancer settle in the lungs to form 'secondaries'. This is the reason that a veterinary surgeon may X-ray a bitch's chest to check for evidence of secondaries before operating to remove a mammary tumour.

INFECTIOUS DISEASE

Infectious diseases occur when an infectious agent manages to establish itself on or in an animal despite all the defences that the animal puts in its way. Infectious agents may be regarded as either opportunist or true pathogens. Opportunist pathogens are normally associated with animals and usually cause no harm. For example, *Staphylococci* are normal bacterial inhabitants of a dog's skin. If the relationship is upset, the dog's defences fail to prevent the bacteria from entering the skin and dermatitis results. Infections with pathogens, such as rabies or distemper, will normally result in disease.

All infectious agents, on or in the dog that they infect, are considered to be parasitic. This is because, by attaching themselves to the dog, they gain a home and the food that they require to live. However, the term 'parasite' is normally reserved for the bigger infectious agents, such as the protozoa, helminths and arthropods. The smaller organisms – the bacteria, fungi and viruses – are normally referred to by their specific name, or simply as bacteria or viruses.

The structure of bacteria and virus organisms is fascinating because the appearance often determines the characteristics of the organism. It determines, for example, whether it can survive in the environment, or, if it is very fragile, whether it relies on immediate transfer from animal to animal.

Each virus particle is about one ten-thousandth of the size of a pinhead. They are far too small to be seen with a normal microscope, so veterinarians detect their presence using 'indirect' tests. These tests often examine blood or serum for evidence of the infectious agent itself or for a response by the animal to the specific infection. Rather than seeing the organism itself, the test produces a signal if the sample is positive – often this signal is a colour change in the sample. Viruses that cause disease in dogs include distemper, rabies, canine infectious hepatitis and parvo viruses.

Bacteria are larger than viruses (about one-thousandth of the size of a pinhead), and may be seen with a microscope. Bacterial diseases in dogs include kennel cough, which is caused by several different factors (see Chapter Six).

There are just a few fungi that infect dogs, and the most common of these is ringworm. Once introduced on to the skin, ringworm grows outwards, leaving an area of bald skin in the centre and a characteristic ring of active infection around the outside. Ringworm needs specific anti-fungal treatment to eliminate it. Take care not to rub against the infected area, as ringworm is zoonotic (infectious to humans). Other fungal infections include Candida, which is a yeast fungus that occasionally infects areas such as the mouths of pups, and Aspergillus, which may infect inside the dog's nasal passages. Fortunately, both of these infections are relatively uncommon.

WORMING REGIMES

THE NEW-BORN PUP

As pups normally acquire *T. canis* infection from their dams, all pups should be wormed at intervals up to weaning, starting at two weeks of age. Starting at two weeks is the best way of ensuring that your pups do not pass large numbers of *T. canis* eggs into the environment. There are a number of products available, and the more modern preparations tend to have better levels of efficacy. Manufacturers' recommendations for treatments should always be followed.

THE WEANED PUP

Most owners obtain their pup when he is about eight weeks of age. Try to find out the details of the pup's worming history – if, for example, he has already been treated with fenbendazole at 50mg/kg/day for three days when two, five and eight weeks of age, there is no need to re-treat until

ROUNDWORMS (NEMATODES)

Endoparasites live within the organs and tissues of the host. The majority are parasitic worms (helminths).

Roundworms are invertebrates, which have a smooth, cylindrical body, tapered at both ends. Parasitic forms may have a toothed mouth, used for tearing at tissues. In animals and humans, infections can take place in various sites of the body (e.g. intestines, lungs, blood and eyes).

TOXOCARA CANIS

This is the largest nematode found in the alimentary tract of the dog. It is capable of causing significant disease in young puppies and can also affect man. Females can measure 7 inches (18 cms) in length.

Toxocara has a complex lifecycle. When a dog ingests an egg containing an infective larva, the larva hatches in the small intestine and passes through the gut wall, travelling

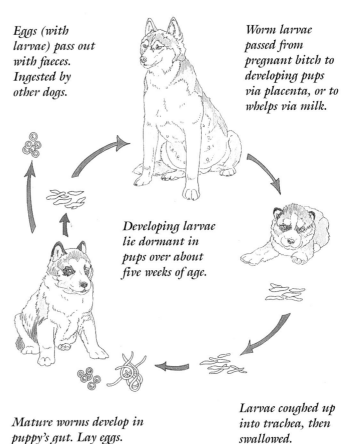

ROUNDWORM LIFECYCLE

Eggs (with larvae) pass out with faeces. Ingested by other dogs.

Worm larvae passed from pregnant bitch to developing pups via placenta, or to whelps via milk.

Developing larvae lie dormant in pups over about five weeks of age.

Mature worms develop in puppy's gut. Lay eggs.

Larvae coughed up into trachea, then swallowed.

to the lungs via the bloodstream, liver, heart and pulmonary artery. Once in the lungs, the larvae begin a second developmental stage, which is then coughed up and swallowed, travelling back to the intestines. This is where the final stages of development occur. Adult worms in the gut produce eggs that are passed out in the faeces.

This nematode is mostly found in puppies, which become infected by the mother. The immature larvae are passed via the placenta or mother's milk. Once aboard their new host, they mature in the intestine and begin producing large numbers of eggs. The eggs are protected by a thick coat, allowing them to survive in the environment for long periods of time. In the bitch some of these larvae become active about three weeks prior to whelping, when they migrate across the placenta to infect the pups. These worms then mature in the pups, becoming adult worms by three weeks of age. Pups should therefore be wormed beginning at two weeks of age. Adult dogs can be infected by eating eggs, or mice, or other prey containing larvae. In the older dog, the larvae often migrate into tissues where they remain for extended periods.

If humans ingest a large number of infected eggs, they migrate throughout the body to major body organs, causing a condition known as visceral larval migrans (VLM), which is associated with damage to the organs. When only a few are ingested, they migrate through the body causing few signs of illness although, if they find their way to the eye (ocular larval migrans – OLM), they will cause blindness.

TREATMENT AND CONTROL

It is better to prevent illness due to *T.canis* than to cure infection.
• Bitches can be wormed from day 40 of pregnancy with fenbendazole.
• Worm pups regularly from 14 days of age, following manufacturers' recommendations.
• Worm your dog regularly at the intervals recommended by your veterinarian.
• Pick up after your dog has defaecated.
• Encourage children to wash their hands after handling dogs or pups, and after playing outside.

TOXOCARIS LEONINA
This is a variant that can infect both dogs and cats. It is not thought to be zoonotic and large burdens are well tolerated.

WHIPWORM
Trichuris vulpis is commonly seen in dogs that have permanent access to grass runs. It has an infected first-stage larva, which develops inside the egg and does not hatch out until inside a suitable host. It is very resilient and can survive in the environment, providing a real risk of re-infection. A heavy burden can cause diarrhoea and repeated treatment may be necessary to control the problem, particularly if it is not possible to remove the dogs from the source of the infection, e.g. the grass run.

BLADDER/LIVER WORMS
Collectively known as *Capillaria* species. *Capillaria plica* worms live in the bladder and eggs are passed in the urine. They are rarely seen in the U.K.

LUNGWORM
There are a number of species of worm that may infect the lungs of dogs. Found in the air passages of domestic and wild dogs, Oslerus (Filaroides) osleri embeds in the fibrous nodules of the trachea, causing affected dogs to cough. This worm can cause considerable damage, with debilitated health. Treatment would include using a suitable anthelmintic (e.g. fenbendazole), at the recommended doses.

WHIPWORM LIFECYCLE

The adult Whipworm is embedded in the wall of the large intestine and caecum.

Eggs are passed in the faeces.

Infective larva develops inside the egg but does not hatch unless the egg is swallowed.

Hill's Atlas of Veterinary Clinical Anatomy

---

twelve weeks of age. If, however, you are unable to ascertain for certain what the pup has received, it is best to treat him again, possibly in conjunction with having him vaccinated.

THE GROWING DOG
The growing dog, from three months to a year old, may be at more risk of developing a *T. canis* infection than an older dog, though at less risk than a pup. It is, therefore, worth treating the growing pup at monthly intervals until he is six months of age, and then at three-monthly intervals until he is one year old.

THE ADULT DOG
The adult dog (more than one year old) may acquire worm infections even if he only goes for walks around the park. However, the infections that he is likely to acquire differ from those that dogs with a flea infestation, or those that dogs with access to dead sheep carcasses on hillsides, are likely to acquire. To some extent, then, frequency and type of wormer can be tailored to the needs of the dog:
- Dog in hydatid disease areas (localised areas where hydatid cysts occur in sheep): treat with a compound containing praziquantel at two-monthly intervals. There is a risk to dogs

and humans in these areas.
- Dog that does not hunt and does not have fleas or lice: treat with a broad-spectrum, or simple roundworm, wormer. You could also consider combining flea control prophylactic treatment.
- Dog that eats snails: consider administering a lungworm dose of fenbendazole at regular intervals.
- Dog that may hunt: use a broad-spectrum treatment, at three- to six-monthly intervals, for tapeworms and roundworms.
- Help to prevent tapeworms in dogs by preventing them from eating the intermediate hosts: uncooked meat, dead sheep, rabbits and rodents, fleas and lice.

The above are guidelines only, and your veterinarian, based on his knowledge of your particular dog, is the best-placed person to give advice specific to your dog's requirements.

THE PREGNANT BITCH
Treatment of the pregnant bitch, with anthelmintics at the normal dose-rate, will only affect the worms in her intestine at the time of treatment, and will not affect the *T. canis* larvae migrating to her pups and to her mammary glands.

HOOKWORM LIFECYCLE

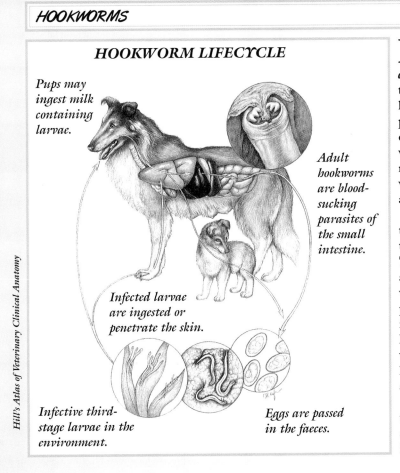

Pups may ingest milk containing larvae.

Adult hookworms are blood-sucking parasites of the small intestine.

Infected larvae are ingested or penetrate the skin.

Infective third-stage larvae in the environment.

Eggs are passed in the faeces.

Hill's Atlas of Veterinary Clinical Anatomy

Hookworms (*Uncinaria stenocephala* and *Ancylostoma caninum*) are a particular problem for the Greyhound and for dogs at hunt kennels. There tends to be a population boom of hookworms during the summer months, when the weather is mild with adequate rainfall. Unpaved dog runs, or those where faecal matter can accumulate, are at a much higher risk of infection.

Adult hookworms have mouthparts that attach to the gut wall, with teeth that damage and then eat the tissue. The female adult produces eggs that are passed out in faeces. Infection with *A. caninum* can occur via skin penetration, and both species can infect via ingestion of larvae. Following skin penetration, the worms then migrate through the new host before developing into mature adults in the small intestine.

Infection can be passed in milk in the case of *A. caninum*, and is usually a problem in warm climates, such as in the U.S.

There is one product licensed to prevent transfer to the pups: this is fenbendazole given at 25mg/kg body weight per day from day 40 of pregnancy up to two days after whelping. This does not prevent the pups from picking up larvae once they are born, so the manufacturers still recommend treatment of the pups in the normal way. It is critical that any product administered during pregnancy is specifically recommended for use during pregnancy and that instructions about the timing and dose-rate are followed carefully.

THE LACTATING BITCH
A lactating bitch should be treated at the same time as her pups, namely at two, five and eight weeks if treating the pups with fenbendazole, or according to manufacturers' recommendations if using an alternative product.

PROTOZOA

COCCIDIA
The very simplest coccidian parasites inhabit the small intestine of the dog and oocysts (eggs) are passed in the faeces. This is an infection of pups and may be associated with diarrhoea.
- **Toxoplasma gondii:** Dogs and humans are infected when they eat cysts or undercooked, infected meat. There is a variety of ways in which infection may manifest itself; these include weak pups if they are infected prenatally. If toxoplasmosis is diagnosed, then a mixture of anti-protozoal drugs may be used and may result in improvement.
- **Sarcocystis:** This parasite infects the lining of the intestine. The resulting oocysts are passed in faeces and, if eaten by a lamb or calf, can cause severe disease. To prevent the cycle, ensure that your dog's food is properly cooked and that his faeces are picked up and disposed of appropriately.
- **Neospora caninum:** This particularly affects young dogs. Signs include paralysis, caused by the presence of parasitic cysts. Diagnosis may be by blood-sampling the affected dog. Some cases may respond to treatment with antiprotozoal drugs.
- **Giardia sp.:** This protozoan parasite infects the intestine of the dog. Infection may be associated with diarrhoea, particularly in young or immunocompromised animals. Fenbendazole is used to treat Giardia, and bedding and exercise areas should be thoroughly cleaned to prevent the possibility of infection.

TAPEWORMS (CESTODES)

Cestodes (*Taenia hydatigena, Dipylidium caninum, and Echinococcus granulosus*) are flattened, segmented worms that obtain their nutrients from the host's intestines. They rarely cause a problem to the final host and are more of a nuisance than a life-threatening parasite.

Tapeworms grow in the dog's intestines, forming chain-like lengths. Segments of these chains break off and pass out of the dog's intestines in the faeces. The segments are often seen in the faeces or attached to the anus, and they are the remnants of the uterus packed with eggs.

When the intermediate host ingests the egg, the shell is digested by the gut to release and activate the first developmental stage (onchosphore). Using its hooks, the onchosphore tears through the mucosa (tissue lining of the alimentary canal and many hollow organs) to

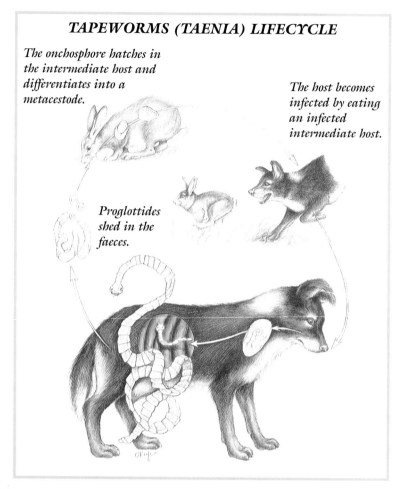

TAPEWORMS (TAENIA) LIFECYCLE

The onchosphore hatches in the intermediate host and differentiates into a metacestode.

The host becomes infected by eating an infected intermediate host.

Proglottides shed in the faeces.

Hill's Atlas of Veterinary Clinical Anatomy

reach the body cavity, bloodstream or lymphatics. Once there, it develops into a larval stage, specific to its species. These are often fluid-filled cysts, which lie dormant in the host's tissue.

When a flea bites a dog, the dog may, in turn, bite the irritated area. If the flea is acting as an intermediate host, the dog also eats the dormant onchosphore. Once inside the dog, the immature-adult tapeworm attaches itself to the dog's intestinal wall, while the rest of the structure is digested. Here the tapeworm matures, producing segments packed with eggs, which are passed into the environment to begin the cycle again.

TAENIA HYDATIGENA
In this type of tapeworm, the onchosphores are carried in the blood of the intermediate host to the liver, before emerging and attaching to the wall of the abdominal cavity. Mature adults can be up to 16 feet (5 metres) in length. Infection often results from eating raw, uncooked meats, offal, or eating prey containing the intermediate stages.

DIPYLIDIUM CANINUM
This is our most common tapeworm. Adults can reach lengths of 20 inches (50 cms) and are transmitted to dogs via the ingestion of a flea or louse intermediate host. Newly-passed segments are active, and can crawl on to the tail region, where they are left in the environment to be ingested by an intermediate host. Here, developmental changes take place, taking from 30 days to several months. Once ingested by the dog (often after grooming), egg production takes only three weeks.

ECHINOCOCCUS GRANULOSUS
This is much smaller than the other tapeworms: the whole tapeworm is about 1 cm ($^1/_2$ inch) long and each segment is so small that it is very unlikely that it will be seen. The intermediate host is the sheep, and dogs are infected when they eat raw sheep liver. The main importance of this parasite is that it can infect man, and, when this occurs, large cysts develop in the person's liver (hydatid diseases). It is therefore extremely important that dogs are not allowed to have access to sheep carcasses.

HEARTWORMS

Heartworm (*Dirofilaria immitis*) is rarely seen in the UK, but it is a regular occurrence in North America and southern Europe. The adult worm can survive for up to five years, producing microfilaria (immature larvae), which circulate in the blood. When a host is bitten by a mosquito, the microfilaria are absorbed, along with the blood. When the mosquito bites its next victim, the worms are then transferred to the new host.

The microfilaria then remain in the connective tissue for up to four months, eventually moving to the heart, where they mature into their adult form. Six to seven months after the intial infection, the newly-adult worm produces more microfilaria.

Adult heartworms cause obstruction in the heart chambers and valves, ultimately leading to right-sided heart failure (see Chapter Five).

Typical symptoms include a cough, and other signs associated with heart failure, such as exercise intolerance. In endemic areas, treatment is a daily (or monthly) preparation from the beginning of, to two months after, mosquito activity (according to manufacturers' instructions).

HEARTWORM LIFECYCLE

Infected mosquitos deposit heartworm larvae into the animal's haemolymph by puncturing the animal's skin.

Mature females release microfilaria into the bloodstream where they are picked up by mosquitoes.

Larvae migrate to subcutaneous tissues where they mature to a young-adult stage.

Young adults migrate to the pulmonary arteries and heart.

Hill's Atlas of Veterinary Clinical Anatomy

ECTOPARASITES: CHEYLETIELLA AND RINGWORM

The mite (*Cheyletiella*) can be seen with the naked eye, appearing as a small fleck of white moving slowly through the coat. The mite is zoonotic, causes mild irritation, and is spread by direct contact.

Signs of infestation include dandruff in the coat, some irritation and small pimply lesions around the head and neck. A non-burrowing mite, it lays its eggs at the base of the hair shafts and completes its lifecycle entirely on the host.
Treatment: Tropical treatments are available from veterinarians. Whilst there are few products with a specific indication for Cheyletiella, a number of preparations containing pyrethroids or fipronil, for example, are effective.

RINGWORM
This contagious skin disease (Dermatophytosis) is caused by the group

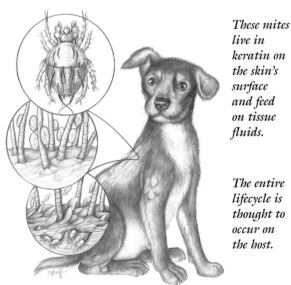

CHEYLETIELLA LIFECYCLE

These mites live in keratin on the skin's surface and feed on tissue fluids.

The entire lifecycle is thought to occur on the host.

Hill's Atlas of Veterinary Clinical Anatomy

of fungi known as dermatophytes. It is a zoonotic disease, easily transferable from animals to humans. Classic lesions are circular patches of alopecia, up to 2 inches (5 cms) in diameter. Any hair that may remain will appear broken off. The lesions are often covered with dry scales or crusts. The infection appears to do no great harm to the animal, but because of its highly contagious nature, all efforts should be taken to prevent further spread. Spores can survive in the environment for many months, making the possibility of re-infection high.

LICE

Lice are host-specific insects (i.e. they do not move between cats and dogs), with transmission occurring only with direct contact. Each louse has claw structures at the end of each leg, to attach to the animal. The eggs laid by lice can be seen with the naked eye.

There are two types of lice: the biting variety and the sucking variety, although both use their mouthparts for feeding.

Lifecycle: This takes place entirely on the host, with the female cementing her eggs (nits) to the dog's hair shafts. Eggs hatch after one to three weeks, and evolve into adults after a further three to four weeks.

Treatment: Lice spend their whole lives on the host, so attention to the environment is not so important. The eggs can be resistant to treatment, which can take three to four attempts before being successful unless a treatment with sustained activity is used. Topical treatment is needed, using an insecticidal wash or spray (such as fipronil).

TICKS

These are blood-sucking parasites with piercing mouthparts to cut the skin and to suck blood. If the tick is removed incorrectly, it can leave its mouthpart behind, causing a raised, inflamed area. Ticks can also transmit disease (e.g. Lyme Disease).

A tick, attached to a dog.

Lifecycle: Ticks, unlike other ectoparasites, attach themselves by their mouthparts firmly to one spot on an animal where they feed and grow in size until fully-fed females look like 'castor beans'. Once fully fed, the tick drops to the ground, where females lay hundreds of eggs. Tiny larval or 'seed ticks' hatch from the eggs and begin to seek a first host. Depending on the species of tick, the larva may stay on the tick for its entire life, or more commonly, feed then drop off, developing to a nymph in the environment. The nymph finds a second host to feed on, feeds and again drops off. The adult stage has then to find a third host for a final feed prior to the engorged females dropping off to lay eggs. There are many species of tick. In the UK, most ticks found on dogs are adult 'hedgehog' *Ixodes hexagonus* or 'sheep' ticks *Ixodes ricinus*, and these are normally active in spring and autumn, staying in the environment during the rest of the year. Occasionally, a premises acquires dog ticks, *Ixodes canisuga*; in this case, all stages of tick may be found on dogs, throughout the year. In warmer climates, other ticks, such as *Rhipicephalus sanguineus*, are common.

Treatment: Ticks require careful removal, to avoid the mouthparts being left behind (see above).

TICK LIFECYCLE

1. Adult ticks lay thousands of eggs, which undergo two moults: larva to nymph and nymph to adult.

2. Larvae, nymphs, and adults feed on blood and lymph.

3. Dermacentor variabilis larvae and nymphs feed on small mammals and drop off between moults.

4. Adults feed on pets.

5. Rhipicephalus sanguineus larvae, nymphs, and adults all feed on pets.

Apply surgical spirit or an insecticide to a swab of cotton wool (cologne or aftershave often works, too). Hold this cotton wool (cotton) in place over the tick, applying firm pressure, for up to one minute. Remove the swab, and, using a pair of tweezers, gently pull the tick from the skin surface. Once removed, examine the insect to ensure that you can see four pairs of legs and the mouthpart. Do not use a cigarette tip to burn the tick – the mouthpart will be left in, and can cause abcesses.

Bathe the area with warm salt water to prevent secondary infection. If the tick is attached on or around the eyelid, seek veterinary advice as products used around this area can cause further harm.

Pets that go to Europe or the U.S. can acquire larger numbers of ticks. Here, treatment with an acaricidal or repellent agent is important.

MAGGOTS

Maggots are the larvae that emerge from eggs laid by the blowfly during the summer months. If undetected, they can cause irreparable damage in a very short space of time. The larvae secrete enzymes that liquify and digest skin and muscle tissue.

This is usually a problem faced by rabbit owners, but it is not unheard of for a dog to be similarly affected, and maggots can be found on old or debilitated animals who have a heavy build-up of organic matter unwashed from their coats.

Maggots need to be removed manually, using an antiseptic solution to prevent secondary infection. They can cause excessive damage deep within tissue layers, affecting important physical structures and even eating their way into the abdominal cavity. In this instance, your veterinarian will be limited in the choice of treatment options available to him.

Clearly, prevention is better than cure – make sure your dog is kept scrupulously clean, particularly around the anal area (and especially if you own a longcoated breed). Be particularly vigilant in the summer months.

MITES

There are two types of microscopic ectoparasites (mites):
• Burrowing: Including the *Sarcoptes scabiei* and the *Demodex canis*.
• Non-burrowing: Including the *Otodectes cyanotis* and *Cheyletiella yasguri* mites.

Mites are related to spiders (arachnids), both having eight legs. They are unable to survive for any lengthy period of time away from the host, so infection usually occurs by direct contact. As with all mites, the chief effect is skin damage and allergic reactions. Skin irritation may be exacerbated by warm temperatures, which increase the mites' activity.

Diagnosis is made by analysis of skin scrapings, coat brushings, swabs, and hair samples. See Chapter Eight for further details.

EAR MITES (OTODECTES CYANOTIS)

These mites attack the external ear, and can be transmitted via close contact. The first signs include excessive shaking of the head, and scratching or twitching of the ears. A thick, dark-brown discharge may also be seen in the ear, which can have a distinctive smell.

If treatment is left too late, secondary infections, perforated eardrums, and middle-ear disease may rarely occur.

LIFECYCLE: The female lays her eggs on the side of the auditory canal, and the eggs hatch within one to three days, producing larvae. The entire lifecycle takes only 21 days.

TREATMENT: Ears should be cleaned twice daily, after which medicated drops can be administered. Treatment should continue for three weeks to ensure that all stages of the lifecycle are treated, or following the manufacturer's recommendations.

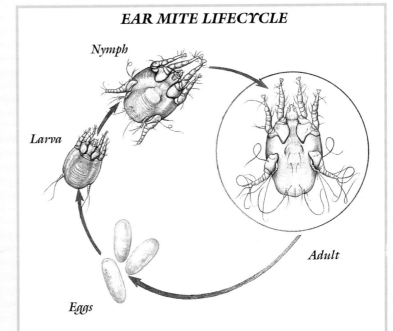

EAR MITE LIFECYCLE

Nymph

Larva

Eggs

Adult

Hill's Atlas of Veterinary Clinical Anatomy

DEMODECTIC MANGE (DEMODEX CANIS)

This mite burrows into the hair follicles. It is thought that all dogs carry this mite, but that it only causes disease in a small percentage. It is often seen in conjunction with debilitated health or in pups.

Demodex mites can be transferred during whelping. They lay their eggs in sebaceous glands, returning to the surface soon afterwards.

SYMPTOMS: Include pustules, secondary bacterial infections, and hair loss (alopecia). It is usually seen in young dogs.

TREATMENT: Veterinary attention is necessary both for the accurate diagnosis and treatment of demodecosis. Treatment may include medicated baths, which will need repeating often. Antibacterial therapy may also be required due to the nature of secondary infections.

DEMODEX LIFECYCLE

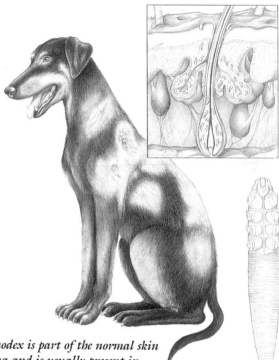

The entire lifecycle is spent on the host in the hair follicles or sebaceous glands.

Adult Demodex mite.

Demodex is part of the normal skin fauna and is usually present in small numbers in healthy animals.

Hill's Atlas of Veterinary Clinical Anatomy

SARCOPTIC MANGE (SARCOPTES SCABIEI)

This mite produces an intense skin inflammation so infected animals are very itchy. Symptoms are normally seen at the edges of earflaps or on elbows, spreading to the limbs. It rarely spreads to the dog's trunk.

The Sarcoptes mite is transferred by direct contact and the incubation period can be up to two months. Stress is thought to be a trigger in some animals, which may have come into contact many months previously and been relatively asymptomatic until diagnosis. Humans can also be affected.

LIFECYCLE: Fertilised females burrow into the dog's skin and lay their eggs in tunnels that they have formed. Eggs are laid on a daily basis over a period of up to two months, with the female dying shortly after laying. The eggs hatch after three to five days, and the emerging larvae make further burrows at right angles to the first, continuing their developmental stages during the next seven to ten days. At the final 'moult', the larvae become either male or female, with the female reproducing after a further two to four days.

TREATMENT: Treatment must penetrate the skin to reach the burrowing mites. Topical treatment with selamectin or baths is the treatment choice. If the infection is localised, topical preparations can be used. Repeated treatment will be necessary.

SARCOPTES LIFECYCLE

Female mites burrow into the skin and lay eggs in the tunnels that they form.

Larvae and nymphs develop in these tunnels.

The patient response is often severe self-inflicted trauma.

Hill's Atlas of Veterinary Clinical Anatomy

The flea is a wingless insect, capable of very rapid movement, although it is visible to the naked human eye. It is brown and has modified mouthparts to assist in piercing and sucking blood. Fleas are responsible for a large proportion of skin conditions (see Chapter Eight).

FLEA-BITE DERMATITIS

The common response to a flea bite is seen as a small, raised, slightly inflamed area on the skin surface. One flea bite is often not enough to cause distress, but the problem occurs when an animal develops a sensitivity to the saliva produced by the flea.

As the flea feeds, it releases saliva into the skin to prevent the blood from clotting. This saliva contains allergens, which leads to a reaction. A sensitive animal will not only be affected by the last bite given, but also to all previous bites. This is why preventative treatment is crucial.

Signs of flea-bite dermatitis include:
- Scratching or biting of the skin
- Self-mutilation due to immense irritation
- Areas of hair loss (alopecia) and secondary skin infections
- Thickened skin, which may become hairless over time, with excessive pigmentation occurring.

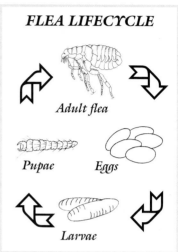

FLEA LIFECYCLE

Adult flea

Pupae *Eggs*

Larvae

LIFECYCLE

A female lays up to 500 eggs in her lifetime. To overcome flea infestations, it is necessary to break the flea's lifecycle:
- The female lays eggs.
- The eggs hatch within 2 to 16 days.
- The larvae feed on dried blood and organic matter, growing to approximately 5 millimetres ($^1/_4$ of an inch). In favourable conditions this can take between 7 and 14 days.
- The mature larvae spin a cocoon, and pupae form, taking up to 2 weeks.
- Each pupa hatches to reveal an adult flea, which continues to seek a new host.
- The flea feeds on the host and the female lays eggs, continuing their lifecycle.

All the developing stages may take considerably longer in cold conditions. Pupal hatch may be delayed when the environment appears devoid of suitable hosts.

DETECTION

Fleas can often be seen moving quickly through the fur, but more often it is the small blackish flecks of flea dirt that are detected. As the dirt mainly consists of blood, it will produce a reddish-brown stain when applied to damp tissue.

TREATMENT

You will need to treat both your animal and the environment. As flea eggs can roll between crevices in woodwork and under furnishings, you may choose to use an effective spray and work systematically through the whole house at least once a year. Make sure that special attention is given to favoured sleeping areas, and do not forget to include the garden shed and the car. By vacuuming carpeted areas before spraying, you can encourage emerging fleas to come to the surface, where treatment will be more effective.

There are several preparations available to treat your dog, including:
- Spot-on treatments: Ensure the correct dosage is given.
- Sprays: Economical for the multi-animal household.
- Flea collars: Provide constant cover.
- Tablets: Given with food to prevent eggs hatching out.

The use of organophosphate compounds for the treatment of parasites is declining. This is due to the development of new chemicals (such as fiprinol, imidacloprid, selamectin), which are safe for long-term use. Coupled with products that work exclusively on insects, such as insect growth regulators, you can be confident that a toxic reaction is unlikely to occur.

Consult your veterinarian for advice on which product is best for your animal. Products purchased at pet stores may produce ineffective results, as the chemical components are not strong enough to contend with an aggressive problem. A veterinarian is licensed to hold stronger preparations, therefore offering better cover.

As a side effect of the installation of central heating in most homes, the problem of fleas is now seen all year round. This means that it may be necessary to treat pets even in winter.

Body temperature can be a valuable indication of the onset of illness. Temperature is most commonly measured in degrees Celsius, but some still use degrees Fahrenheit, or even both.

Normal temperature: 38.9 degrees C (+/- 0.5)
102 degrees F (+/- 1)

MERCURY THERMOMETER
The mercury thermometer consists of a narrow glass stem, along which mercury will rise from the bulb as it expands on contact with body heat. A small kink, just above the bulb, prevents the mercury falling once the thermometer has been removed from your animal. The thermometer must therefore be shaken down, to return the mercury to the bulb, before each use.

Store your thermometer in its original container, to protect it from breakages. After each use, clean it with an antiseptic solution on a cotton wool (cotton) swab.

ELECTRONIC THERMOMETERS
Electronic thermometers show the dog's temperature on a digital display. They do not need to be shaken before use, but, once inserted into the rectum, they are used in the same way. Some models will bleep when ready; others will flash repeatedly.

TEMPERATURE TAKING
Your dog may need gentle restraint during this procedure. Ask someone to cradle the dog's head in their left arm while supporting the dog's tummy with their right arm.
- Shake the end of the mercury thermometer well, then lubricate the end.
- Lift your dog's tail, and gently, with a rotating action, insert the thermometer into the rectum.
- Hold the thermometer at an angle, so the bulb is in direct contact with the rectal wall.
- Hold in place for 30 to 60 seconds before removing. Wipe the thermometer clean. Avoid touching the bulb as this may influence the results.
- Holding the thermometer horizontally, gently rotate it until the mercury line becomes visible, or read the display on an electronic thermometer.
  Read off against the scale and make a note of the temperature.
- Clean the thermometer, using an antiseptic swab, shake down, dry, and place in its cover.
- Wash your hands.

RESULTS
A high temperature may be an indication of:
- Infection
- Heat stroke
- Pain
- Excitement.

A low temperature may indicate:
- Shock
- Impending birth.

Your pet's temperature should be interpreted in conjunction with other signs, and, where possible, you should discuss your findings with your own veterinarian.

SIGNS OF ILL HEALTH

- Dullness (the dog is not as responsive or alert as normal).
- Mucous membranes in the mouth and around the eye are not pink.
- Drinking more or less than normal.
- Unwilling to eat.
- Unwilling to move.
- Faeces passing as abnormal/diarrhoea.
- Abnormal temperature and breathing.
- Signs of injury/abnormal shape/unwillingness to be touched/any unusual smells?
- Straining to pass urine, or increased/decreased amounts passed.
- Discharge from eyes and/or nose.

CHECKING VITAL SIGNS

BREATHING AND HEART RATE
- Get to know your dog's normal pattern of breathing – the rate and depth. A normal resting dog takes 15-30 breaths per minute. This increases dramatically with exercise, but

then should settle down again once exercise is over.

- Get to know what your dog's normal pulse rate feels like. A resting dog's pulse rate is 70-100 beats per minute. Using the tip of your index finger, feel inside the back leg, near the top, close to the groin, and approximately midway between the front and the back. Here, you will feel the femoral artery.

RECOGNISING COMMON PROBLEMS

SICKNESS
Vomiting occurs when the contents of the stomach are returned. This may be because the dog has eaten something disagreeable, such as rubbish, or it may be one sign of an illness. Vomiting must be distinguished from regurgitation, when food is returned before it reaches the stomach.

DIARRHOEA
This occurs when faeces are looser and more frequent than normal, and may be anything from slight looseness to something that looks like coloured water. It may occur after the dog has eaten something unsuitable, or it may be associated with infection or other illness.

LAMENESS
When a dog fails to place equal weight on each leg, he is lame. This may be associated with pain in the leg or foot (see Chapter Four).

COUGHING
Persistent coughing may be associated with a respiratory infection such as kennel cough (see Chapter Six).

Other causes may include: exercise intolerance (when a dog's capacity for exercise is less than that of a similar dog). This diminishes abruptly or gradually over time.

SIGNS RELATED TO REPRODUCTION
For example, bitches in season, prior to parturition, false pregnancy and pyometra (see Chapter Nine).

ITCHINESS OR PRURITIS
This is normally indicated by the dog rubbing and scratching more than normal, or by the appearance of hairless patches. It is usually associated with skin-related illness such as scabies, fleas or allergy (see Chapter Eight).

FIRST AID

GIVING FIRST AID
The following are guidelines for the way to tackle health problems which your dog may develop. Some are genuine emergencies, while others are less serious. If in doubt, always seek veterinary advice sooner rather than later.

Make sure that you record – either mentally or on paper – when a problem begins and how severe it is, so that you can assess its progress objectively and take action if the problem does not resolve itself in a reasonable time. This will also help you to come to a decision that veterinary advice is necessary before 10pm on a Sunday night! You will also be able to give the veterinarian an accurate account of the problem as you have seen it evolve.

When a dog is badly injured or in pain, he may be aggressive, even if he is usually a gentle, placid animal. Make sure that you have the dog sufficiently under control before trying to examine any injury. You can put on a muzzle or apply an ad-hoc muzzle of crepe bandage before examination, because even very small dogs can nip when in pain. However, do not muzzle your dog if he is having difficulty breathing.

SICKNESS AND DIARRHOEA
There are many reasons why a dog may be sick. Where there is no underlying medical cause for the sickness, sometimes simply giving the stomach a rest from food is sufficient to stop the vomiting. This works equally well in cases of diarrhoea. Starve the dog for 24 hours, and after about six hours begin to offer him small amounts of water. When food is reintroduced it should be a small amount and bland, such as chicken and rice. If the dog continues being sick or having diarrhoea, or if he seems to be depressed or unwell, seek veterinary advice.

CUTS, ABRASIONS AND BURNS
Firstly, ensure that you have the dog under control and that you are not in danger of being bitten. Try to examine the injury; cutting hair away from the area around the injury may help you to see the extent of it. Decide if it appears deep or large, if it may need stitches, or if it is bleeding badly. If the answer to any of these questions is yes, then seek veterinary help immediately.

If the injury is minor, clean the area with cotton wool (cotton) dipped in cool, sterile salt water, cleaning from the middle to the outside. Dry very

Your first-aid kit should be adequately stocked to give immediate, emergency attention until a veterinarian can attend to your dog. Keep your first-aid kit in an accessible place with your veterinarian's telephone number taped on the inside lid. Your kit should be regularly checked, to ensure that all materials are within their use-by dates. If you use an item, replace it immediately.

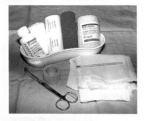

*First-aid kit for the treatment of wounds (left)
and for preventing blood loss (right).*

CONTENTS

- Sterile saline solution or an antiseptic solution to flush wounds, e.g. dilute Savlon 1:20 or use a salt-water solution: 1 gram (0.035 oz) for every 100 mls (3.5 fluid oz) of water.
- Antiseptic swabs to clean wounds.
- Dressings to protect and cover wounds.
- Cotton wool (cotton) or Gamgee for padding and protecting pressure points. Can also be used for swabbing.
- Cool pack to reduce inflammation.
- Curved, blunt-nosed bandage scissors.
- Mercury or digital thermometer.

- Gloves.
- Petroleum jelly to lubricate thermometer and to protect skin sores.
- Washing soda crystals to induce vomiting (as instructed by your veterinarian).
- Forceps to remove thorns and grass seeds.
- Bandages:
  - 2 conforming materials (see below): one 2 inches (5 cms) wide and one 2.5 inches (7 cms) wide.
  - 1 elastic, adhesive bandage.
  - 2 sterile wound dressings, 2 square inches (5 square cms).

gently with more cotton wool and then apply antiseptic cream. Do not let the dog lick at the wound – it does not help to clean up the wound and there is a risk that licking will hinder healing.

If your dog burns himself, remove him from the source of the injury, and apply cold tap water liberally to the burn site. If the burn is anything other than very minor, ring the veterinarian and arrange to take the dog to the practice. Continue the cold water treatment for up to 15 minutes. Once finished, allow the area to dry and prevent the dog from licking at it.

ROAD TRAFFIC ACCIDENT (RTA)

Take care, as the dog will be frightened and possibly injured. If he gets up and walks, get him under control, phone the veterinary practice, and gently get the dog into a car, taking care to avoid pressing against any areas that appear injured. Take the dog to the veterinary practice for a check-up – even if he appears fine – as there may be internal injuries.

In situations where the dog is unable to stand and walk, ensure that you have the dog under control, lift him very carefully and gently on to a blanket and lift the blanket into the car. Ring the veterinary surgery to warn them that you are bringing in an RTA and go there immediately.

ANAL GLAND PROBLEMS

These are the small sacs that empty into the anus. Sometimes they become full and cause the dog some irritation. Signs of discomfort include the dog rubbing his bottom across the floor ('scooting'). The anal glands can be emptied by squeezing below the anus at about 'five and seven o'clock'. Ensure that you have the dog under control while doing this, wear gloves, and hold a large pad of kitchen towels or cotton wool (cotton) – the contents of the anal glands stink! If unsure, or if you do not succeed, ask your veterinarian to demonstrate the procedure.

DROWNING

Get the dog out of the water (without endangering yourself). Hold the dog upside down to drain the water out of his lungs. Take him immediately to the veterinarian for a check-up, telephoning beforehand, if possible, to alert them to expect you.

ELECTROCUTION

Turn off the electrical supply, then remove the dog and take him immediately to the veterinary practice. If it is impossible to turn off the electricity, do not touch the dog directly but instead use an object that is a non-conductor (such as a wooden pole) to drag him away from the electrical supply.

EYE INJURIES

Eye injuries can be very painful, so you will need to ensure that the dog does not try to scratch the affected eye. Eye injuries injuries should always receive immediate veterinary attention.

HEAT STROKE

Heat stroke is a killer, as dogs are unable to self-regulate their body temperature effectively in heat. Cool down the dog using cold water (a hosepipe, for example). Then take the dog to the veterinarian for a check-up.

VETERINARY ADVICE

All veterinarians in the UK are obliged to offer a 24-hour service. This is not so in North America, although, in most urban areas, there are now emergency clinics that open when the day practices close. These may be situated separate from the day practices, or be part of them, and serve a number of local practices.

It is often more costly to take a dog to the veterinarian during unsocial hours, so try to reserve only real emergencies for the night. It is normal to take a dog to the veterinary practice in an emergency, just as you would go to the accident and emergency department of your local hospital. This is because the veterinarian will have all the necessary equipment: X-ray, drips, etc. Moreover, if the dog needs observation, he can be hospitalised.

The following lists of symptoms are split into those where immediate veterinary advice is imperative and those where it is very unlikely to be an acute emergency situation, so a routine appointment can be made. In the latter case, keep an eye on your dog, and, if he seems to become worse, do not hesitate to ring the practice to ask for an emergency appointment.

URGENT CASES
- Acute, bloody diarrhoea
- Acute vomiting
- Suddenly distended abdomen
- Road traffic accident
- Collapse/unconsciousness
- Prolonged fitting
- Snake bite
- Acute swelling in facial/neck area
- Ingestion of rat bait or your medication

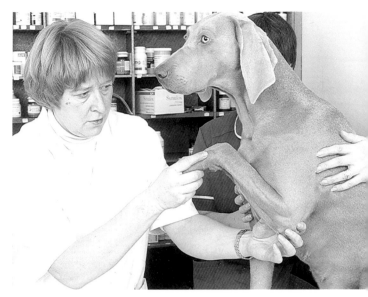

If you are concerned about your dog's condition, do not delay in seeking veterinary advice.

- Severe back pain
- Inability to use back legs
- Deep or long wound
- Profuse bleeding/bleeding that will not stop
- Suddenly not putting any weight on a limb
- Choking
- Swollen eyeball(s).

CASES TO CHECK UP
- Stiffness/unable to move as normal into all positions
- Loss of appetite
- Marked weight loss, with or without going off food
- Yelps/growls with pain when moved or touched
- Smells – could be dermatitis, teeth, diarrhoea, ear infection, etc.
- Coughs or gags
- Has a small wound (remember that a large shard of glass can leave a small entry hole and can remain inside the animal)
- Increased thirst (check that this is not simply due to hot weather, increased exercise, or a change to a dry diet). If an unspayed bitch begins to drink more, check when she was last in season. If she is developing a pyometra, it is important that she is examined without delay.

You might need to apply a bandage to your dog in order to:
• Protect an area from constant licking, scratching or self-mutilation.
• Prevent infection of a wound while seeking veterinary advice.
• Hold in place a cold compress or wound dressing.
• Restrict the movement of a limb during transportation to your veterinarian following an accident.

Your veterinarian may use a bandage to:
• Protect a surgical site.
• Provide support to reduce swelling and pain, improve mobility, or to support a recently-repaired fracture site.

TYPES OF DRESSING

• *Non-adherent contact layer:*
  A non-stick, sterile dressing to go directly over a wound.

• *Padding material:*
  Such as cotton wool (cotton). This is essential for foot dressing, where the toes need padding to prevent sores. Where padding is required to stem haemorrhage or to provide support, Gamgee (cotton wool sandwiched between two layers of gauze) is useful.

• *Conforming bandage:*
  This is applied over wound dressings or padding to hold them in place. Containing elastic properties, conforming bandages allow movement of a body part while maintaining support, so can be used for limb and body dressings. They should not be applied too tightly, as circulation may be cut off.

• *Cohesive bandage:*
  This has self-adhesive properties, meaning a comfortable dressing can be applied with maximum support, without the discomfort that adhesive tape may cause when applied directly to fur.

• *Tape:* Standard 1-inch (2.5-cm) adhesive tape can anchor an end of bandage material while you apply the next layer.

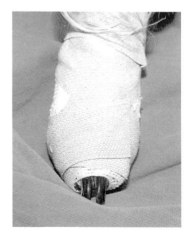

BANDAGE CARE
Your dog will tolerate a bandage much better if it is comfortable and not applied too tightly. The dressing should be kept dry and should be checked regularly by your veterinarian.
• When walking a dog with a foot dressing, place a strong plastic bag over the bandage and secure it with a thin strip of adhesive tape (not elastic bands).
• Commercial socks with rubber soles are also available. On arrival home, remove the bag to prevent the foot from sweating inside the bandage.
• If your dog keeps interfering with the bandage, use a commercial bitter spray on the bandage.
• Alternatively, put a 'lampshade' collar (available from your veterinarian) on to your dog to prevent him from reaching the bandage.
• If you notice any swelling, discharge, pain, or smell around the bandage, you should inform your veterinarian immediately.

Foot dressings will require protection when taking your dog outdoors.

EAR BANDAGE

Used to protect a ripped earflap or aural haematoma (blood blister).

- Place a square of Gamgee or cotton wool (cotton) to the top of the head.
- Bring the tip of the affected ear up on to the Gamgee. The position should be as natural as possible, not held at an awkward angle.
- Place a second square of Gamgee on top of the earflap.
- Starting at the top of the head, roll the conforming material clockwise around the head, making sure that it is not pulled too tightly around the throat.
- The dressing material is taken in front of, and then behind, the free ear on each alternate circle of the head. You may wish to cover the ear canal entrance with the dressing material. This will depend on whether you will need to gain access to the ear canal at a later stage.
- Secure the dressing on the top of the head using a piece of adhesive tape.
- Add a light but firm cohesive dressing by rolling the material clockwise around the head.
- Using a felt pen, mark the position of the earflap on the outside of the dressing – you do not want to cut the earflap accidentally when removing the bandage.

◀ *Position the ear as naturally as possible, and cushion it with cotton-wool.*

Use a light ▶ gauze bandage and wind it clockwise round the head.

◀ *The bandage should be well clear of the eyes.*

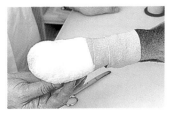

The bandage ▶ is secured with adhesive tape.

FOOT/LOWER LIMB BANDAGE

If the bandage is used in an emergency to arrest haemorrhage, you will need to apply adequate pressure during application. In a routine foot bandage, you would need to pad out the toes (to absorb sweat and to prevent sores); in an emergency this can be omitted.

- Place the cotton wool or absorbent material around the foot, including between the toes, pads, and underneath the dewclaw. Extend this layer above the hock or wrist.
- Apply a conforming material. Start at the stopper pad and come down and around to the front of the foot. Then come back on your first layer and around to take in the corners anticlockwise (figure-of-eight pattern). Take the dressing material up the leg, ensuring that you overlap each subsequent layer by about half to two-thirds.
- Secure the end with a small piece of tape.
- Cut a 4-inch (10-cm) piece of cohesive material, and apply this longitudinally to the foot. Starting at the bottom left-hand corner of the foot, use the rest of the roll to work in a figure-of-eight action until the foot is adequately covered, and then slowly work up the leg until the conforming layer is covered. Extend 2 inches (5 cms) beyond the edge of the conforming material so the bandage stays in place.

Place cotton-wool around the foot and between the toes.

Start bandaging the foot and then move up the leg.

The bandaged leg should look like a close-fitting sock.

The bandage is secured with adhesive tape.

Medicines come in various forms:
• Oral preparations: Tablets, capsules, powders or granules, liquids, syrups and pastes.
• Topical preparations: Eye drops, ear drops, and skin creams.
It is important that you follow all instructions given with your dog's medication; failure to do so could lead to the drugs being ineffective or causing harm to your pet (some anti-inflammatory drugs can cause gastric ulceration if not given with food). It is also important that your dog finishes the prescribed course of treatment.

ORAL PREPARATIONS
Where possible, oral medications are manufactured with palatability in mind, but this is not always enough to outsmart your canine friend.

CAPSULES
These are made of gelatin, and dissolve in the stomach and release their contents. Capsules can be split easily into two halves, and the contents sprinkled on to warmed, highly-flavoured food, if required. Alternatively, the contents can be mixed into a water-filled syringe and given as a liquid. Check with your veterinarian before giving medication this way, as some drugs have to be swallowed in a capsule to be absorbed properly.

POWDERS
These are very good when treating young dogs, as they are usually tasteless and odourless, but you should still use a highly-flavoured food, just in case. There is no hard-and-fast rule to giving this type of medication. Subterfuge is often most successful, but there will always be those animals that defy even the experts among us.

LIQUIDS/SYRUPS/PASTES
This type of medication is best administered via a syringe, which can be obtained from your veterinarian.
• You may need to restrain your dog, as when giving tablets.
• Gently tilt your dog's head back.
• Insert the syringe nozzle into the side of the mouth, behind the canine teeth.
• Slowly release the contents of the syringe towards the back of the throat.
• Gently stroke the throat to aid swallowing.

As with tablets, always ensure that you follow the instructions carefully and that any applicators, which may already be included with your dog's medicine, are used correctly.

Most dogs readily accept some liquids and pastes and therefore these can be added to food, in the same way as tablets. By drawing as little attention as possible to giving medication, your dog should be less likely to react in an inappropriate manner. Forcing the issue can be your undoing.

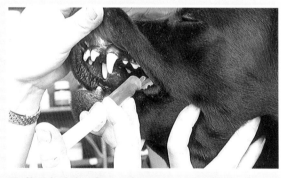

Enlist the help of an assistant, to restrain the dog and to tilt his head upwards.

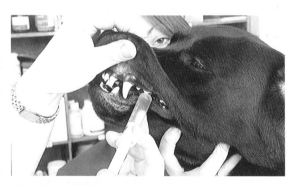

Lift the dog's upper lip and slowly release the contents of the syringe into the back of the mouth.

TABLETS

Most tablets are coated to disguise an unpleasant taste. It is, therefore, vital that the tablet goes down either whole or as heavily disguised as possible, so that your dog does not become 'difficult' at his next dose.

- Take a small amount of your dog's meal ration and add the tablet.
- Ensure that the tablet is sufficiently covered.
- Offer the food to your dog.
- Give the remaining amount of food once the tablet has been eaten.

Your dog may eat around the tablet and then refuse anything else offered at a later date. By giving a small amount first, you can ensure that it has been eaten and then offer the remaining amount of food as a reward.

There are several products designed to hold tablets, which can be purchased from either your veterinary surgery or your pet shop. Alternatively, bread and butter (or a piece of cheese), with the tablet sandwiched in between, rarely fails.

You may hear advice to give tablets in snack-sized chocolate bars and there is certainly no doubt that the tablet will go down successfully, but theobromine in chocolate, especially dark chocolate, is potentially lethal to all dogs and therefore should be avoided.

Some medications are designed to be given on an empty stomach. If your dog will not take them unless coated in food, don't panic – a small amount of food is preferable to no medication at all.

If your dog refuses to eat food that has a tablet disguised in it, you will need to put the tablet directly into his mouth. It can often be useful to train your dog from an early age to accept tablets being given this way (practise using a pleasant food item, such as a dog treat).

- You may need a hand to restrain your dog. If so, get your helper to cradle your dog's head in their one arm while the other arm is gently placed around his hindquarters (get your dog to assume the sitting position).
- Place one hand across the dog's muzzle, gently inserting your thumb and forefinger into the space located behind the canines or fangs.
- With your other hand, hold the tablet between your thumb and forefinger. With your index finger, push down the lower jaw, while still keeping hold of the tablet.
- Place your hand into the dog's mouth, keeping the lower jaw pressed down, and place the tablet at the base of the tongue.
- Close your dog's mouth and gently stroke his throat to encourage him to swallow. Keep his mouth held closed until you have seen him swallow several times.

Hold the top jaw in one hand, hold the tablet in the other hand, and apply light pressure behind the canine teeth.

Some dogs are experts at holding a tablet in their mouths while appearing to have swallowed. If this is the case, have a water-filled syringe at the ready, gently tilt the head back, apply the syringe nozzle to behind the canine teeth, and administer the water.

In theory, if the tablet is placed as far back on the tongue as possible, it should go down first time. Ask your veterinarian or nurse to demonstrate if you are unsure.

Ease the mouth open, holding the tablet ready.

If you are unable to find a helper, a quiet corner can become your greatest ally when giving a pill to an unwilling patient. This will prevent him from moving backwards. Alternatively, sit behind your dog, so that his hindquarters are restrained between your knees, and administer the tablet from behind.

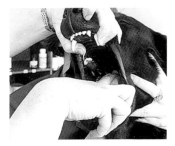

The tablet must be placed at the back of the mouth so that the dog cannot spit it out.

These are medications that are applied to external surfaces. They sometimes contain steroids, so you should always ensure that you wash your hands thoroughly after applying them, or, where possible, wear gloves.

EYES
- Gently tilt your dog's head back, holding the eye open with your thumb and forefinger.
- If using drops, apply a single drop to the centre of the eyeball.
- If using ointment, apply a thin strip to the inside lower lid.
- Allow your dog to blink to take up the medication.
- Re-apply drops if a multiple amount is required.

Don't touch the surface of the eye with the applicator nozzle. This can damage the eye surface and may introduce infection.

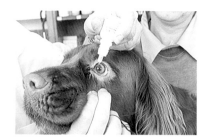

Tilt the head back, holding the eye open with your thumb and forefinger, and apply a single drop to the centre of the eyeball.

EARS
- Hold the earflap firmly in one hand.
- Using the other hand, place the nozzle of the ear-drop bottle down the ear canal.
- Apply the stated amount and remove.
- Still holding the earflap, gently massage the base of the ear.
- Take a piece of cotton wool (cotton) and wipe away any excess.

SKIN
Most dogs will tolerate the application of skin cream or ointments, but will lick them before they have had time to absorb. This can be overcome by applying the medication before a meal or a walk, thereby distracting your dog and giving ample time for absorption. Where this fails, an 'Elizabethan' or 'lampshade' collar may be the solution.

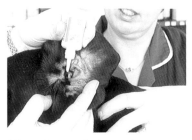

Place the nozzle down the ear canal, and apply the stated amount.

NURSING THE SICK DOG

The following is intended as a guide only, and should not replace the specific guidelines given by your veterinarian.

GENERAL CARE
- Make sure that the dog is able to go out to relieve himself every few hours, helping him to get out if necessary.
- If your dog's appetite is reduced, consider offering smaller meals of particularly tasty, tempting food. The veterinarian may suggest a special diet with the nutrients in the best balance for convalescence.
- Ensure that water is always within reach of your dog.
- If the dog is not moving about as normal, he may need a warm environment and/or heat pads to keep him warm.
- Make sure that he has somewhere quiet and peaceful to rest.
- Ensure that both the dog and his environment are kept clean.

WOUND CARE
- If the wound has been dressed by a veterinarian, leave the dressing on, or change it as instructed.
- Do not bandage too tightly and always include the paw in a limb bandage, otherwise you risk restricting blood flow.
- Modern dressings often provide a moist environment for healing to occur while removing dead tissue.

EXERCISE
Animals tend to recover from surgery more quickly than we do, and so may want to exercise as they feel better. However, it is often necessary to restrict exercise until healing has had a proper chance to occur. Follow the veterinarian's instructions carefully about the amount of exercise that is appropriate for your dog's recovery.

FOOD

Unless stipulated by your veterinarian, you should provide your sick dog with first-class proteins (e.g. chicken, fish, and eggs). These will aid repair of the body and should be given little and often throughout the day. Rice, pasta, toast etc. are low-residue foods, meaning less faeces are produced. Feeding this type of diet will prevent frequent trips to the back garden.

You may need to tempt your dog's appetite by adding chicken or fish to his meal.

STIMULATING THE APPETITE

If your dog appears uninterested in his food, there are several ways to coax him to eat.

- Warm the food slightly. This will increase the aroma, making the food more appealing.
- Add a small amount of chicken or fish to the normal food, which tempts most appetites. You should decrease the amount added as your dog's appetite returns or you may end up with a dog that will no longer eat his normal food. Chicken and fish are great for short-term use, but are not well balanced enough to sustain good nutrition by themselves.
- If the normal food is a dried, complete diet, soak it in warm water, draining off the excess after around five minutes.
- Add a meat or soya extract product to the food (e.g. Bovril, Vegemite). Adding a stronger-tasting flavour to the food may make your dog regain some of his appetite.
- Encourage your dog to eat by hand-feeding him. Again, this can become a luxury that some dogs may not want to give up. Once your dog has started eating, encourage him to continue on his own, by talking to and reassuring him.
- In extreme cases of anorexia, you may need to syringe-feed your dog. You can purchase specially-balanced foods that can be given in this way.

FLUID

Increasing fluid intake during a time of illness can help to flush toxins from the body, and can also help prevent dehydration and constipation. Glucose-based drinks are available from your veterinary surgery and may form part of the medication dispensed. These can help balance out minor body-water deficiencies in an animal that may be reluctant to eat or drink properly. If your dog is regulating his own drinking sufficiently to cope with illness, substitute his normal water with a glucose substitute. If not, syringe fluids gently into his mouth four to six times a day. Tip: clear chicken soup is highly recommended by many intensive care specialists.

WARMTH

Place your dog's bed in a quiet, draught-free area. Fleecy veterinary-type beds are ideal, as they are easy to clean and provide good warmth. Heat can be provided in several ways, but you will need to monitor your dog to ensure a comfortable temperature is maintained. With heated pads and hot-water bottles, make sure that scalding does not occur because your pet may not be able to move away from the heat source. Space blankets (made of highly reflective material to conserve heat) may well be a good investment for a long-term recumbent animal, as they reflect the dog's natural body heat without requiring an additional heat source.

If your dog is likely to remain immobile for a long period of time, a thick bed (veterinary bedding underlaid with a non-flammable foam material) is ideal. This can ▶

Warm, fleecy veterinary bedding is ideal for a canine patient.

help to prevent pressure sores from developing on bony prominences (elbows and hocks). These are areas of inflamed skin, which can ulcerate and become infected, if neglected. Preventative treatment is preferable as, once established, they can be difficult to treat.

Beanbag-type bedding can be useful to prevent pressure sores. A small shift in the bodyweight can cause changes in the distribution of the beanbag; creating a constantly changing bedding. This means that no single area is constantly under pressure at any one time.

MEDICATION
Must be given in accordance with your veterinarian's instructions (page 40).

EXERCISE/TOILETING
A sick dog's exercise is usually governed by the rate of his recovery, so devise a tailor-made regime, using common sense.

An animal with debilitated health may have little need for walks, but would benefit immensely from being led into the garden every four to six hours. Not only will this allow access for toileting, it also gives your dog some fresh air. It will allow sight, sound and smell senses to rejuvenate themselves, and generally gives your dog a pick-me-up.

Grooming is an important part of convalescent care.

During your dog's recovery, it is important to strike a balance between fresh air, rest, and mental stimulation. An active mind is often keener to repair itself than an idle one. By stimulating the body senses, you can actively encourage a sense of wellbeing.

Toileting itself should not be overlooked, and you should be certain to take your dog into the garden regularly. If he is unable to walk, place a large towel underneath his abdomen and support the rear end as he walks forwards. Good toilet hygiene is essential. The dog's perineal area and abdomen should be thoroughly washed with soap and water (do not use antiseptics), and carefully dried and dusted with talcum powder.

GROOMING
This is often overlooked in the recovering animal, but it is a good way of stimulating the senses. Regular grooming also helps to improve coat condition, which often becomes dull during times of illness.

PHYSIOTHERAPY
Physiotherapy can be a good tool in a long-term recumbent animal. Decreased exercise can result in muscle wastage, and physiotherapy works these muscle groups individually, thereby actively discouraging fatigue. You can massage leg muscles and feet to stimulate the circulation. You may need to check with your veterinarian to ensure the suitability of this for your dog's particular needs (see also Chapter Twelve).

3 FEEDING AND NUTRITION

Dogs have a common ancestry with, and are still often classified as, carnivores. However, from a nutritional point of view, they are actually omnivores. This means that they can obtain all the essential nutrients they need from animal or plant material. As far as we know, dogs can be fed a 'vegetarian' diet, provided that their protein requirements are met.

Being opportunistic eaters, dogs have developed anatomical and physiological characteristics that permit the digestion of a highly-varied diet.

THE DIGESTIVE SYSTEM

The function of the digestive system is to take in food (prehension), break it down (digestion), remove nutrients from the food (absorption), and eject the waste material (elimination). The digestive system can be divided into seven main parts:
• Mouth and teeth
• Oesophagus
• Stomach
• Small intestine (subdivided into duodenum,

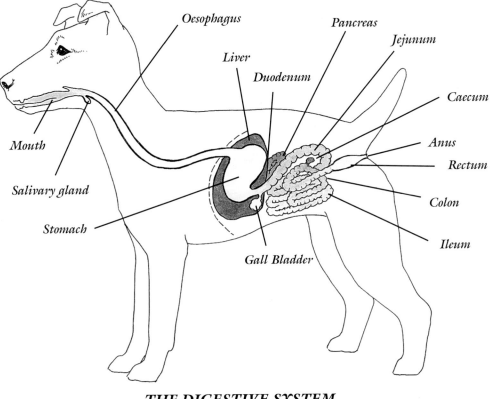

THE DIGESTIVE SYSTEM

jejunum and ileum)
- Large intestine (subdivided into caecum and colon)
- Rectum
- Anus.

MOUTH

The function of the mouth is to take in food and reduce its size. This not only aids swallowing, but it also increases the surface area of the food, which enhances the digestive process.

The tongue forms a small 'ball' of food (bolus) and pushes the food to the back of the mouth to be swallowed. As the dog chews on large pieces of food, saliva is produced. This moistens and lubricates the food and aids swallowing into the pharynx and on into the oesophagus.

See pages 20-21 for details on teeth.

OESOPHAGUS (ESOPHAGUS)

This is a muscular tube that connects the pharynx (throat) with the stomach. The presence of food within the oesophagus stimulates muscular contractions of the oesophageal wall that propel the bolus of food towards the stomach. This is termed peristalsis. The hallmark of oesophageal disease is regurgitation, often of undigested food. Hard rough foods, especially bones, can cause damage to the delicate lining of the oesophagus, and should be avoided.

STOMACH

Due to the intermittent nature of the dog's natural diet, the stomach must be able to expand markedly to accommodate the dog's entire daily food intake in one large meal. The size of the stomach varies with breed size from 1 litre (1.75 UK pints/2 US pints) to 9 litres (16 UK pints/ 19 US pints). Since the components of dog food are complex large molecules and the gut is only able to absorb small molecules all nutrients (with the exception of water and very simple substances) must be broken down into smaller molecules prior to absorption. This process is called digestion.

The digestion process begins in the stomach. The acid environment helps to activate an enzyme called pepsin, which begins the digestion of protein. However, little or no absorption of nutrients occurs within the stomach. The composition of the diet will influence the rate at which the stomach empties. This regulation of emptying ensures a constant supply of nutrients and calories to the small intestine. So, despite irregular feeding intervals, the

THE STOMACH

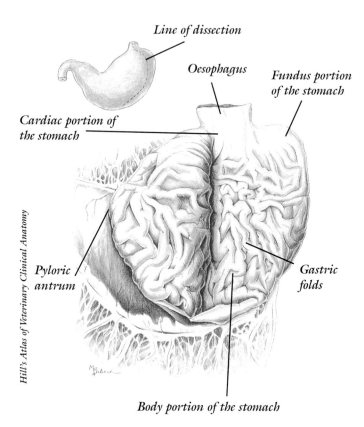

Line of dissection

Oesophagus

Fundus portion of the stomach

Cardiac portion of the stomach

Pyloric antrum

Gastric folds

Hill's Atlas of Veterinary Clinical Anatomy

Body portion of the stomach

dog has a fairly constant supply of nutrients. Diets that are very high in fat are emptied from the stomach more slowly. This can be important in breeds predisposed to bloat (see page 59).

SMALL INTESTINE

The small intestine is divided into three main parts: the duodenum, the jejunum and the ileum. Food passes from the stomach through a muscular sphincter, called the pylorus, into the first part of the small intestine (the duodenum). It is here that the vast majority of nutrient digestion and absorption occurs. The environment within the small intestine is very different from that of the stomach. The digestive enzymes working within the small intestine require an alkaline environment; hence the hydrochloric acid from the stomach is neutralised by bicarbonate produced by the pancreas.

To improve absorption, the surface area of the small intestine is very large. This is achieved partly by the sheer length of the small bowel, but also by the fact that the intestinal wall is thrown into a series

THE SMALL INTESTINE

THE COLON

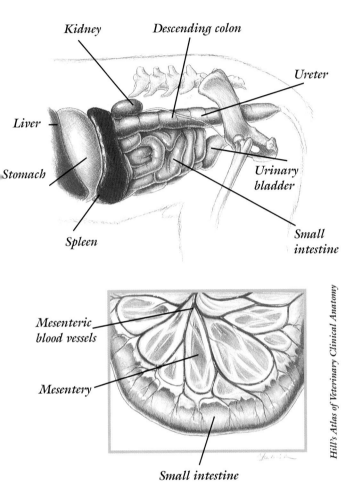

Kidney

Descending colon

Ureter

Liver

Stomach

Urinary bladder

Spleen

Small intestine

Mesenteric blood vessels

Mesentery

Small intestine

Hill's Atlas of Veterinary Clinical Anatomy

CROSS SECTION OF THE SMALL INTESTINE

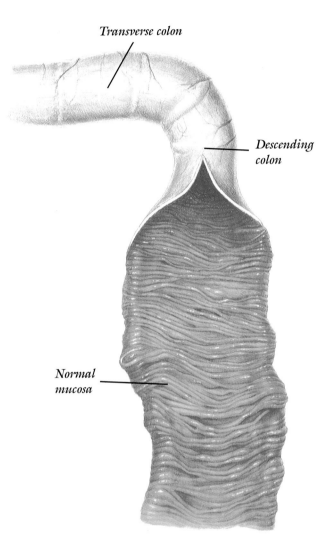

Transverse colon

Descending colon

Normal mucosa

of folds (called villi), which are like fingers. The surface of each of these 'fingers' is covered with even smaller folds called microvilli. Under the microscope these microvilli look like hairs and are called the 'brush border'.

LARGE INTESTINE

The main function of the large intestine is the absorption of water and electrolytes (salts) from the faeces. The last part of the large intestine (the rectum) is adapted to lubricate the faeces with mucus, which allows easier defecation. The rectum is lined with cells that produce this mucus. When a dog has an inflamed large bowel (colitis), mucus is

often overproduced and can be seen in the faeces (like jelly).

The speed at which the faeces pass through the large bowel can determine their consistency. If they move too rapidly, there is little time for the water to be absorbed and so the dog will have diarrhoea. If they move too slowly, then nearly all the water is absorbed and the faeces will be dry and hard to pass (the dog will be constipated). This rate is called the transition time and can be influenced by the level of fibre in the diet. Fibre is insoluble (indigestible) carbohydrate. If the transition time is too rapid, fibre can slow it down, and, if the transition time is too slow, fibre can act to speed it up.

NUTRITIONAL REQUIREMENTS

Diet is an important part in maintaining optimum health, and research into canine nutrition has allowed the development of diets for different breeds and activities of individual dogs. The correct diet plays a major role in producing a healthy puppy, in maintaining the health of an adult dog and in the management of many diseases.

NUTRIENTS

A nutrient is any food component that helps to support life. A balanced diet contains the correct levels of all nutrients. Any nutrient required by the dog, and that cannot be synthesised in the body, is called an essential nutrient. It must be present in the diet. If any essential nutrient is missing, or present at too low a level, then the diet as a whole is inadequate.

Nutrients are divided into six basic classes:
- Protein (page 49)
- Fat (page 49)
- Carbohydrate (page 50)
- Minerals (page 50)
- Vitamins (page 51)
- Water (page 52).

ENERGY

In addition to providing specific nutrients, food also provides energy. Energy in dog food is measured in kilocalories (kcal).

The energy content of the diet is derived solely from the fats, proteins and carbohydrates, and the proportion of these energy-producing nutrients in the diet will determine its energy content (or energy density).

Dietary fat supplies $2\frac{1}{4}$ times as much energy per gram as protein or carbohydrate, and so high-fat diets are high-energy diets. Water has no energy value and so a diet with high moisture content will contain a low energy density.

A dog's energy intake must be controlled carefully, since excess energy can lead to obesity and growth abnormalities, but inadequate energy intake leads to poor growth and weight loss.

Dogs eat to satisfy their energy requirements unless a diet is excessively palatable – in which case overeating may occur. In a balanced diet, when a dog has consumed the correct amount to meet his energy needs, the requirements for all other nutrients should also have been met.

Each dog has unique and individual energy requirements that vary according to:

- Age
- Breed
- Sex
- Activity level
- Reproductive status
- Environment
- Health status.

CALCULATING YOUR DOG'S ENERGY REQUIREMENTS

The basal energy requirement (BER) is the amount of energy expended while asleep, 12-18 hours after feeding in a thermoneutral environment (where the dog does not have to pant to lose heat, or shiver to gain heat).

The maintenance energy requirement (MER) is the amount of energy required by a moderately active animal in its daily search for and utilisation of food. It does not include the energy required for growth, repair, pregnancy, lactation or work.

To calculate your dog's BER, multiply his body weight (in kg) by 30 and add on 70. MER in dogs is approximately twice that of BER (for dogs over 2 kg).

DAILY MAINTENANCE ENERGY REQUIREMENTS

Dog's weight in		Kcals needed	
kgs	lbs	kgs	lbs
3	6.6	110	242
6	13.2	85	187
10	22.0	75	165
>25	55.0	65	143

Conditions	Energy requirements
Full day's work	1.5 x MER
Gestation (last 3 weeks)	1.3 x MER
Peak lactation	2 to 4 x MER
0-3 months old	2 x MER
Sub-freezing temperatures	1.7 x MER
Tropical heat	2.5 x MER
Resting	0.8 x MER
Obesity	0.6 x MER
Geriatric	0.6 x MER

CALCULATING ENERGY DENSITY

By knowing your dog's daily energy requirements, you can calculate how much of a certain food you should be feeding per day. The table below shows you how to calculate the energy content in each ration of food. Remember, the energy in the diet is only provided by the protein, fat and carbohydrate. Most manufacturers will have already done this calculation for you, and this forms the basis of the feeding guide found on the bag or can of food. Remember, this is only a guide; you should adjust the amount you feed your dog to achieve and maintain optimum body weight and condition, since all dogs are individuals.

Analysis	Per cent of nutrient	Multiply	Kcal/g	Total Kcal/100g
Protein	22	X	3.5	77
Fat	9.0	X	8.7	78.3
Fibre	3.0	X	0	0
Moisture	10	X	0	0
Ash	5.0	X	0	0
Carbohydrate	51	X	3.5	178.5
TOTAL				333.8

FOOD GROUPS

PROTEINS

Proteins consist of many amino acids. The quality of a protein varies with the number and amount of essential amino acids it contains. The quality of a protein is referred to as its biological value.

There are only 23 amino acids but they can be arranged in any combination. This creates an almost infinite variety of naturally occurring proteins, each with its own characteristic properties, e.g. hair, skin, muscle, hormones, antibodies. A dog needs all 23 amino acids but only 10 are termed essential, meaning they must be provided in the dog's diet. If these are present, then the remaining 13 amino acids can be synthesised. The essential amino acids are:

- Phenylalanine
- Valine
- Tryptophan
- Threonine
- Isoleucine
- Methionine
- Histidine
- Arginine
- Leucine
- Lysine.

Proteins are essential components of all living cells. They have several functions, including the regulation of metabolism and a structural role in the production of cell walls and muscle fibres. They are important for tissue growth and repair and so the protein requirement is greatest in the young, growing puppy or following an injury or illness.

Proteins may also be used as a source of energy in the diet, but exercise and work do not increase a dog's protein requirement. In fact, feeding excess protein may be more detrimental. Very active dogs actually need more fat or carbohydrate and *not* more protein.

Dietary protein in excess of the dog's requirements cannot be laid down as muscle but is broken down by the liver (through a process called deamination). The waste product of protein breakdown is urea. This is transported to the kidneys for excretion in the urine. Excess dietary protein may therefore be damaging to dogs with liver and kidney problems – hence the control of dietary protein is prudent in the ageing dog.

Protein deficiency is very rare as most dogs are fed commercial dog food that contains a plentiful supply of protein. However, if the dog has a very unusual home-made diet, or he is not consuming enough food to obtain his required level, then a deficiency could occur. Signs of protein deficiency include:

- Poor growth or weight loss
- Dull coat
- Muscle wasting
- Increased susceptibility to disease
- Oedema (fluid under the skin, in the abdomen, or in the lungs).

FATS

Fats are required in the diet for many reasons:

- To provide energy
- To aid absorption of the fat-soluble vitamins (A, D, E, and K)
- To enhance palatability
- As a source of essential fatty acids.

Inadequate dietary fat may lead to fatty acid deficiency and/or energy deficiency. There are three essential fatty acids:
• Linoleic acid
• Arachidonic acid
• Linolenic acid.

Fatty acids are needed as constituents of cell membranes, for the synthesis of certain chemicals needed by the body, and for controlling water loss through the skin. Essential fatty acid deficiency may result in impaired reproductive performance, impaired wound healing, a dry coat, and scaly skin. This can predispose the skin to bacterial infection and eczema 'hot spots'. Essential fatty acid deficiency occurs most commonly in dogs receiving low-fat, dry dog foods containing beef tallow, or dry food that has been stored too long, especially under warm or humid conditions. Fatty acids become rancid and lose their nutritional value. This oxidation is hastened by high temperatures and humidity. Oxidation of fats is prevented by the inclusion of substances called antioxidants, such as vitamin E.

CARBOHYDRATES

There are three main groups of carbohydrates:
• Monosaccharides (e.g. glucose, fructose)
• Disaccharides (e.g. maltose, sucrose, lactose)
• Polysaccharides (e.g. starch, glycogen and fibre).

Carbohydrates provide the body with energy, which can be converted to body fat. All dogs have a metabolic requirement for glucose, but, provided the diet contains sufficient glucose precursors (substances which can be converted to glucose, such as amino acids and glycerol), they can synthesise enough glucose to meet their metabolic needs, without dietary carbohydrate.

DIETARY FIBRE

Dietary fibre, or roughage, consists of a group of indigestible polysaccharides (carbohydrates) such as cellulose, lignin and pectin. They are the main constituents of plant cell walls and are relatively indigestible within the gut of dogs. The role of fibre in the diet is to provide bulk to the faeces, regularising bowel movements and helping to prevent constipation and diarrhoea. Fibre also has therapeutic uses in the treatment of fibre-responsive diseases. Since fibre is largely indigestible, it decreases the energy content of the diet and so has a role in the correction and prevention of obesity.

MINERALS

Minerals are sometimes referred to as 'ash'. You may find this term used on pet food labels. Minerals are divided into macro-minerals, which are needed in larger amounts, and trace elements, which are needed in smaller amounts.

Macro-minerals	Trace elements
Calcium	Iron
Phosphorus	Copper
Magnesium	Zinc
Sodium	Cobalt
Chloride	Selenium
Potassium	Iodine

Electrolytes are minerals in their salt form and these are found in body tissues and fluids. The absorption of different minerals is often linked, so that an excess intake of one mineral can lead to a deficiency of another. This is important, since supplementation of one mineral can cause deficiency of another.

CALCIUM AND PHOSPHORUS

Calcium and phosphorus are the major minerals involved in maintaining structural rigidity, as they are components of bone and teeth. The minimum

Excess calcium can be responsible for skeletal abnormalities, such as Wobbler Syndrome, a condition seen in some Dobermanns.

ratio of calcium and phosphorus for growth is 1:1. Imbalance in this ratio leads to skeletal deformities.

Calcium deficiency occurs most commonly in diets that are high in phosphorus (high meat and offal diets) and in lactating bitches it can cause eclampsia (see Chapter Nine). Calcium excess most commonly occurs when additional calcium supplementation is added to a growth-type diet for large-breed puppies. Many skeletal abnormalities have been attributed in part to excess calcium, including osteochondrosis (OCD) and hip dysplasia (see Chapter Four), and 'Wobbler' Syndrome (see Chapter Seven).

MAGNESIUM

Magnesium is required for the normal function of heart and skeletal muscle. Magnesium deficiency can cause muscular weakness but it is very rare, seen only in dogs fed inadequate home-made diets.

SODIUM AND CHLORIDE

Sodium and chloride are the major electrolytes in the body water. They are needed for acid/base balance and for the regulation of the concentration of body fluids. A deficiency can arise from excessive fluid loss, such as occurs in vomiting and diarrhoea. Signs include exhaustion, an inability to control water balance, dry skin and hair loss.

When selecting a food it is prudent to meet, but not significantly exceed, both sodium and chloride requirements. This is because uncontrolled high blood pressure may lead to kidney, eye, brain, and heart disease. A food containing 0.15-0.4 per cent sodium, on a dry matter basis, will meet but not exceed the recommended intake level. Some commercial foods exceed this recommended level and are best avoided. An excess will cause an increased fluid intake and may predispose dogs to high blood pressure (hypertension) and therefore heart and kidney problems.

IRON, COPPER AND ZINC

Iron is an essential component of haemoglobin (the oxygen-carrying pigment of the blood), and myoglobin (the oxygen-carrying pigment found within muscle). Iron deficiency causes anaemia and fatigue. It may occur if milk is fed to pups for too long or as a secondary complication following severe blood loss.

Copper is needed for the formation of red blood cells and in the normal pigmentation of skin and hair. Copper deficiency may occur when zinc and iron are in excess. Copper toxicity, due to an inherited condition, occurs mainly in Bedlington

Terriers, West Highland White Terriers and Dobermanns. These breeds are prone to a defect that causes liver disease (cirrhosis) and elevated copper levels.

Zinc maintains a healthy skin and coat. High-calcium diets can increase a dog's need for zinc. The most common presentation of zinc deficiency is poor skin, hyperkeratosis (skin-thickening and crusting, especially of the nose and pads) and a sparse coat.

POTASSIUM

This is the most abundant mineral within the cells, and the third most abundant in the body. Potassium has a number of functions, including:
• Maintaining acid/base balance
• Maintaining water balance
• Aiding muscle contractions
• Transmitting nerve impulses.
Potassium is not stored in the body and must be provided daily in the diet. Excess intake is very rare (unless excretion by the kidney is impaired). The recommended daily intake for dogs is 0.6 per cent dry matter basis (DMB) in all life stages. Rich sources of potassium include soya and grain.

VITAMINS

Vitamins can be divided into two main groups. The water-soluble vitamins are the B-complex, and vitamin C. The fat-soluble vitamins are A, D, E, and K.

Most vitamins cannot be synthesised in the body and so must be present in the diet. Since the water-soluble vitamins are readily lost via urine and are poorly stored in the body, a daily supply must be available in the diet. Fat-soluble vitamins are more readily stored and so a daily intake is not so important. However, toxicity arising from excessive intake of fat-soluble vitamins is more common.

There is not any daily dietary requirement for vitamin C (ascorbic acid) in dogs since they can synthesise all they require from glucose.

FUNCTIONS OF COMMON VITAMINS

Vitamin	Main function
A	Vision
D	Absorption of calcium from gut
E	Antioxidant
K	Blood-clotting
B-complex	Many varied functions

If a dog is dehydrated, the skin will stay in a ridge when it is lifted up.

WATER

Water is the most important nutrient of all, making up about 70 per cent of a dog's body weight. Dogs can lose almost all their fat and half their protein and they will still survive. However, a 15 per cent loss of body water would result in death. It is vital that good-quality water should always be available, except when a dog is persistently vomiting.

Water is needed for many different functions including:
- Temperature regulation
- Saliva production
- Replacing water lost in breathing
- Maintaining blood volume
- Dissolving nutrients into a solution to allow absorption
- Production of urine and hence removal of toxic waste products from the body
- Milk production in the lactating bitch.

There are several factors that can increase water intake. These include:
- Habit
- Increased salt intake (especially salty treats)
- Increased water losses (e.g. bleeding, diarrhoea, lactation, increased body temperature).

The amount of water a dog should consume per day in millilitres is roughly equivalent to his daily energy intake in kilocalories. For example, 2000 ml (70 fl oz) of water should be consumed on a 2000-calorie diet.

LIFESTAGE NUTRITION

The concept of lifestage nutrition is now widely accepted as the optimum method for feeding dogs. The days of feeding a single proprietary food from 'womb to tomb' are long gone, and most people agree that different lifestages have differing nutritional requirements. There are even specialised foods for larger breed dogs, and foods marketed as being most suitable for a single breed have recently been launched in the US.

The five main lifestages are:
- Growth
- Adult maintenance
- Neutered/Light/Less active
- Performance or active
- Senior.

FEEDING THE GROWING PUPPY

Achieving optimum growth in a puppy is a great step towards achieving a healthy adult dog. Optimum growth is a balance between the puppy's genetics, the environment, and nutrition. Puppies need relatively more energy, protein, calcium and phosphorus than adult dogs (i.e. in relation to their body weight) but too much of any one of these nutrients can be harmful. When it comes to nutrition, more is not better!

ENERGY

Growing puppies need twice as much dietary energy, on a per-kilogram basis, as do adults. This need is greatest just after birth and then decreases as the dog matures. Excessive dietary energy may support a growth rate that is too fast for proper bone development, resulting in an increased frequency of skeletal disorders in the large and giant breeds. Because fat has twice the calorie density of protein or carbohydrate, dietary fat is the primary contributor to excess energy intake.

Not only does excess energy result in rapid growth, but dietary energy in excess of the puppy's needs will be stored as fat and hence predispose the dog to juvenile obesity. Fat puppies will increase the number of fat cells they have (called fat cell hyperplasia) and are then predisposed to obesity for the rest of their lives.

Body condition scoring (BCS) evaluates body-fat stores, confirming if the energy intake is suitable. Maintaining a proper BCS during growth not only avoids juvenile obesity but also helps to control excessive growth rates. Limiting food intake, while avoiding deficiencies, to maintain a lean body condition will not impede a dog's ultimate genetic potential, but it will reduce food intake, faecal output, and obesity, as well as lessening the risk of skeletal disease.

ENERGY REQUIREMENTS

Energy requirements for the healthy adult dog are, of course, highly individual, but they are largely affected by the individual's:
• Breed
• Activity level
• Sex
• Age
• Environment.

The amount of food fed (and therefore the calorie or energy intake) should be varied to achieve a healthy, lean body condition.

FAT REQUIREMENTS

The minimum amount needed for healthy adult dogs is at least 5 per cent DMB (dry matter basis), with at least 1 per cent DMB being linoleic acid (an essential fatty acid for dogs). By increasing the amount of fat in the food, palatability can be enhanced and the essential fatty acid level increases. This can be beneficial in improving skin and coat condition.

PROTEIN

Although puppies need more protein than adult dogs, any protein in excess of what is needed for growth may be converted to energy, and so increase the growth rate. Protein deficiency during growth has been shown to be harmful. The minimum,

Good nutrition plays an important part in achieving optimum growth in puppies.

adequate level of dietary protein will depend upon its digestibility, its amino-acid profile, and its ratio of essential amino acids. A growth food should contain at least 22 per cent protein (on a dry matter basis) of high biological value. Once the puppy reaches maturity, this level may be reduced.

The amount of protein in commercial foods for healthy, adult dogs varies widely (15 to 60 per cent DMB). Once the individual's amino-acid requirements are met, there is no benefit to be gained from additional protein. Remember that excess protein, above the amino-acid requirement, is not stored as protein, but is detoxified by the liver and kidneys. A food containing protein levels of 15-30 per cent DMB, will provide adequate protein for the healthy, adult dog.

MINERALS

The intake of too much calcium is more common than the intake of too little. This is because of the tendency to overfeed and to supplement the diet with additional minerals and vitamins in the form of powders, tablets and capsules. Adding high-calcium foods (such as milk, bone meal, and treats) also affects the growth ratio.

A high intake of calcium has the effect of inhibiting the natural remodelling process of bone that has to occur during development in response to the changing stresses on the skeleton. Over-nutrition may result in skeletal disorders in adulthood, especially in large breeds.

Optimum skeletal development for a puppy is achieved by feeding a minimum level of 1 per cent calcium on a dry matter basis. This level is desirable for larger-breed puppies whose adult body weight will be more than 25 kgs (55 lbs). For smaller-breed puppies the maximum recommended level is 2.5 per cent.

FEEDING METHODS

FREE-CHOICE FEEDING

This is an effortless way to feed growing puppies. Frequent trips to the always-full food bowl may help to limit boredom. Timid or non-thrifty animals have less competition when eating, as they can choose to feed at quieter times. However, free-choice feeding encourages overeating, which increases the risk of developmental bone diseases. Therefore, free-choice feeding methods are not recommended for all 'at-risk' breeds until they have reached skeletal maturity (12-18 months of age, or at least 80 per cent of their adult weight and height).

The at-risk breeds include: Bernese Mountain Dog, Bulldog, German Shepherd Dog, Golden Retriever, Great Dane, Labrador Retriever, Mastiff, Rottweiler, and crosses involving these breeds.

TIME-LIMITED FEEDING

This feeding method can be used for most breeds. The food is only available for a set period two or three times daily, leading to a reduced intake in most breeds. This slightly reduced intake results in slower growth rates but does not diminish the adult size achieved. Close attention should still be paid to the total amount of food consumed, since certain individuals (greedy feeders) are still able to consume large amounts of food during this limited time period. If this method is chosen, it is recommended to allow three 5- to 10-minute feeding periods for the first month after weaning, reducing to two per day after that.

FOOD-LIMITED FEEDING

This is the best method for feeding puppies to maintain optimum growth rate and body condition. Food-limited feeding involves giving a measured amount of food based on a calculated energy requirement. This will have been done by the manufacturer and is indicated in the feeding guide.

Clinical monitoring of growth and adjustment of feeding amount are critical. Large- and giant-breed dogs grow rapidly and thus have steep growth

Weighing out rations ensures your puppy maintains good growth and body condition.

curves. Their intake should be monitored closely and will have to be adjusted more frequently than that for dogs of smaller breeds. These at-risk breeds should be weighed, evaluated and have their feeding amount adjusted every two weeks. This is still an uncommon approach to feeding many puppies. Many owners do not want the bother of calculating feeding amounts on such a regular basis, but in many cases it can be a valuable step towards a healthier puppy.

Regardless of a food's nutrient profile and how it is fed, the ultimate measurement of appropriate intake is the physical condition of the puppy. The ribs should be palpable with a thin layer of fat between the skin and the bone. The bony prominences should be easily felt with a slight amount of overlying fat. Animals over six months of age should have a pronounced abdominal tuck when viewed from the side and a well-proportioned lumbar waist when viewed from above.

Nutritional management alone will not control developmental bone diseases since they are multi-factorial and include the dog's genetic make-up. However, skeletal diseases can be influenced during growth by feeding technique and nutrient profile. Dietary deficiencies are of minimal concern now that most dogs consume commercial foods specifically prepared for young, growing dogs. The potential harm comes from over-nutrition – from excess consumption and oversupplementation. It is not only important to feed the appropriate food, but to feed the food appropriately.

FEEDING THE ADULT DOG

Depending upon the breed, adult dogs are those that are fully grown (over about 14 months old) but not yet 'seniors' (7.5-12 years). The role of the diet in the healthy adult dog is to maintain a healthy, shiny coat and to maximise longevity and quality of life.

ORAL HEALTH

Periodontal (dental) disease is the most common disease in dogs of this age. It is a common myth that simply by feeding a dry food, oral health is improved. Typical dry dog foods actually contribute very little to dental cleansing and bones break more teeth than they clean. Regular dental checks should be carried out by your veterinarian, and tooth-brushing should be part of your dog's regular routine (pages 20-21). Research has demonstrated that feeding a maintenance dog food with specific textural and process properties (Hill's*Prescription

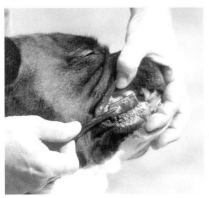

Tooth-brushing should form part of your dog's regular grooming routine.

Diet* Canine t/d*) can significantly decrease plaque and tartar accumulation and help in maintaining oral health.

FEEDING THE NEUTERED DOG

Obesity occurs twice as often in neutered and spayed dogs as in 'entire' ones. Very little is known about why this is so. Spaying does not have a marked impact on the resting energy requirements (RER) of female dogs, but it may increase food intake, possibly due to a reduction in the activity of the appetite-suppressing hormone oestrogen.

A decrease in activity is also thought to occur in most dogs after neutering. This may play an important role in the onset of obesity in neutered males, since they will have a decreased tendency to roam.

The daily energy intake of neutered dogs should be lowered to prevent rapid weight gain. Levels of 0.6 x MER are suitable starting points, but some breeds and individuals may need even lower levels.

Many manufacturers produce diets suitable for obesity control, marketed as 'light/lite' diets. Those based on a decreased fat intake, but increased crude fibre level (to maintain satiety), can be very successful.

FEEDING THE SENIOR DOG

The ability to respond to dietary changes decreases with age, and the daily food ration of older pets should meet nutritional requirements more rigorously and consistently than food given to younger animals.

Many factors, such as genetics, exercise and environment, combine within one individual dog to determine how rapidly the ageing process advances, and nutrition is another important factor.

WHEN IS A DOG OLD?

The chart below is a guide to the age at which dogs are often considered to be geriatric (see table at bottom of page).

Small-breed dogs live significantly longer than large and giant breeds. One survey revealed a 12:1 ratio of small- to large-breed dogs at the age of 17 years or more. We can consider a dog as being older around the time he reaches half of his life expectancy. Therefore, a change of diet (to a 'senior' variety) would be considered around the age of five for large- and giant-breed dogs and around seven years for small dogs.

Careful nutritional management can help to keep a veteran in peak condition.

Size of dog	Weight (lbs)	Weight (kgs)	Age in years
Small	0-20	0-9	11.5 +/- 1.9
Medium	21-50	9.5-23	10.2 +/- 1.6
Large	51-90	23-41	8.9 +/- 1.4
Giant	>90	>41	7.5 +/- 1.3

It is important to consider that older dogs are a mixed population and that we cannot make a single dietary recommendation for aged dogs in general. It is good advice to carefully monitor food intake in very old dogs, since, in very old people, it is known that low food intake increases the risk of vitamin and trace-element deficiencies. Feeding smaller meals frequently increases nutrient utilisation and may improve food intake.

PROTEIN REQUIREMENTS

Protein requirements of elderly dogs are controversial. Lean body mass decreases with age, and muscle mass is replaced by fat. Many older dogs may have early kidney problems, and, by controlling protein, the intake of phosphorus is also controlled. Reducing the phosphorus intake in dogs with kidney disease slows the rate at which the kidneys deteriorate. A diet containing 18 to 20 per cent protein (percentage DMB), of good quality and digestibility, will provide sufficient protein.

ZINC

Zinc acts as an essential cofactor in more than 100 enzymes of protein metabolism, and zinc supplementation has been associated with enhanced immune response. One study showed that blood levels of zinc and copper start decreasing in dogs over 7.5 years of age, and age may influence the blood levels by up to 20 per cent. This may indicate a decrease in availability of zinc or an increase in losses, resulting in higher nutritional needs. When a food is given with high levels of calcium, phosphorus, phytates, or certain soluble fibres, the zinc availability may be decreased even further. Zinc should be considered whenever dietary supplementation of ageing dogs is contemplated. Please note: over-zealous mineral supplementation could be dangerous, so seek veterinary advice before giving supplements.

FAT

A relatively low fat content would be beneficial to prevent obesity in middle-aged dogs. Later in life, however, old dogs show a tendency to lose weight. Therefore, a good balance should be maintained between prevention of obesity and providing enough calories. As a general guide, the diet for an older dog should contain a minimum of 10 per cent (DMB) fat, with a maximum of 20 per cent (DMB).

FIBRE

The intestinal transit time may be prolonged in older animals, and constipation is one of the most common digestive complaints in older dogs. Increasing the fibre content of the diet can help to correct the transit time. Cellulose has the advantage that it affects availability of both minerals and trace elements (especially copper and zinc) to a lesser extent than other fibre sources (such as beet pulp and pea fibre). This is important for older dogs, who may already have a higher need for trace elements.

CALCIUM AND PHOSPHORUS

Osteoporosis, similar to the condition in humans, is not common in dogs. Degenerative joint disease is a more common, typical geriatric condition, and may be secondary to excessive weight gain and chronic repeated low-grade trauma. It is therefore important to monitor body weight and to prevent obesity in older dogs.

There is no special need for calcium or vitamin D_3 in older dogs. A food that offers a correct level for adult maintenance and the correct calcium: phosphorus ratio will meet the needs of older dogs. However, because of a possible decrease in kidney function, older dogs may already have higher blood levels of phosphorus, and excesses of both minerals, but particularly of phosphorus, should be avoided. For older dogs, a food with relatively low levels of phosphorus (around 0.5 per cent) and a correct calcium: phosphorus ratio (page 50) is recommended.

SODIUM

There is no nutritional need for the levels of sodium found in some pet foods today. This is even more important for older and geriatric dogs, in which the incidence of clinical heart disease is relatively high, and increases with age. High blood pressure may be more common than previously expected. Hypertension becomes particularly important in animals affected by diseases that are more frequently seen in older dogs, such as obesity and chronic renal disease.

The minimum requirement for sodium in dogs is around 4 mg per kg BW (body weight), whereas the recommended amount for adult dogs is generally stated between 25 and 50 mg per kg BW, or 6 to 12 times more. Many dog foods given to older dogs provide up to more than 160 mg per kg BW. An older dog should not receive more than the recommended intakes of 25 to 50 mg per kg BW, provided by a food that contains approximately 0.2 to 0.35 per cent sodium DMB.

VITAMINS

Dogs receiving a complete and balanced commercial pet food are unlikely to become deficient of any vitamin. Home-made diets may be low in vitamins if they are not supplemented. Because of the increased risk of excessive drinking due to kidney disease, diabetes mellitus, or hyperadrenocorticism (Cushing's Disease), it may be a good idea to increase the dietary intake of water-soluble vitamins in older dogs.

ALTERNATIVE EATING

- **Rubbish eating**: This is probably a normal behaviour, and many dogs prefer decomposed food. There is a possibility that it may be unhealthy due to ingestion of toxins, so prevent access to garbage.
- **Grass eating**: Grass eating is a normal behaviour.
- **Begging for food**: Encouraging begging behaviour often leads not only to antisocial behaviour, but also to overfeeding the dog, and obesity. Begging can be difficult to stop but it must be ignored. Keep your dog out of the room when you are preparing and eating food.
- **Pica**: If a dog develops a perverted appetite (i.e. he craves non-food items), it may be due to mineral deficiencies, blood disorders, organ failure, toxicity, or anxiety. Veterinary advice should be sought.
- **Coprophagy**: This involves the dog eating his own or other animals' stools. Bitches normally eat their puppies' faeces during the first three weeks of life. Coprophagy can be responsible for the spread of dangerous diseases, such as parvovirus, parasites, and bacterial disease.

CLINICAL NUTRITION

In modern veterinary practices, dietary management plays an important role in treating many clinical conditions. Proprietary dog foods are now available to aid in the management of many canine diseases.

OBESITY

More than 50 per cent of dogs are over their optimum body weight. Obesity increases the risk of the dog developing many other diseases and conditions, including:
- Skeletal problems (especially intervertebral disc rupture, cruciate rupture, osteoarthritis)
- Increased surgical and anaesthetic risk

Most veterinary surgeries hold weight-loss clinics, and the results can be dramatic.

This overweight poodle looks a different animal after shedding excess pounds.

- Respiratory problems
- Decreased exercise tolerance
- Cardiovascular disease (especially hypertension, thromboembolism)
- Skin disease (especially in the folds of fat by the vulva, the axilla or armpit, and the pinnae or earflaps)
- Diabetes mellitus
- Lower life expectancy
- Poor quality of life.

There are many factors that contribute to the development of obesity:
- Temperament
- Environment
- Age
- Sex
- Neutering
- Activity level
- Juvenile obesity (a 'roly-poly' puppy develops extra fat cells, which leave him prone to obesity for life)
- Breed (certain breeds are known to be genetically predisposed to obesity)
- Metabolic diseases (e.g. hypothyroidism)
- Feeding practices (e.g. flavour rotations, human food, treats, ad-lib feeding methods).

However, the simple fact is that an excessive intake of calories will lead to excess energy being stored as fat. Clinical diets, used for the management of obesity, usually restrict calorie intake by reducing fat and increasing fibre intake (to about 17-15 per cent DMB). This additional fibre does not contribute calories but provides a satisfying 'full-up' feeling. This helps to prevent begging and can maintain owner co-operation.

Recent research has shown that obese dogs benefit from diets containing supplemental L-carnitine. This water-soluble amino-acid cofactor speeds up the rate of weight reduction by facilitating the use of fat in the production of energy.

DENTAL DISEASE

Dental disease is an epidemic among dogs. It is estimated that some 80 per cent of dogs over the age of three have dental disease that requires veterinary treatment within 12 months.

Dental disease causes tooth loss, dental abscesses, oral pain and systemic bacteraemia (bacteria in the bloodstream). This can cause secondary systemic disease, such as heart and kidney problems (Chapter Five). Cosmetic consequences of dental disease include loss of those teeth required to maintain a

normal facial appearance, and halitosis. In addition, teeth impart considerable strength to the jaws, so loss of teeth therefore weakens the jawbone, increasing the risk of fractures.

The clinical signs of dental disease include:
- Halitosis (bad breath)
- Plaque
- Stained teeth
- Tartar
- Gingivitis (sore or bleeding gums)
- Oral pain
- Poor chewing of food
- Loose teeth
- Swelling under the eye (abscess).

The treatment of dental diseases involves mechanical cleansing (scaling) by a veterinary professional. Anaesthesia, assessment of teeth, scaling and polishing and surgical manipulation of teeth and gums may be required. Follow-up treatment may involve antibiotics and painkillers.

TOOTH CARE

Regular home care is essential (see pages 20-21). Hill's *Prescription Diet* Canine t/d is designed to reduce the build-up of plaque, stain and tartar by wiping the surface of the tooth clean each time the dog eats. Its larger kibble size has also been shown to reduce gingivitis and halitosis.

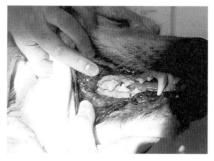

Severe build-up of tartar on the teeth.

KIDNEY DISEASE

Kidney disease is a common problem, especially in older dogs, and it is a major cause of illness and death. By controlling the intake of protein, phosphorus and sodium, the severity of the clinical signs can be decreased, and both the quality and length of life improved.

GASTROINTESTINAL DISEASE

There are many different types of gastrointestinal disease depending on which part of the gastrointestinal tract is primarily affected. These include:

GASTRITIS

This is an inflammation of the stomach. Dogs vomit readily as a protective mechanism against this condition, which is due to their natural scavenging nature. If they eat spoiled or rancid food, they are able to vomit and so prevent illness. This is not a problem in the wild dog, but it can be a concern when the dog decides to vomit on your new carpet!

BLOAT

This acute condition of the stomach is often fatal. It is also called gastric dilatation and volvulus (GDVC). It commonly affects large, deep-chested breeds, especially the following breeds: Boxer, Great Dane, Gordon Setter, Irish Setter, Irish Wolfhound, St. Bernard, Standard Poodle, Weimaraner.

The cause is unknown but risk factors include:
- Increasing age (dogs over 7 are twice as likely to succumb)
- Obesity
- Body conformation (particularly a narrow, deep chest in Irish Setters and a narrow, deep abdomen in Great Danes)
- Diet (especially high-cereal diets)
- Stress
- Aerophagia (swallowing air during eating)
- Lax gastric ligaments (large volume, bulky cereal-based diets may predispose to this)
- Over-drinking (again, this may stretch the stomach ligaments)
- Post-prandial exercise (exercise just after eating).

Dilatation (enlargement of the stomach due to the accumulation of gas) precedes volvulus (twisting of the stomach). Following dilatation, the stomach wall and muscle undergo potentially irreversible damage due to a lack of blood supply. Treatment of GDVC involves immediate decompression, surgical

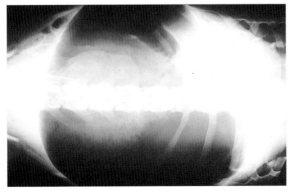

X-ray showing gastric dilatation.

GASTRIC DILATATION WITH TORSION

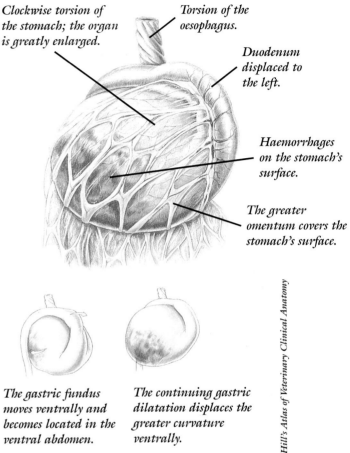

Clockwise torsion of the stomach; the organ is greatly enlarged.

Torsion of the oesophagus.

Duodenum displaced to the left.

Haemorrhages on the stomach's surface.

The greater omentum covers the stomach's surface.

The gastric fundus moves ventrally and becomes located in the ventral abdomen.

The continuing gastric dilatation displaces the greater curvature ventrally.

Hill's Atlas of Veterinary Clinical Anatomy

correction of the twisted stomach, and fluid therapy to counter the shock. This situation is a true veterinary emergency.

It is controversial whether diet affects the incidence of recurrence. Most experts recommend feeding a meat-based, canned, highly digestible diet at least three times daily. Avoidance of post-prandial exercise and competitive feeding may also help reduce aerophagia. At-risk dogs should not be competitively fed, as this may increase the ingestion of air. Very greedy dogs should have a large stone placed in the feeding dish to slow down the feeding rate. Some people also advocate soaking dry food prior to feeding, again to help slow down the rate of eating.

ENTERITIS

This is an inflammation of the small intestine. The most common sign of small intestinal disease is diarrhoea, and gut rest is the classic treatment. A short (24-48 hour) period of starvation, during

CHRONIC COLITIS

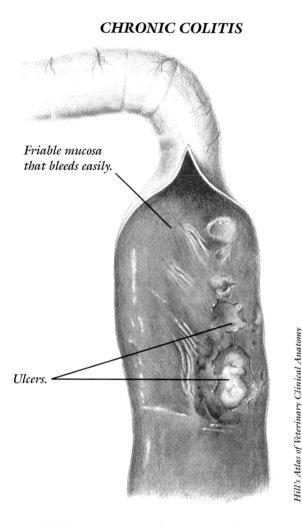

Friable mucosa that bleeds easily.

Ulcers.

Hill's Atlas of Veterinary Clinical Anatomy

which fluids are given (either orally or into the vein), is followed by small, low-fat, highly digestible meals.

As the diarrhoea improves, the dog can be slowly transitioned back on to the normal diet (over a 5- to 7-day period). If the diarrhoea does not resolve in 48 hours, veterinary advice should be sought to obtain a correct diagnosis.

COLITIS

The most common clinical signs of colitis (inflammation of the large intestine) are watery diarrhoea, often containing blood and mucus (jelly), together with excessive straining and often a dramatic increase in the number of bowel movements passed each day.

The affected dog may be constantly trying to pass faeces, but only achieving a small amount of bloodstained mucus. Dogs with colitis often benefit from diets containing an increased amount of fibre.

CONSTIPATION

Constipation refers to too slow a passage of faeces through the large bowel, causing the difficult passage of hard, dry stools. This may be common in older dogs, partly due to decreased physical activity. Since fibre is able to increase the rate of passage of stools through the intestines, diets that contain higher levels of fibre have proven beneficial in dogs suffering from constipation. Results are best if the fibre is finely gound and an integral part of the diet, not sprinked on to the usual food.

DIABETES MELLITUS

Chapter Seven covers this disease in detail (pages 131-132).

Dietary modification, combined with insulin therapy if appropriate, has been shown to be effective in the management of both insulin dependent diabetes and non-insulin dependent diabetes. Since many dogs with non-insulin dependent diabetes are obese, a major part of the treatment regime should be the restoration of a normal body weight with the use of a low-fat, low-energy diet food.

When managing diabetes, care should be taken, not only with regard to the nutritional composition of the diet, but also over the physical food type selected (see chart on opposite page).

CANCER

Cancer is the leading cause of death among dogs over the age of seven. There are many different types of cancer and each has a different degree of severity. Common forms of cancer in dogs include mammary

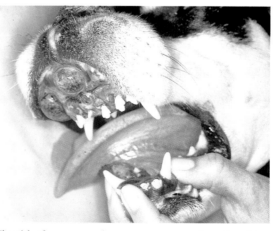

The risk of recurrence in some cancers can be reduced by careful dietary management. Pictured: mouth tumour (fibrosarcoma of the upper jaw).

CANINE DIABETIC DIETARY REQUIREMENTS	
Nutrient	**Desired level and reason**
Water	As desired by your dog, fresh water should be readily available to prevent dehydration due to urine losses.
Energy	Feed to normalise body weight. If obese, your dog requires an energy-restricted, low-fat diet. If he is too thin, he needs a lower-fibre, high-energy food.
Protein	Affected dogs are losing amino acids through their urine. Avoid restricting proteins in the diet, and try to provide highly digestible proteins.
Fat	Avoid excess fat as many dogs suffering from diabetes have high cholesterol levels in the blood.
Carbohydrate	Avoid simple sugars which are readily absorbed and will worsen hyperglycaemia.
Fibre	Increase fibre levels to slow absorption of glucose and to reduce hyperglycaemia (in obese or normal-weight dogs).
Food type	Avoid semi-moist foods as they often contain high levels of simple sugars.

cancer, ovarian cancer, lymphoma, skin tumours (certain breeds such as the Boxer are more prone to these types of cancer) and tumours of the spleen.

Lymphoma (also called lymphosarcoma) is a cancer of the lymphatic system. In the most common form of lymphoma you may notice that the dog's lymph nodes ('glands') become enlarged.

The most common presenting sign of cancer in pets is the appearance of an abnormal swelling. Some forms of cancer affect the blood or organs inside the body and so the swelling may not be obvious to the naked eye.

Tumours may be benign (grow locally, and do not invade and spread) or malignant (they invade and spread to other parts of the body). It is only called cancer if the tumour is malignant.

COMMON SIGNS OF CANCER
- Abnormal swellings that persist or continue to grow
- Sores that do not heal
- Weight loss
- Loss of appetite
- Bleeding or discharge from any body opening
- Offensive odour
- Difficulty eating or swallowing
- Hesitation to exercise or loss of stamina
- Persistent lameness or stiffness
- Difficulty breathing, urinating or defecating.

(Source: Veterinary Cancer Society).

PREVENTION FOODS
The aim of dietary management of the canine cancer patient is to address these metabolic abnormalities and so prevent cancer cachexia. The main metabolic abnormalities are:

- Altered carbohydrate metabolism
- Altered protein metabolism
- Altered fat metabolism.

These metabolic abnormalities have been shown to persist even during remission and apparent recovery from cancer.

Hills Prescription Diet Canine n/d is the only diet proven to be beneficial in dealing with cancer.

BLADDER DISEASE
The development of stones (uroliths) and crystals in the bladder is a common occurrence in many dogs. The two most common presenting signs of bladder crystals and stones are the appearance of blood in the urine (called haematuria) and straining to pass urine. In rare cases, a dog may be totally unable to pass urine. This is more common an occurrence in male dogs than in bitches because the male urethra (the tube connecting the bladder to the end of the penis) is much narrower and therefore will block more easily. This is an emergency situation and you should seek immediate veterinary assistance.

Common canine bladder stones include:
- Struvite (magnesium ammonium phosphate)
- Calcium oxalate
- Ammonium urate
- Cystine.

The role of nutrition in the management of bladder stones and crystals is vital. The correct diet can help to dissolve bladder stones and prevent their recurrence. The first step to successful treatment, is the correct identification of the mineral type involved. See also page 102.

FOOD ALLERGIES
See Chapter Eight, pages 149-151.

4 CANINE STRUCTURE

When discussing the dog in motion, it is essential to take into account the differences in the sizes and shapes of the countless breeds now in existence.

The various gaits used by big dogs differ from those adopted by toy breeds and those that have developed a specialised shape of skeleton, such as the Dachshund. The main differences are due to the different proportions of the length of the back to the length of the legs.

The sighthound breeds use their hindlegs and backs to a great advantage over the 'chondrodystrophoid' breeds such as the Basset Hound and the Dachshund. Nevertheless, when one studies, by means of slow-motion cameras, these two extremes of breed shapes, one sees that the basic patterns of the gaits remain, much more than one might expect when one stands the two side by side.

BONES

A dog's skeleton is the scaffolding of his body. This framework not only protects and supports the internal organs, but it is also an organ in itself.

THE PRENATAL SKELETON

Bones develop from a cartilage model. Their formation starts at specific sites within those models – the ossification centres. Some centres develop before the puppy is born, while others appear in early puppyhood.

After birth, the various cartilage models grow, and, during that growth, there is a 'laying down' of young bone (ossification) in those models.

For mainly the sake of the theme of this chapter, we shall deal with the bones of the appendicular skeleton – the front and hindlimbs.

POSTNATAL DEVELOPMENT

A puppy has a lot of growing to do before he reaches adulthood. As in any other mammal, that growth is achieved by two basic means: appositional and longitudinal growth. Appositional growth may be likened to the increase in girth that a tree acquires as it grows upwards. That increase in girth is, of course, necessary to support the increase in the height and weight of the growing animal. According to the particular bone in question, longitudinal growth occurs at one or both ends of long bones. These areas add length to long bones, but that increase in length has to take place at a site that is close to, but not part of, the joint. These special sites are known as growth plates. Each growth plate is programmed to close at a particular time in the life of the young animal. When the last one has closed, the dog's skeleton has virtually ceased to grow. Only a little appositional growth takes place after 14 months of age. Some owners might dispute that statement. Nevertheless, most of the growth seen after that time is due to increases in muscle mass, which adds to the animal's apparent height.

THE ADULT SKELETON

The skeleton continuously adapts to the forces to which it is subjected. The bones are splendidly designed to withstand these variations, provided the forces are not excessive – if they are excessive, the bone breaks or fractures.

Different functions are reflected in the various shapes and sizes of the bones. It is customary to divide bones into four classes:
- **Long bones**: These possess a marrow cavity and their length exceeds their breadth. Most limb bones are long, and are involved in locomotion.

THE ADULT SKELETON

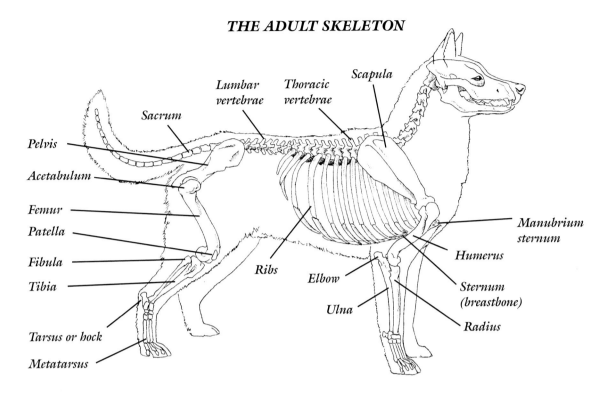

- Pelvis
- Acetabulum
- Femur
- Patella
- Fibula
- Tibia
- Sacrum
- Tarsus or hock
- Metatarsus
- Lumbar vertebrae
- Thoracic vertebrae
- Scapula
- Ribs
- Elbow
- Ulna
- Manubrium sternum
- Humerus
- Sternum (breastbone)
- Radius

• **Flat bones**: These possess very little marrow cavity and have large areas for the attachment of muscles. They also afford protection of adjacent structures, such as the bones of the skull, the shoulder blade (scapula) and the pelvic girdle.
• **Short bones**: Examples include the wrist (carpus) and the hock (tarsus).
• **Irregular bones**: An example is the spinal vertebrae.

BONE STRUCTURE

A typical bone is made up of two distinct types of bony tissue: cortical and cancellous. The junction between the two is not acute but a melding of one with the other. Cortical bone makes up the dense outer layer. It is characterised by an ability to support great loads. This strength is determined by its cellular structure. In cortical bone, the cells overlap, rather like bricks in a wall.

Cancellous bone is the inner 'coral-like' network of cells. It absorbs and transmits loads as well as forming the lattice for the marrow. The marrow itself helps in cushioning the loads. It also has very important roles in the various biochemical systems of the dog's body.

The major difference between the two types of bone is the difference in the density of the tissue.

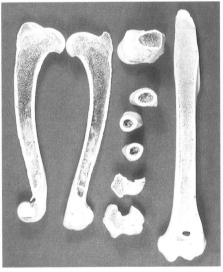

Bone bisection, showing the inner coral-like cancellous bone, and the outer cortical bone.

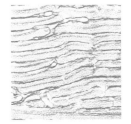

Microscopic section of cortical bone, showing the strong, brick-like structure of the cells.

Cancellous bone is about four times more porous than cortical bone and it has a greater capacity to absorb energy in compression. A combination of these two types of bone gives strength and rigidity, while remaining light and resilient. A typical long bone is 85 per cent as strong as cast iron but it is only one third of the weight.

In order to remain alive, as with all other tissues, bones require a blood supply. In the case of long bones, many small arteries penetrate the bone at both ends through fine tunnels (foramen). However, the major supply is via one or two arteries, known as nutrient arteries, which penetrate the midshaft. The blood circulates within the marrow where it deals with various cellular and biochemical responsibilities and then leaves the bone in two ways. Most leaves via a very complex series of fine tunnels that pass outward from the core – a centrifugal flow – while the rest leaves via nutrient veins through the major tunnels.

In addition, at particular points where muscles and ligaments attach to the bone, there is a blood supply provided by those same tissues that goes part-way into the bone and then leaves via a parallel route. All these various routes of flow meld with one another – they are not cut off like separate railway lines.

INDIVIDUAL BONES OF THE SKELETAL SYSTEM

The canine skeleton is divided into two areas:

- **Axial skeleton**: Skull, spine (including the tail), ribs and sternum.
- **Appendicular skeleton**: All of the bones of the four limbs.

As with all species, the bones of the dog are grouped according to their origin, shape, function, structure and position.

DIFFERENT SKULL TYPES

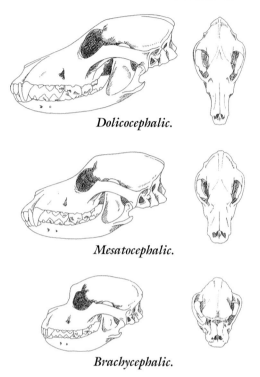

Dolicocephalic.

Mesatocephalic.

Brachycephalic.

AXIAL SKELETON

The skull, spinal column, ribs and sternum make up the axial skeleton. In dogs, the skull is differently shaped from one breed to another. The rounded head and face of breeds such as the Pug and the Bullmastiff have a skull shape known as brachycephalic. The elongated skull of the sighthounds is termed dolicocephalic, whereas the 'average' shape of the 'average' skull of the species is termed mesatocephalic.

The vertebral column is formed by approximately 50 vertebrae. This comprises 7 cervical, 13 thoracic, 7 lumbar, 3 sacral, and 20 coccygeal (according to the breed). The first two cervical vertebrae are

Total average number of bones in the canine skeleton		
Axial skeleton	Vertebral column	50
	Skull and hyoid bone around the larynx	50
	Ribs and sternum (breast bone)	34
Appendicular skeleton (limbs)	Pectoral (front) limbs	90
	Pelvic (hind) limbs	96
Heterotopic skeleton	Os penis (male)	1
	Total	321

N.B. The first digits of the hindfeet (dewclaws) are not included.

Attention to feet and nails should be part of the routine care of your dog. Regular care will often stop problems developing.

- Young puppies can easily scratch their mother while feeding. Most breeders will trim the puppies' nail tips, using nail scissors.
- Accustom your puppy to having his nails clipped from an early age; he will then learn to accept the procedure.
- As a dog gets older, the nails become stronger and more difficult to cut. Most owners find that guillotine-type nail-clippers work best.
- Dogs that are walked on hard surfaces will wear down their nails naturally. However, in many cases, human intervention is needed to keep the nails trim.
- It is essential to trim the tip of the nail only. If you cut into the 'quick' (the nail's nerve and blood supply), it will bleed profusely. If you cut into the quick accidentally, apply a little potassium permanganate or a stypic, which will stem the bleeding.
- The pads should be checked for cracks or soreness. If you are walking in the countryside, it is especially important to inspect the pads for thorns or grass seeds that may have become embedded.
- Longhaired breeds tend to grow hair between their pads, and this can become matted and uncomfortable; keep the hair trimmed.

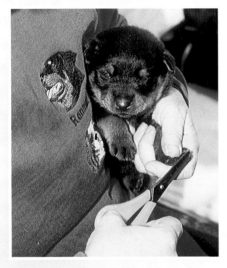

A puppy's nails need to be trimmed so that he does not scratch the dam when he is feeding.

Adult nails can also get overgrown.

Trim the tip of the nails only.

The hair from the underside of the pads may need trimming in long-coated breeds.

The neat appearance of newly-trimmed nails.

MUSCLES

The movement of the bones and joints is brought about by messages from the brain being transmitted, via the nerve pathways, to the muscles. Three types of muscles are recognised:

- **Smooth muscles**: These are present in the various organs and blood vessels within the body.

- **Cardiac muscles**: These make up the heart.

- **Skeletal or striated muscles**: These are involved in the movement of the limbs, and hence in locomotion.

Striated muscles consist of cells that make up long fibres and collectively form the individual muscles. They are also known as 'voluntary muscles' as the brain instructs the muscles to respond to its signal.

The smooth muscles and the cardiac muscles are described as being involuntary, in that they are perpetually contracting and relaxing in their functions within the body.

Skeletal muscles consist of a belly (the general area comprising millions of muscle fibres), which represents the 'meat' of the muscle, and the tendon. The latter part is the termination of the muscle, which is a 'cord-like' extension of the belly. It is strong and transmits the force of contraction of the belly to the point of insertion lower down the limb.

The junction between the belly and the tendon is not acute; it is a melding of the muscle fibres into the fibres of the tendon. In conjunction with the ligaments of a joint, the tendons play a major role in stabilizing the joints.

MUSCLE GROUPS

Generally speaking, a group of muscles will flex a joint and an opposing group extends the same joint. Whether a muscle extends or flexes a joint, and the effect it has on a particular bone, depends upon where its tendon – the extension of the contractile belly of the muscle – is inserted.

Although not totally accurate, one may say that the muscles in front of a joint swing the limb forwards, in the swing phase (protraction), and those behind pull it backwards in the stance phase (retraction).

In some cases, a particular muscle will have a double action – to extend one joint and to flex a neighbouring one. The bicep is one such muscle, as it extends the shoulder joint and flexes the elbow.

MAJOR MUSCLE GROUPS

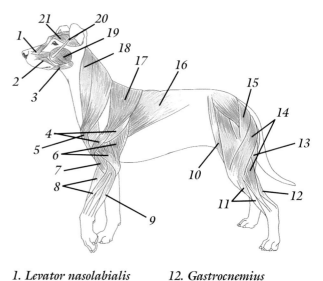

1. *Levator nasolabialis*
2. *Buccinator*
3. *Digastricus*
4. *Deltoids*
5. *Biceps brachii*
6. *Triceps*
7. *Branchialis*
8. *Extensors of the elbow*
9. *Flexors of the elbow*
10. *Sartorius*
11. *Extensors of the stifle and flexors of the hock.*
12. *Gastrocnemius*
13. *Flexors (stifle)*
14. *Biceps femoris*
15. *Gluteals*
16. *Latissimus*
17. *Trapezius*
18. *Sterno-occipitalis*
19. *Masseter*
20. *Zygomaticus*
21. *Scutularis*

GAITS

In order for the reader to understand the various gaits that dogs employ, it is necessary for some terminology of gait analysis to be understood. We speak of the 'lift point' and the 'contact point'. The lift point is when the paw leaves the ground, and the contact point is when the paw first touches the ground. However, a stride is not the distance between those two points. So that all of the movement may be taken into consideration, the term 'stride' covers the whole locomotive cycle, from one point in that cycle back to the same point again. Therefore, it is usually best to consider the lift point as the beginning of the stride and the end of the stride – the point at which the same foot touches the ground again.

During movement, the forelimbs arrest and support the body and the hindlimbs initiate deceleration. This latter attribute is very easily observed when a dog suddenly slows after galloping, particularly if he has found an item which he was chasing, e.g. a Frisbee.

Walk.

NORMAL LOCOMOTION

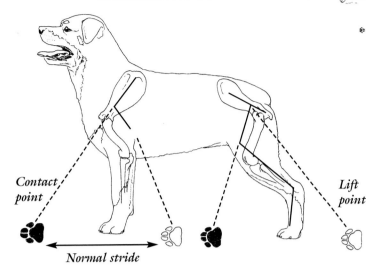

Contact
point

Lift
point

Normal stride

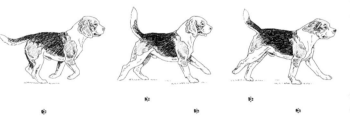

Flying trot.

WALK

During the walk, two, three or four legs may be supporting the dog at any particular point in the stride.

FLYING TROT

Due to strong and fast propulsion, the dog's feet leave the ground.

CANTER/LOPE

There are three beats to each stride sequence: two diagonal legs move as a pair and the two other legs move separately. When a dog lopes and 'leads' with the right front leg (RF), the left front (LF) leg moves on co-ordination with the right back (RB) leg, the left back (LB) leg acting on its own (see figure). If the dog changes to 'lead' with the left leg the sequence is reversed to: LF alone, RF and LB, RB alone.

Canter/lope.

GALLOP

In the gallop – the dog's fastest gait – there is a sequence of one of few occasions where the feet touch the ground: left hock, right hock, left front and right front (when the right front is the 'leading leg'). The opposite sequence occurs when the left front is the leading leg. When all four feet are under the dog, it does not have any contact with the ground.

PACE

Here, the front and back legs on the same side support the dog. It is often adopted by large dogs and it is said to save energy over long distances. The

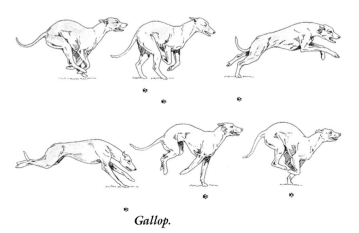

Gallop.

Because ED has a significant inherited component, the incidence of the disease in the population can be minimised by breeding from unaffected dogs.

Radiographic screening programmes operate across Europe, Australia and in the US.

In the UK, animals have to be 12 months old to be submitted for the screening programme run by the British Veterinary Association and Kennel Club. The Orthopedic Foundation for Animals in the USA screens at a minimum of two years. Although the number of radiographs required varies between schemes, the grading is the same:

> Grade 0: Normal
> Grade 1: Mild osteoarthritis
> Grade 2: Moderate osteoarthritis
> Grade 3: Severe osteoarthritis.

Grading depends on the size of secondary osteophytes (bony proliferations) around the joint and on the presence of any primary lesions. It is recommended that dogs with grade 2 or 3 elbows are not used for breeding.

In addition to national schemes, an International Elbow Working Group has been established. This group meets annually to further current knowledge and research into this important condition.

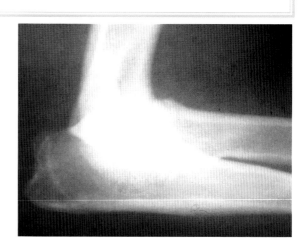

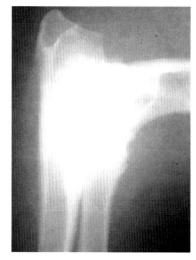

▲ *A lateral radiograph of a normal Bullmastiff elbow.*

◀ *A lateral radiograph of the elbow of a St. Bernard with elbow dysplasia, due to a fragmented medial coronoid process.*

ELBOW DYSPLASIA (ED)

The term 'elbow dysplasia' describes the abnormal development of the elbow joint. The most common primary lesions are ununited (fragmented) coronoid process, osteochondritis dissecans (see Osteochondrosis, pages 78–80) and ununited anconeal process. These defects arise during puppyhood.

The elbow is a close-fitting articulation between the humerus, radius and ulna. It does not tolerate any incongruity and responds to primary defects by rapidly developing secondary osteoarthritis. This gradually progresses and can affect a dog for his entire life.

Elbow dysplasia is being recognised more often and occurs worldwide. It affects mainly the large and giant breeds, particularly Bernese Mountain Dogs, Retrievers, Rottweilers, German Shepherd Dogs and the St. Bernard.

Causes: Ununited coronoid process and osteochondritis dissecans are polygenic disorders with a significant heritability. Much like hip dysplasia, factors such as nutrition, obesity and level of exercise may also contribute to the condition.

Signs: Foreleg lameness, often starting at four to five months of age, is one of the first signs of this condition. If both elbows are affected to the same extent, there may be stiffness rather than obvious lameness. Another symptom is that the dog will resent full flexion of the elbow. The diagnosis can be confirmed by radiography.

Again, much like hip dysplasia, lame dogs are just the tip of the disease iceberg – many more dogs will have abnormal elbows but show no signs of lameness. However, these dogs still carry susceptible genes and are more likely to produce clinically affected puppies if they are used for breeding. Therefore, it is as important to identify those dogs with subclinical disease as it is to treat the clinically affected animals.

Treatment: A period of controlled exercise, possibly with the use of painkillers, should be tried first. Body weight should also be carefully controlled. Often, owners can find an individual exercise routine that the dog copes with well. If this conservative approach does not work, the alternative is surgery to remove any loose fragments from the joint. The osteoarthritis tends to progress irrespective of treatment, however, and dogs may have persistent or intermittent locomotion problems.

NORMAL HIP JOINT

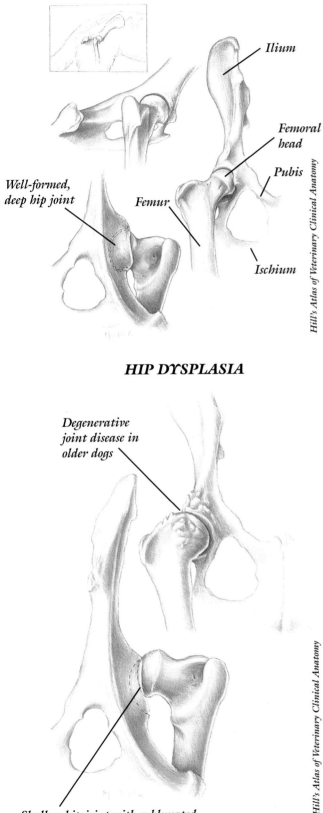

Ilium

Femoral head

Pubis

Femur

Ischium

Well-formed, deep hip joint

Hill's Atlas of Veterinary Clinical Anatomy

HIP DYSPLASIA

Degenerative joint disease in older dogs

Shallow hip joint with subluxated femoral head in younger dogs

Hill's Atlas of Veterinary Clinical Anatomy

HIP DYSPLASIA (HD)

Hip dysplasia is a common problem, particularly in dogs with an adult weight of more than 44 lbs (20 kgs), although it has been reported in almost every breed. The literal translation of the Greek word 'dysplasia' is abnormal growth. In affected dogs, there is abnormal development of the hip joint, with increased laxity and incongruity between the articular surfaces.

In the normal hip joint, the contours of the femoral head and the acetabulum of the pelvis closely follow each other, the joint space being narrow and even. If this congruity is lost, the femoral head tends to subluxate (or luxate in severe cases) out from the acetabulum. Defects leading to instability and joint laxity include an abnormally shallow acetabulum, a deformed femoral head (as in Perthes disease) and an incorrect angle between the femoral head and the shaft of the femur. Over time, the unstable joint responds by laying down new bone to try to increase the congruity. This often improves the situation for several years, but, in old age, chronic osteoarthritic changes become more pronounced and affect movement.

Importantly, HD shows a spectrum of disease. Indeed, many animals are subclinically affected – they show no clinical signs but nonetheless are dysplastic. These dogs can produce offspring that show signs of HD. In severe cases, where both hips are affected, dogs can be totally incapacitated.

Causes: HD has a moderate heritability and is polygenic (i.e. more than one gene contributes to the condition). It can be minimised by adopting suitable breeding strategies. However, because environmental and other factors also contribute, the condition cannot be totally eliminated. Factors linked to HD include rapid growth rate, overfeeding, obesity, over or underexercise, and poor pelvic muscle development.

Signs: In the case of clinically affected dogs, there are two peak times for lameness, namely five to eight months (while the dog is maturing) and in middle/old age (due to the long-standing degenerative changes within the joint). Between these two times, lameness often diminishes, the hip joint remodels, and it may function well.

Other signs include difficulty getting up steps or stairs, or jumping into the back of vehicles, bunny-hopping (running using both hindlegs together) and a tendency to throw weight forward on to the forelegs. On examination, there is pain on hip manipulation. Crepitus (a feeling and sound of the bones grinding on one another) may be felt when

The dog is placed on his back with his hindlegs bent, stifles together and pointing straight up. Slight downward pressure (to subluxate the joints) is put on the stifles and the legs are then allowed to open. There will be a palpable and audible 'clunk' as the femoral head clicks back in to the acetabulum in dysplastic animals.

BARDON (HIP LIFT) TESTING

The dog is placed on his side. One hand is placed over the hip and the femur is lifted parallel to the table. There will be excessive movement in dysplastic hips.

the joints are moved. Under sedation or general anaesthesia there is a positive Ortolani test and Barden (hip lift) sign (see above).

Treatment: Many dogs can be successfully managed by controlling exercise (frequent, gentle exercise is best), reducing body weight and using painkillers when necessary. Physiotherapy can also help. Unless lameness is severe, the dog should not be rested completely as an important element of treatment is building and maintaining a good muscle mass.

A number of surgical interventions are available for young dogs:

- **Pectineal myectomy**: The pectineus muscle runs over the inner aspect of the hip joint. Transecting the muscle is a simple surgical technique, and it is suggested that this reduces pressure on the joint capsule, so relieving pain. The procedure is often sufficient to allow young dogs enough time for the joint to stabilise naturally.
- **Excision arthroplasty**: Removal of the femoral head and neck gives excellent results in dogs under 33 lbs (15 kgs). It is also effective in heavier dogs, but the outcome is less predictable (see Perthes disease, page 80).
- **Triple pelvic osteotomy**: Cuts are made in the three bones of the pelvis – the ilium, ischium and pubis – to free the acetabular segment. This section is then rotated so that it better covers the femoral head. It is held in place by a plate.
- **Intertrochanteric varisation osteotomy**: A wedge of bone is removed from the base of the femoral neck to reduce the angulation of the femoral head. This allows it to better fit into the acetabulum. A plate is needed to hold the femoral neck in place while the osteotomy site repairs. In adults, the options are:
- **Excision arthroplasty**: This is much the same procedure as in younger dogs.
- **Total hip replacement**: This is available at specialist centres. Most implants consist of a metal femoral component and a polymer acetabular cup. The outcome is usually excellent, with dogs being able to lead active lives.

HIP DYSPLASIA TREATMENTS

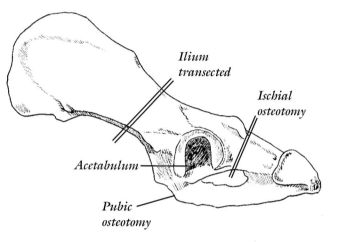

Several treatment options are available for hip dysplasia, including triple pelvic osteotomy (above) and intertrochanteric varisation osteotomy (below).

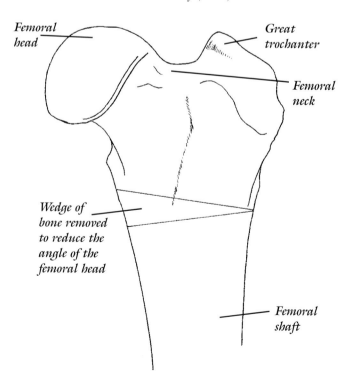

US SCHEME

In the USA, the Orthopedic Foundation for Animals (OFA) runs radiographic screening for HD and a registry. Animals should be sedated or anaesthetised as they must be accurately positioned on their back and remain still. A ventrodorsal view of the pelvis is required. For screening, an animal must be at least two years of age. However, dogs showing clinical signs of HD can be radiographed before this time.

Hips are graded as:
Grade 1: Excellent/normal
Grade 2: Good/normal
Grade 3: Fair/normal
Grade 4: Borderline
Grade 5: Mild dysplastic
Grade 6: Moderate dysplastic
Grade 7: Severe dysplastic.

Dogs in categories one to three are given an OFA number and the results are available to the public. Results are withheld from publication for categories four to seven unless the owner has given permission for the results to be posted in the open registry.

UK SCHEME

A joint scheme is operated in the UK by the British Veterinary Association and the Kennel Club. Animals must be a minimum of one year of age. Submitted radiographs are scored, each hip having a possible total of 53 points. The total score is out of a possible 106, with the higher scores showing a more dysplastic hip. Breed averages are published on an annual basis, and it is best to breed from dogs that have scores better (i.e. lower) than the breed average.

With both schemes, it is important to screen as many offspring as possible (i.e. both good and bad examples) so that the true breed average is known. Benefit will only be obtained if breeding from the better animals is maintained over several generations.

CANADIAN SCHEME

In Canada, an official kennel club-sanctioned certification scheme does not exist; however, the major certification organisation in that country is the Ontario Veterinary College (OVC). In addition, as with the USA, hip dysplasia certification is offered by a number of specialist radiologists, primarily practising in the veterinary schools. In Canada, the OVC classifies hips as normal or as being grade 1 to 4 hip dysplasia, with grade 1 being the least severe, and grade 4 being the most severe.

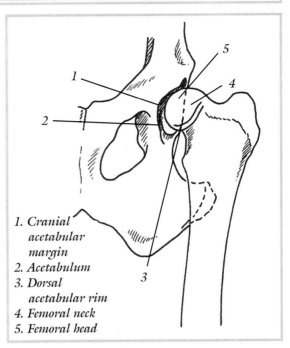

1. Cranial acetabular margin
2. Acetabulum
3. Dorsal acetabular rim
4. Femoral neck
5. Femoral head

Outline diagrams of the hip joint, showing the component parts that are assessed in evaluation for hip dysplasia.

A radiograph of the pelvis of a Labrador Retriever demonstrating normal hip joints.

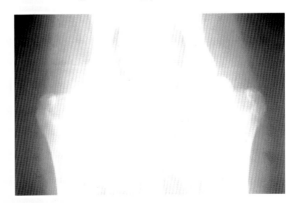

A radiograph of the pelvis of a Golden Retriever affected with hip dysplasia. The femoral heads are subluxated, the acetabulae are shallow, and the cranial acetabular margin is straighter than normal.

The Fédération Cynologique International (FCI) is an umbrella organisation for most of the European kennel clubs, and many kennel clubs around the world (notable exceptions being Great Britain, Australia and New Zealand).

The FCI recommends that hip certification is made at one year of age for most breeds and at 18 months for giant breeds. There is no upper limit at which dogs cannot be evaluated.

The FCI recommends five categories from A to E, with A being normal, B borderline, C representing mild hip dysplasia, D hip dysplasia, and E severe hip dysplasia.

METAPHYSEAL OSTEOPATHY

Known also as hypertrophic osteodystrophy or Barlow's disease, this is a developmental disease seen in rapidly growing dogs of the large and giant breeds.

Causes: The cause is unknown, although the condition has been associated with excess dietary supplementation. A region of bone, next to a growth plate, dies (particularly around the carpus or wrist). The area becomes inflamed and reactive new bone may be deposited.

Signs: The condition normally becomes apparent at three to six months of age, when the pup develops painful, hot swellings in the carpal region. Dogs are reluctant to move and may have a raised body temperature. They often go off their food and are reluctant to exercise. There is moderate lameness that tends to subside gradually over several days. Repeated bouts can occur but they reduce as the animal matures. The condition is confirmed by examining radiographs of the affected regions.

Treatment: Any dietary excesses should be corrected. Non-steroidal, anti-inflammatory drugs (NSAIDs) may be required to reduce the inflammation and to provide pain relief. The pup should be rested until lameness improves.

NUTRITIONAL DISEASES

Nutritional diseases are rare nowadays, as most dogs are fed commercially-available, balanced diets. However, it should be remembered that dietary excesses may be as damaging as deficiencies, particularly in the growing dog. Indeed, research shows that high levels of dietary supplements increase the incidence of many skeletal disorders such as hip dysplasia, Wobbler Syndrome, and osteochondrosis. As a general principle, dietary deficiencies or excesses can be avoided by feeding a commercial diet to maintain a healthy body condition. In this case, additional supplementation should not be necessary. If a home-made diet is fed, a basic supplement may be required at the recommended dosage.

Examples of possible nutritional disorders affecting the locomotive system include:
• **Rickets**: This is due to a lack of vitamin D/phosphorus, which results in poor mineralisation of the skeleton. Puppies with rickets have swelling of the long bones close to the joints (most noticeable at the carpus or wrist joint) and their bones may bend. Nodules commonly develop over the ribs too. The condition can be confirmed radiographically. Standard treatment involves improving the diet to create the correct vitamin balance, and resting the animal until his skeleton strengthens.
• **Osteoporosis**: This is due to a lack of calcium. It is most likely to occur if puppies are fed an all-meat diet. Affected pups are reluctant to move and may be lame. The bones appear thin and fragile on radiographs, and they are more prone to fractures than their normal counterparts. As with the treatment for rickets, the diet should be corrected and the pup rested.

OSTEOCHONDROSIS

As the limb bones of the young dog lengthen, so the joint surfaces have to enlarge to carry the increasing body weight. Immediately beneath the articular cartilage of the joint is a highly active area, similar to a growth plate in a long bone (see page 62), where cartilage is replaced by bone matrix. This bone deposition allows the joint surfaces to expand. In osteochondrosis, there is a failure of this ossification process. Cartilage is retained and thickened areas form at specific sites in the joints. The deeper layers of cartilage die, and, under the stresses of normal movement, cracks develop. When these fissures extend up to the joint surface, a flap of cartilage forms – this is the classical 'osteochondritis dissecans' lesion (OD or OCD). As the flap lifts away, nerve endings are exposed in the subchondral bone, causing pain and lameness. In some cases, the cartilage flap may detach completely and can slowly calcify and enlarge in the joint. This is called a joint mouse. These can reach a considerable size and impede joint movement.

Causes: Osteochondrosis is a problem mainly in the large and giant breeds – different breeds have a predisposition for specific joints to be affected. The condition has been shown to have a moderate heritability in the shoulders of Bernese Mountain Dogs. It is also inherited in the elbow, where it is an important cause of elbow dysplasia (see pages 73-

OSTEOCHONDRITIS DISSECANS

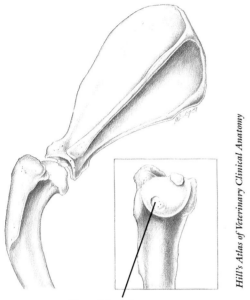

Hill's Atlas of Veterinary Clinical Anatomy

Site of detachment

74). Environment and nutrition may also play a role. The shoulder, elbow, stifle and hock are the joints affected, although the condition has also been reported infrequently at other sites, such as the hips and vertebrae.

Signs: The first sign tends to be mild to moderate lameness, beginning when the pup is as young as three to four months. The condition is often bilateral, and, if both joints are affected to a similar degree, the dog may not show overt lameness but will instead have a stiff and stilted gait. The affected joint may have a mild effusion. The affected joint may be mildly swollen due to increased production of synovial fluid. Range of movement is reduced and the dog may show signs of discomfort when the joint is manipulated.

The condition is confirmed on radiographs, which will show irregular joint contours or secondary osteoarthritis.

SHOULDER OSTEOCHONDROSIS

The shoulder joint is affected in Border Collies, Great Danes and other large breeds. A cartilage flap develops on the caudal aspect of the humerus and can be 0.75 inches (2 cms) or more in diameter. The treatment of choice is surgical removal of all loose cartilage. This creates an even larger defect initially, but the ulcer is encouraged to granulate and to fill in with fibrocartilage. The outcome is usually extremely good, with little long-term damage. Affected dogs should not be used for breeding.

ELBOW OSTEOCHONDROSIS

The elbow is the joint most commonly affected by osteochondrosis. Retrievers, Rottweilers and Bernese Mountain Dogs are prime candidates for the disease, although many other large breeds are affected too.

The lesions are seldom seen on radiographs because of the superimposition of bony structures in all views of the elbow. However, the elbow rapidly develops a secondary osteoarthritis and these changes can be seen, with the primary lesions being inferred. Occasionally, flaps may be seen if they have mineralised.

Mild or intermittent lameness can be managed conservatively, but many dogs require exploration of the elbow to remove fragments. The prognosis is always guarded because the osteoarthritic change tends to gradually progress. Many affected dogs can happily lead pet lives, but prospects for serious canine athletes are reduced.

STIFLE OSTEOCHONDROSIS

Giant breeds are affected by stifle osteochondrosis, but this is the least common form of osteochondrosis. Lesions develop on either the medial or lateral side of the femoral condyle. Conservative treatment may be tried for a few weeks but dogs that fail to respond require arthrotomy (surgical opening of the joint) to curette (scrape away) the defects. The outlook is fair, but the stifle often becomes osteoarthritic in the long term.

HOCK OSTEOCHONDROSIS

In the hock, the dissecting lesion classically develops on the medial trochlear ridge of the talus. Again, lameness begins in puppyhood and the most

Obvious distension of the hock joint in a dog with osteochondrosis. OCD is just one of many causes of swollen joints.

commonly affected breeds are Bull Terriers, Mastiffs and Retrievers. Mild cases may be managed conservatively but many require surgical removal of cartilage fragments from the joint. The outcome is generally fair. Similar to the elbow, the hock does not tolerate injury – the joint remains stiff and osteoarthritis develops.

PANOSTEITIS (EOSINOPHILIC PANOSTEITIS, EO-PAN)

Causes: Panosteitis is a common cause of lameness in puppies, but it is poorly understood. Fortunately, it usually wears off as the dog matures, and leaves no permanent damage. It affects mainly German Shepherd Dogs, Retrievers and other large/giant breeds. The condition is thought to be due to inflammation and necrosis (death) of a fatty region of bone marrow, possibly caused by alterations in blood supply.

Signs: Panosteitis typically gives rise to lameness that tends to wax and wane – any leg may be affected in a shifting pattern. Most dogs will suffer their first bout at four to six months of age. The lameness will gradually subside over several days, but may recur later in the same leg or elsewhere. There is pain when pressure is applied over the middle of the affected bone, which, in some cases, can be quite pronounced. The diagnosis can usually be confirmed by taking radiographs, where the affected area will show up as a mottled patch, described as a thumbprint lesion. The most common site affected by panosteitis is the mid-humerus (forearm), but it also occurs in the radius, ulna, tibia and femur.

Treatment: Analgesics and non-steroidal, anti-inflammatory drugs are used during an attack to control the pain. Bouts of lameness gradually become less frequent and less severe, and have usually stopped by the time the dog is 12 to 18 months, although in occasional animals the episodes will continue for several years. There is no long-term damage.

LEGG-CALVÉ-PERTHES DISEASE

This is an aseptic necrosis (death) of the femoral head (an important component of the hip joint). It is a common disease that affects breeds under 33 lbs (15 kgs), such as the West Highland White Terrier, the Toy Poodle, and the Jack Russell.

Causes: The necrosis and collapse of the femoral head is due to impairment of the blood supply to the region. The cause of this change in blood supply is not known. There is an equivalent condition in children from which the disorder gets its name.

Signs: Hindleg lameness becomes apparent from four to six months of age. There is pain when the hip is manipulated. Radiographs confirm the deformity – usually only one hip is affected. The femoral head is flattened and misshapen.

Treatment: Some mildly affected dogs will respond to a period of rest, although this may be required for several weeks and can be difficult with a young pup that wants to socialise. Over time, the hip will remodel but it is likely to develop an early osteoarthritis. Most animals require surgery – removal of the femoral head and neck. After surgery, the dog forms a fibrous joint between the femur and

PANOSTEITIS

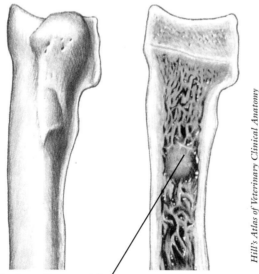

Hill's Atlas of Veterinary Clinical Anatomy

Lesions of panosteitis in the proximal radius

This West Highland White Terrier puppy is favouring a hindleg, throwing most of his weight forward and on to the normal hindleg. The affected limb is rested behind the dog.

pelvis. Animals are rapidly pain-free and function extremely well.

UNUNITED ANCONEAL PROCESS (UAP)

The anconeal process of the ulna is a large bony prominence that helps to stabilise the elbow and to prevent overextension of the joint. As the limb is straightened, the process rides up into the trochlear groove of the humerus. By four to five months of age, the process should be completely fused to the ulna, but with UAP, this fusion fails. As the powerful triceps muscle mass inserts on to the process, the fragment is pulled away from the ulna. Great Danes, German Shepherd Dogs, and Basset Hounds are the breeds most commonly affected.

Causes: The exact cause is unknown, but it is likely to have a moderate inherited component. It has been suggested that the ulna notch is too small to take the distal humerus, thus putting additional stress on the process in affected dogs.

UNUNITED ANCONEAL PROCESS

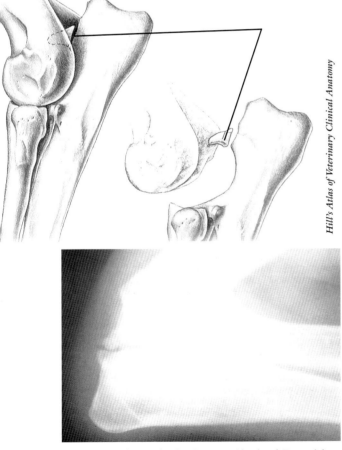

Hill's Atlas of Veterinary Clinical Anatomy

A lateral radiograph of a German Shepherd Dog with an ununited anconeal process.

Signs: Lameness from four months of age onwards. The elbow is often noticeably distended and painful, and has a reduced range of movement. The diagnosis is confirmed on radiography. Both elbows should be examined as the condition is often bilateral.

Treatment: Some dogs may respond to conservative treatment (rest and painkillers) and this can be tried for a few weeks. Many cases require surgical removal of the detached process.

ADULT LOCOMOTIVE DISORDERS

CRUCIATE DISEASES

There are two strong ligaments within the stifle joint, running from the femur to the tibia, namely the cranial (or anterior) cruciate and the caudal (posterior) cruciate ligaments. These substantial, fibrous bands are important stabilisers of the joint, preventing the tibia from slipping forward when the dog bears weight, and limiting rotation. The caudal cruciate is rarely injured, but partial tearing, or complete rupture, of the cranial cruciate is a common orthopaedic problem.

Causes: Three different groups of dog suffer from cranial cruciate rupture:

- **Group 1, any breed, any age**: Where rupture is associated with a traumatic, rotational or hyperextension injury, such as catching a foot in a rabbit hole while running at speed.
- **Group 2, old dogs, often overweight**: The cruciate ligament undergoes degenerative ageing changes that weaken it so much it may rupture after relatively mild trauma.
- **Group 3, young adult dogs of large/giant breeds**: Breeds such as Rottweilers, Bernese Mountain Dogs etc., are predisposed to a premature ageing of the cruciate ligament. Dogs with a very straight stifle – such as the Chow Chow – may also be predisposed. Many dogs become lame as early as two to three years of age. Both stifles are likely to be affected by degenerative changes in the ligament, so even if the worst leg is treated, the other may be affected in the future.

Signs: Marked lameness is the most common presenting sign. When examined, the joint is distended with excess amounts of synovial fluid. This can be felt as soft swellings to either side of the patellar tendon. Radiographs may also be taken to check for any other damage and to assess the degree of secondary osteoarthritis that is inevitably associated with joint instability.

CRUCIATE LIGAMENT

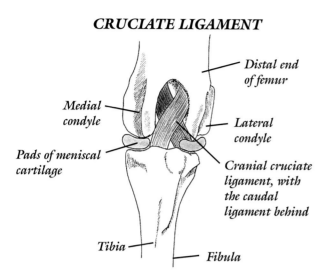

Distal end of femur

Medial condyle

Lateral condyle

Pads of meniscal cartilage

Cranial cruciate ligament, with the caudal ligament behind

Tibia

Fibula

RUPTURED CRUCIATE LIGAMENT

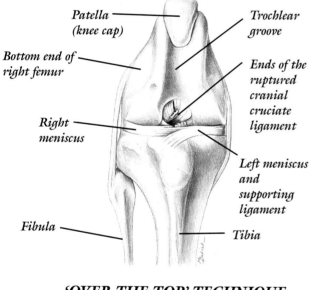

Patella (knee cap)

Trochlear groove

Bottom end of right femur

Ends of the ruptured cranial cruciate ligament

Right meniscus

Left meniscus and supporting ligament

Fibula

Tibia

'OVER THE TOP' TECHNIQUE

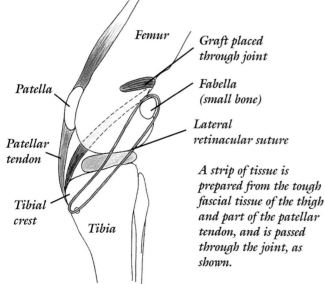

Femur

Graft placed through joint

Patella

Fabella (small bone)

Lateral retinacular suture

Patellar tendon

Tibial crest

Tibia

A strip of tissue is prepared from the tough fascial tissue of the thigh and part of the patellar tendon, and is passed through the joint, as shown.

Hill's Atlas of Veterinary Clinical Anatomy

Treatment: Several different options are available. Small dogs weighing under 22 lbs (10 kgs) often respond well to conservative measures, with a period of strict rest for four to six weeks. Heavier animals require surgical intervention. The joint is opened and the frayed remnants of the ligament are removed, along with any damaged cartilage.

Repair techniques are used for the torn techniques. Strict rest is required post-operatively. The outcome is usually fair, although the joint inevitably has limited movement and develops osteoarthritic changes.

EHRLICHIOSIS
Causes: This is an infective arthritis caused by the rickettsial organism *Ehrlichia canis*. The organism is transmitted by the dog tick and is endemic in many parts of the US.
Signs: Clinical signs of this condition are diverse, and include anorexia, depression and fever, with stiffness, limb oedema (swelling), and variable lameness. Blood tests may demonstrate the presence of the organism or antibody levels to confirm diagnosis.
Treatment: Most cases respond well to treatment with the antibiotic tetracycline. Ticks should be controlled, especially during the warmer months, to minimise the risk of spreading the disease.

BORRELIOSIS (LYME DISEASE)
Causes: This is an infective arthritis caused by the spirochaete organism *Borrelia burgdorferi*. The organism is spread by ticks, although lameness and illness may occur several weeks after tick infestation.
Signs: Affected dogs suddenly become lame, with one or more joints affected. They also have a fever and anorexia. In some cases, the kidneys and nervous system may be affected too.
Treatment: The disease normally responds well to a course of antibiotics. A vaccine is available where the condition is common (e.g. parts of the USA). Tick control is also important.

EOSINOPHILIC MYOSITIS
Also known as masticatory muscle myopathy, this relatively common muscle disease affects the large chewing muscles of the skull – the temporal and masseter muscles – but, although recognised for many years, it remains poorly understood.
Causes: Unknown.
Signs: Sudden, painful swelling of the masticatory muscles. Affected dogs find it difficult to open their mouths and they may show signs of pain if forced to

do so. The inflammation gradually subsides, but repeated bouts can occur. In time, the muscles atrophy (wither) and are reduced to fibrous bands. The bony ridges of the skull become more prominent, which gives dogs an aged appearance. The animal may need to be fed a soft diet if jaw movement is permanently restricted.

Treatment: Corticosteroids help to control the inflammation and to limit the damage caused by this disease. Some dogs require jaw traction under anaesthesia to free the jaw. Most animals manage to cope with the condition.

OSTEOARTHRITIS

Osteoarthritis (OA) is also referred to as degenerative joint disease (DJD) and osteoarthrosis. It is the most common form of arthritis found in many species, including man, dogs and horses. It is the body's response to long-standing joint instability and damage.

Causes: Osteoarthritis is invariably secondary to an injury or joint abnormality, such as hip dysplasia, osteochondrosis, or patellar luxation. Although the most obvious changes are bony and can be seen on radiographs, it is important to remember that *all* the tissues of a joint are affected by OA. There will be pathological changes in the articular cartilage, joint lining, synovial fluid, supporting muscles, ligaments and tendons, as well as in the bone.

An osteoarthritic joint is likely to have weakened cartilage, with areas where the cartilage is eroded, flaking or cracking. In areas where the cartilage is completely eroded, underlying nerve endings in the bone will be exposed – giving rise to pain.

A joint responds to chronic instability by laying down more bone, in an effort to restabilise the articulation. This commonly manifests itself as new bony spurs around the edges of the joint – known as

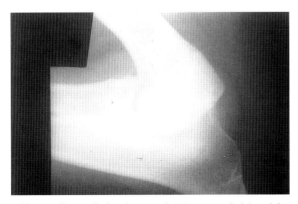

Elbow radiograph showing grade III osteoarthritis, with 'new bone' being laid down all around the joint.

periarticular osteophytes. In addition, some areas of bone that are exposed to increased, abnormal forces, respond by thickening and becoming more dense. Although this seems a logical and useful response, these areas are poor shock-absorbers and increase the amount of joint damage in the long term.

In the osteoarthritic joint, there is also proliferation of the synovial membrane, which initially produces large volumes of thin, watery joint fluid. The joint may be obviously distended on examination. This fluid is not as good a lubricant as normal synovial fluid, however. With time, the amount of fluid produced diminishes, and, very often, joints at the final stages of the condition will be dry.

Over time, the joint capsule thickens, which limits normal joint movement. In addition, muscles may atrophy (wither) due to reduced use, and ligaments will weaken also.

Signs: Initial signs include stiffness and lameness that has an insidious onset and is often worse after a period of rest and improves (warms up) with exercise. The lameness tends to worsen over time, and cold, damp weather may exacerbate the situation. Severe lameness may flare up periodically if there is additional trauma to the joint. On examination, there is a reduced range of movement in the joint. Crepitus (grating) may be felt. There is also pain associated with joint movement.

Treatment: There is no cure, but several treatments are available. Therapy needs to be carefully tailored to each individual animal. The objectives are to control pain, to maintain good muscle support around the joint, while also minimising trauma (wear and tear). Steps to take include:

- **Weight reduction**: Excess weight will increase the stress on the joints. In mild cases, weight loss may be all that is required.
- **Exercise control**: Rest the dog for a few days if lameness flares up. Most owners can find a level of regular exercise that the dog copes with. Short, frequent walks on the lead are better than longer free runs. There may be certain types of exercise that have to be avoided e.g. chasing balls. Exercise should be consistent – the dog may not be able to cope with little exercise during the week and hill walking on the weekend.
- **Physiotherapy and swimming**: Both these gentle forms of exercise are useful.
- **Non-steroidal, anti-inflammatory drugs (NSAIDs)**: These are the mainstay of treatment. Many are available and you should be prepared to try several to find the one that best suits your dog.

They can be administered as tablets or liquid, and can be given for many months. Note that only animal preparations should be used – human drugs can cause serious gastric ulcers in dogs.

- **Corticosteroids**: These are potent anti-inflammatory and analgesic agents, but they may hasten cartilage degradation. Therefore, they should be used sparingly, and are best reserved for short courses during acute flare-ups of lameness.
- **Injections**: Synthetic synovial fluid, injected directly into the joint, can be given by veterinarians to provide some relief.
- **Chondroprotective agents**: These are a recent advance and can be given by injection under the skin. These help to reduce inflammation and to stimulate cartilage repair. They are usually given at weekly intervals for a month.
- **Treatment of primary disorders**: Treating any primary joint disorders, e.g. repairing the ruptured cranial cruciate ligament, may alleviate the symptoms.
- **Joint curettage and flushing**: Removing flaking cartilage, drilling into the bone to improve the blood supply, and flushing debris from the joint, can be beneficial.
- **Excision arthroplasty**: Removal of one of the bony components of the joint can provide a good result, e.g. as an option for Legg-Calvé-Perthes disease or to treat hip dysplasia.
- **Arthrodesis**: Severely affected joints – such as the elbow, shoulder and stifle – can be surgically fused (arthrodesis). This is a major surgical procedure, where the articular surfaces are removed, the area is packed with bone graft, and a plate is put across the joint to fix it at the normal angle. As the joint can no longer move, this has an effect on gait.
- **Joint replacement**: Hip and elbows may be replaced with prosthetic joints in some cases. However, this treatment is not appropriate in all cases.

PATELLAR LUXATION

This is a dislocation of the kneecap (patella). It is one of the most commonly encountered orthopaedic problems. The displacement of the patella can be either medial or lateral. It is medial, towards the inside of the leg, in toy and bow-legged breeds such as the Staffordshire Bull Terrier. The patella luxates laterally in large breeds with a tendency to knock-knees e.g. the Great Dane. To understand how the problem arises and how it can be treated, the anatomy of the hindleg has to be understood.

Causes: In the normal hindlimb, the hip, stifle and hock joints are all aligned along the same axis. The patella, an extremely hard, dense bone, is located within the tendon at the far end of the quadriceps muscle mass. This block of muscle sits on the cranial edge of the femur and acts to straighten the leg. It exerts an extremely strong pull, which is directed down the limb by the patella, which rides in a groove (the trochlear groove) at the distal end of the femur. A short tendon runs from the distal patella to a bony prominence at the front of the leg (the tibial crest).

In many small and bow-legged breeds this anatomy is altered. The femur and tibia are curved so that the angles of the hip and stifle are changed, making the patella more likely to slip medially. The trochlear groove is often abnormally shallow, increasing the likelihood of patellar slippage. The tibial crest is placed more medially so that the pull of the quadriceps is redirected.

In large breeds, where the patella tends to luxate laterally, the femur and tibia are angulated in the opposite direction and the tibial crest is displaced laterally. Again, the trochlear groove can be abnormally shallow.

Signs: The main symptom is lameness, of varying severity, depending on the extent of the anatomical

PATELLAR LUXATION

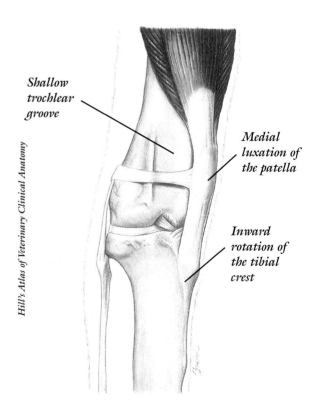

Shallow trochlear groove

Medial luxation of the patella

Inward rotation of the tibial crest

Hill's Atlas of Veterinary Clinical Anatomy

TYPES OF LUXATION

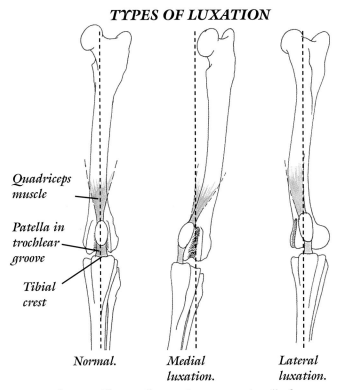

Quadriceps muscle

Patella in trochlear groove

Tibial crest

Normal.   *Medial luxation.*   *Lateral luxation.*

changes. The patella may luxate occasionally for a few strides – many people will be familiar with small dogs such as Jack Russell Terriers who hitch up a hindleg and skip for a step as they run – or it may be permanently out of place. Gait abnormality can start in puppyhood or may only become apparent in later life. On examination, the patella is felt slipping out of the trochlear groove as the stifle is flexed and extended, or it can be displaced by slight pressure.
Treatment: Mild cases may be managed with controlled exercise as necessary. However, most dogs require surgery (see panel). There are several repair

techniques that are used in combination until the joint is stabilised. The outcome is usually excellent, although the stifle joint will be prone to developing secondary osteoarthritis.

ROCKY MOUNTAIN SPOTTED FEVER (TICK-BORNE FEVER)
Causes: This fever is an infective arthritis caused by the organism *Rickettsia rickettsii*. It is spread via tick bites.
Signs: As in ehrlichiosis and Lyme disease, the illness is characterised by lameness affecting one or more joints, fever, anorexia and depression. Nervous signs have been reported, and retinal bleeding can occur. Blood tests, to demonstrate antibodies to the disease, confirm diagnosis.
Treatment: Antibiotics and supportive nursing, along with tick control, are the best forms of treatment.

TENDON RUPTURE
Tendons are tough, fibrous structures that attach muscle to bone. They transmit the 'pull' of muscles to move joints.
Causes: Tendons may be severed by sharp objects, such as stepping on glass.
Signs: Sudden, marked lameness and a wound are the main symptoms.
Treatment: Surgical repair, sewing the two tendon ends back together, is required and is best carried out as soon as possible after the injury. There are several suture patterns that are designed specifically for tendons. The whole area then has to be immobilised during healing – until the tendon is strong enough to withstand the large forces placed upon it again. This will take several weeks.

SURGICAL CORRECTION FOR PATELLAR LUXATION	
Tibial crest transplant	If the tibial crest is displaced, it is freed and swung back to its correct midline position. It is secured with 1 or 2 small pins.
Trochleoplasty	The trochlear groove is deepened by cutting out a wedge of cartilage and underlying bone. This allows the patella to sit more deeply within the groove.
Tissue release	Any restraining tissues to the side of the luxation are cut to free the patella so it can be returned to the midline position.
Imbrication suture	A 'tuck' is taken in the joint capsule and surrounding tissues on the opposite side to the release.
Corrective osteotomy	In dogs with severe angular defects where the above techniques prove insufficient, wedges of bone may need to be removed from the distal femur to realign the stifle joint.

TUMOURS (NEOPLASIA)

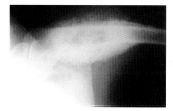

Radiograph showing the presence of an osteosarcoma of a dog's leg bone.

An ulcerating tumour on the paw.

TUMOURS (NEOPLASIA)

Many different types of tumour can affect the locomotive system. Some of the common ones are listed in the panel. Benign tumours tend to grow slowly and remain localised to one area. If they are removed, they are unlikely to recur. Malignant tumours, however, are more aggressive and can spread to other distant sites such as the lungs. If they are removed, they often recur. Many tumours are confirmed by radiography – and the chest is often X-rayed too, to check for evidence of any spread to the lungs. Sometimes the tumour is biopsied (a small portion is removed) to identify it accurately.

The most common tumour of the bone is the primary osteosarcoma. It occurs most often in the distal radius (near the carpus) and in the proximal humerus (near the shoulder). Large and giant breeds are more frequently affected than smaller dogs.

Signs: The signs depend on the site and nature of the tumour, but common symptoms are swelling, and lameness that gradually worsens. Sometimes an obvious lump can be felt.

Treatment: Treatment is individualised but it includes:

- **Surgical removal**: This may involve extensive resection (removal) of large areas of bone, which then need bone grafting and reconstructing.
- **Chemotherapy**: This is often combined with surgical removal of the mass.
- **Radiation therapy**.
- **Amputation of the affected limb**.
- **Palliative use of painkillers**: This is normally administered in untreatable, terminal cases. Pain control is given until the quality of life is impaired to such an extent that the dog requires euthanasia.

OTHER CONDITIONS

These conditions occur at any age.

CARPAL HYPEREXTENSION

The carpus (wrist) is a complex series of joints. If the structure is damaged, the carpus will sink towards the floor when the dog tries to bear weight on the limb.

Causes: Falling from a height.

Signs: Lameness, with sinking of the carpus and overextension. Radiographs are taken to see exactly which level of the carpus has been affected.

Treatment: Surgery is usually required. The affected joint is fused, by removing the articular cartilage from the bone ends, packing the joint with a bone graft and putting a plate across. Even though movement in the carpus is reduced, the outcome is usually good.

FRACTURES

A fracture is a break in a bone. Any bone in the body may be affected, including the skull and spine.

Causes: Fractures are caused by direct trauma, such as a road traffic accident, a shotgun injury or a fall.

Signs: Symptoms of a fractured bone include a reluctance to use or to move the affected area – a limb will be carried and will have an altered angulation. There may or may not be an obvious wound. The fracture site will be hot, swollen, and you may hear or feel grating. If a fracture is suspected, the animal should be moved as little as

COMMON TUMOURS OF THE LOCOMOTIVE SYSTEM		
Tissue type	**Benign form**	**Malignant form**
Bone		Osteosarcoma
Muscle	Rhabdomyoma	Myosarcoma
Joint lining		Synovial sarcoma
Cartilage	Chondroma	Chondrosarcoma
Fibrous tissue	Fibroma	Fibrosarcoma

Amputation of a limb is often as a result of severe trauma (e.g. road traffic accident) or disease (e.g. bone tumours). Contrary to most owners' initial reactions, animals will tolerate the loss of a limb exceptionally well, even though it can be a difficult time for all those involved in the decision.

Scars can be a constant reminder of the traumatic illness that the pet has had to endure. In time, though, these scars will be covered from view, as the fur grows back, and it is at this stage that owners often become more comfortable with the decision that has had to be made.

Initially, your veterinarian may keep your pet in the hospital under observation. This is primarily to manage his pain threshold and to administer pain-killing injections as soon as they are required. Once the wound has settled down and your pet is eating and able to stand without assistance (usually within 24 hours), he will be discharged home to you.

POST-OPERATIVE CARE
You will be given simple post-operative instructions, which will almost certainly contain information regarding the animal's immediate and future exercise and dietary requirements. In these first few weeks, you may find that providing extra bedding will cushion the surgical site and provide extra comfort and support.

EXERCISE
Exercise will largely be required little and often until your pet has mastered his new physique. Becoming aware of his new centre of balance will become second nature within a short period of time.

FOOD
Obesity is a problem encountered by a growing number of our dog population and it is even more important for an amputee not to become overweight. This would place extra strain on both the hips and other joints of the body, which are already compromised through loss of a limb. Carrying extra weight can also put additional pressure on the heart and the work it needs to do. See Chapter Three for information on weight loss and control.

LONG-TERM CARE
This is simply a matter of balancing the right intake of food with the correct amount of exercise, and your veterinary surgery can help you with this.

A healthy amputee will continue to lead a normal life and enrich his owners' lives as before.

---

possible and only with extreme care, as the dog may bite due to the pain. Seek immediate veterinary attention and remember that every time the fracture fragments move, they do more damage to the surrounding tissues.

Treatment: Radiographs are required to assess the exact nature and extent of the fracture. Repair can be postponed for several days if the animal is in shock or has other life-threatening injuries. During this time, a haematoma (collection of blood) will form around the broken bone ends. However, if the fracture is left too long, the muscles around the injury will contract, making repair more difficult. Repair is urgent where fractures extend along a bone into a joint. In this case, it is important rapidly to restore the normal joint surface in order to avoid long-term problems such as osteoarthritis.

There are many repair techniques, depending on the fracture site, type and other factors such as the age of the animal. However, the basic principles remain the same:

FEMORAL FRACTURE

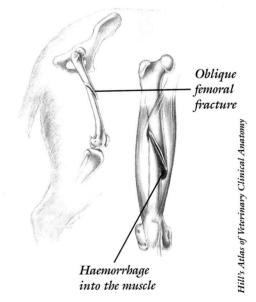

Oblique femoral fracture

Haemorrhage into the muscle

Hill's Atlas of Veterinary Clinical Anatomy

5 LIFE SUPPORT SYSTEMS

CARDIOVASCULAR SYSTEM

Blood passes around the dog's body about two times in every minute. The heart is the centre of the system, and the arteries, capillaries and veins transport the blood to the vital organs. The heart is regulated by a well-developed control system in the brain. Together, these various elements make up the cardiovascular system.

CIRCULATORY SYSTEM

The circulatory system has two circuit loops, rather like a figure of eight race track. One circuit leaves the left side of the heart by the dorsal aorta. This circuit is responsible for supplying the body with oxygen, nutrients and hormones, etc. Once these vital supplies have been delivered, the blood returns to the right side of the heart, via the veins. En route, it removes carbon dioxide and other waste products from the body's tissues.

The second circuit starts from right side of the heart, via the pulmonary artery and into the lungs. Oxygen and carbon dioxide are exchanged in the lungs, with the newly-oxygenated blood returning to the left side of the heart via the pulmonary vein.

There is a third, slower-moving, drainage circuit called the lymphatic system (see page 92).

THE HEART

There are four pumping chambers (the right atrium, the right ventricle, the left atrium, and the left ventricle), each of which has its own set of non-return valves propelling blood away from the heart with each contraction.

STRUCTURE OF THE HEART

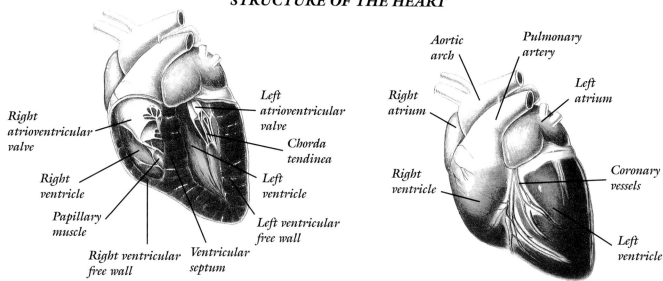

Right atrioventricular valve

Right ventricle

Papillary muscle

Right ventricular free wall

Ventricular septum

Left atrioventricular valve

Chorda tendinea

Left ventricle

Left ventricular free wall

Aortic arch

Pulmonary artery

Right atrium

Left atrium

Right ventricle

Coronary vessels

Left ventricle

Hill's Atlas of Veterinary Clinical Anatomy

90

ARTERIES AND VEINS

The arteries have elastic walls. With every beat of the heart, blood is forced down the arteries, and the arterial walls stretch to help propel the blood between each heartbeat. If an artery is cut, blood will spurt from it with each beat of the heart.

Arterioles are smaller arteries. The wall of the arterioles also has a smooth muscle that can constrict or dilate depending on the need to direct blood to a particular organ. For example, in a state of shock, or after major blood loss, blood can be directed to vital areas, such as the dog's brain, the kidneys, and the heart muscles. The blood flows from the main arteries to the arterioles, eventually reaching the even smaller capillaries, after which the arterial system of circulation terminates.

Capillaries are the tiny channels which feed blood to the body's tissues, with oxygen, glucose, and the other substances carried in the blood. Once the body's myriads of cells have been fed their fresh blood supply, the blood returns to the heart via the veins. Small veins remove the 'used' blood from the tissues. The blood then travels through increasingly large veins until it reaches the heart. The veins do not have muscles and the blood pressure in the veins is low. However, there is a series of one-way valves in the veins that prevent the blood from flowing backwards. The body muscles around the veins squeeze the blood in the right direction and this is why exercise, even gentle walking for the sick or elderly dog, helps the circulation.

BLOOD

There are three major components of blood:
- **Red blood cells**: Carry oxygen around the body.
- **White blood cells**: Fight infection.
- **Plasma**: Carries the antibodies as part of the serum proteins of the blood.

Blood is bright red when it leaves the heart because it is full of oxygen. Blood returning to the heart through the veins is a blueish-red colour. This is because it has given up most of its oxygen content to the body's tissues. Plasma consists of water, mineral salts that help to keep up the blood pressure, plasma proteins, foodstuffs, gases (e.g. the carbon dioxide removed from the tissues), antibodies against infection, hormones, enzymes, and waste products such as urea.

RED BLOOD CELLS

Red blood cells live for about four months, after which they are removed and broken down in the spleen or lymph nodes. New red cells are produced by bone marrow.

In dogs that have suffered blood loss or anaemia, (see panel, below), more red blood cells are needed

---

ANAEMIA

Anaemia is a condition in which the blood has reduced amounts of haemoglobin, the oxygen-carrying protein within the red blood cells.

In its acute form, anaemia is seen most often after sudden blood loss:
- Bleeding after an accident or a deep cut
- Rupture of the spleen or other internal organ
- Cancer where a tumour bursts (haemangiosarcoma)
- Warfarin poisoning or a blood-clotting disorder.

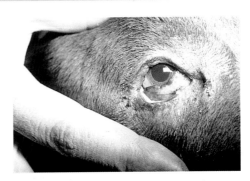

Anaemia (and haematoma) seen in the eye.

Slow bleeding is more difficult to detect, and may not be noticed until a lethargic dog is blood-tested for anaemia. Causes of slow bleeding include:
- **Internal bleeding**: Common sites of internal bleeding are the bladder (indicated by blood in the urine), and the intestines (indicated by black stools). Stomach ulcer bleeding may be recognised by blood in the vomit.
- **Parasites**: Hookworms in the intestine suck blood and will only be discovered if eggs are looked for in the faeces. Babesiosis (common in southern Europe) may occur in dogs bitten by ticks. The dog's blood supply is infected with a parasite when the dog is bitten. This parasite destroys the dog's red blood cells.
- **Immune-mediated haemolytic anaemia**: An auto-immune disease where the dog's body attacks his own blood cells.
- **Bone marrow disease**: This delays the formation of new red blood cells as the older ones are removed.
- **Kidney disease**: This creates a deficiency of the hormone erythropoietin.

very quickly. If the body is short of oxygen, the kidney produces a substance that stimulates bone marrow to produce extra red blood cells.

WHITE BLOOD CELLS

There are various forms of white cell.
- **Neutrophils and monocytes**: attack and destroy invading bacteria or other foreign material in the blood.
- **Lymphocytes and plasma cells**: produce antibodies (the immunoglobins) which destroy or neutralise toxins and invading organisms.
- **Eosinophils**: produce chemicals, e.g. histamine, to cause inflammation to combat parasites and allergens.

PLATELETS

These are the tiniest of the blood cells that clot the blood to prevent an animal from bleeding to death. Provided that no major artery has been severed, blood should clot within two to four minutes.

LYMPHATIC SYSTEM

The fluid that travels through the lymphatic system is known as lymph. It is a clear fluid, not normally seen, except for when fat is digested and the lymph carries small fat droplets in lacteals from the intestine to the liver.

LYMPHATIC SYSTEM

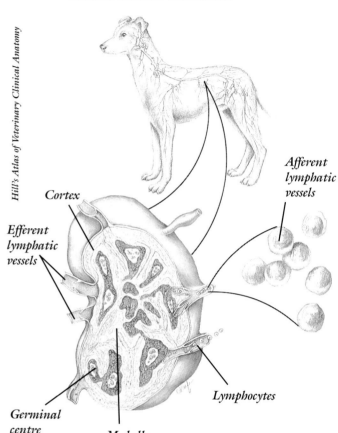

Hill's Atlas of Veterinary Clinical Anatomy

Cortex

Afferent lymphatic vessels

Efferent lymphatic vessels

Lymphocytes

Germinal centre

Medulla

HAEMOPHILIA AND THROMBOCYTOPENIA

There are various reasons why there may be prolonged internal bleeding or blood loss from the gums, or even from the bladder. Failure in the normal blood-clotting mechanism is one of the most likely causes.

HAEMOPHILIA

Haemophilia is an inherited bleeding disease which occurs in breeds such as the German Shepherd and Dobermann. Carriers of the disease do not necessarily display any symptoms, so it is not possible to be sure that any bloodline in an affected breed is free of the disease.

Haemophilia may be diagnosed following sudden, severe bleeding, which normally causes death within hours. Alternatively, the disease may become apparent only after an injury (e.g. road accident) or an operation. Tests on blood-clotting ability can be performed, and wise surgeons do these before undertaking any routine surgery in breeds known to be involved. Von Willebrand's disease (see Chapter Ten) is one of the best-known dog haemophilias.

THROMBOCYTOPENIA

In this condition, a shortage of small blood platelets leads to excessive blood loss. If the condition is not recognised, the dog will become very weak and anaemic. Some forms of thrombocytopenia are the result of auto-immune problems, where the body attacks its own cells. In such cases, treatment with steroids over a long period of time seems very effective.

Sometimes, drugs used to treat other conditions can cause thrombocytopenia. This is especially true of chemotherapy. Blood samples will be taken regularly from any dog undergoing chemotherapy, to monitor blood cells.

Transfusions of plasma are preferable to 'whole' blood in patients with clotting defects. Where severe blood loss leads to anaemia, the most effective treatment is a transfusion of whole blood, with other necessary medication directed at the cause of thrombocytopenia.

LEUKAEMIA

Leukaemia is the presence of excessive cancerous white cells in the blood. Leukaemia is easy to diagnose from blood smears. The disease means 'white blood'; under a microscope, there are many abnormal white cells crowding out the much more frequent red cells.

The signs of canine leukaemia include weakness, loss of appetite, pale gums or bleeding at the gums' margin with the teeth, and pinpoint haemorrhages. Nervous signs, involving the eyes or other nerve-supplied organs, may also develop.

LYMPHOMA

Lymphoma is the term used to cover various forms of cancer affecting parts of the body that contain lymphoid tissue. Cutaneous lymphosarcoma is one of the worst forms to see, as non-healing skin ulcers develop on the body and spread to other parts of the skin. Lymphoma may also start in the spleen, the liver or the tonsils. The bone marrow is another area that may be affected and only when this happens is leukaemia recognised. The disease known as myeloma may first be diagnosed as anaemia, with a shortage of red cells that have been crowded out by the lymphoid cells multiplying inside the bones.

Treatment involves the use of cytotoxic agents (cancer treatments), used in various combinations. The prognosis is good for chronic cases, but unfavourable for acute leukaemia.

The lymphatic system plays a major role in fighting against infection. As lymph travels through the lymphatic system, it is filtered through a series of lymph nodes (glands). Any foreign proteins that are filtered in this way are then examined by the immune system to see if they pose a threat to the dog's health. The lymphatic system also filters blood through the spleen and the thymus.

The spleen is a major centre for the production of lymphocytes, and it functions similarly to the lymph nodes, removing bacteria and other foreign substances. The spleen is also a reservoir of red blood cells, storing fresh cells and removing exhausted cells from circulation.

The thymus is an organ found in the chest, close to the heart. This organ is largest in the younger puppy and it shrinks after the first few months of life. In a puppy, the thymus acts to fight off infection. As the dog matures, the lymphoid tissue in the thymus is replaced by fat, as other organs take over its work. A significant proportion of lymphocytes are produced in the thymus.

The tonsils are full of lymphoid tissue, defending against infections entering the mouth. There is also lymphoid tissue on the inner surface of the third eyelid, which is important in dealing with eye infections.

HEART DISEASE AND FAILURE

The overall incidence of heart disease in dogs is approximately 10 per cent. Unlike humans, coronary heart disease and thrombosis of the heart are rare in dogs. The main problems are due to valvular incompetency, weakening heart muscle or irregular heart rhythms.

Heart disease can be classified into defects that a dog is born with (congenital) or diseases that arise during adult life (adult heart disease). The majority of dogs suffer from adult heart disease, although 1 per cent of dogs present with signs of congenital heart disease.

Some congenital heart diseases are known to be hereditary. Other congenital disorders are probably also hereditary in view of the known breed predispositions, although not proved. It is also quite possible that some adult-onset heart diseases are hereditary, such as dilated cardiomyopathy (page **XX**).

SIGNS

Heart disease is usually present before the dog displays any overt signs, or even before he is actually suffering from heart failure. Your veterinarian will often be able to detect signs of heart disease by listening for heart murmurs and rhythm abnormalities.

CAUSES OF HEART FAILURE

ADULT-ONSET DISEASES
- Mitral and/or tricuspid valve disease (endocardiosis)
- Dilated cardiomyopathy
- Pericardial effusion
- Heartworm disease
- Palpitations.

CONGENITAL DISEASES
- Patent ductus arteriosus
- Aortic stenosis
- Pulmonic stenosis
- Mitral valve dysplasia
- Tricuspid valve dysplasia
- Ventricular septal defect
- Atrial septal defect

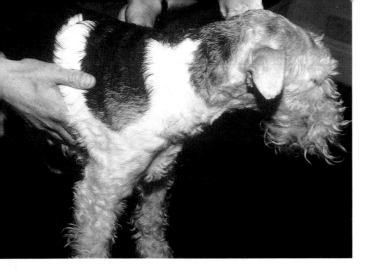

Feeling for a heartbeat and checking for vibrant murmurs – both part of a routine cardiac examination.

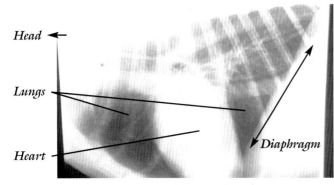

Head ←

Lungs

Heart

Diaphragm

Radiograph of a normal heart and lungs.

DIAGNOSING HEART DISEASE

HISTORY AND CLINICAL EXAMINATION
Often, your veterinarian will be able to make a presumptive diagnosis based on the dog's symptoms, combined with a clinical examination and any predisposition to heart disease (e.g. breed, age, etc.). For example, a Cavalier that developed a murmur at six years of age, presenting two years later with breathlessness, a cough, and a much louder murmur, is likely to have progressed into congestive heart failure (page 95). Likewise, a six-year-old male Dobermann that presents with rapid-onset breathing difficulties and coughing, in which an abnormal heart sound can be heard, is likely to have CHF due to dilated cardiomyopathy (pages 96 and 97). However, in many instances, if the diagnosis is uncertain, additional tests need to be performed.

RADIOGRAPHY
The most valuable diagnostic tool is a chest X-ray. X-rays show the outline of structures in the chest (e.g. the shadow of the heart), providing an overall appreciation of the heart size and shape. The lungs can often also be evaluated to check for any lung congestion or thoracic fluid, which greatly aids in deciding on which drugs and what dosages are required for treatment.

ELECTROCARDIOGRAPHY (ECG)
An ECG shows the electrical activity of the heart. A stretched and dilated heart is often under considerable strain, resulting in palpitations (abnormal electrical activity). An ECG is used in these situations to diagnose the type of electrical fault and to ascertain whether the abnormality can be treated with medication.

HEART RHYTHM

Arrhythmias are abnormalities in the electrical activity of the heart or its electrical wiring. Normally, there is a sequence of electrical activity through the heart, which stimulates the heart muscle to contract in the correct order and with the correct squeeze. There are essentially two types of electrical abnormalities.

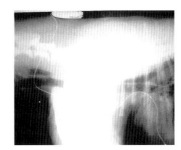

Radiograph of a dog with a pacemaker and its lead running inside the heart.

- **Extra electrical activity**: An extra electrical spark (palpitation) causes the heart to jump and contract out of sequence, resulting in little blood being pumped. If these palpitations are only occasional, drug treatment is not normally required. However, palpitations can be a symptom of a heart under strain. If the palpitations occur frequently and rapidly, the heart can go into spasms, pumping little or no blood for the duration of the palpitations. These can lead to weakness or collapse. The cause needs to be diagnosed and the primary problem treated, or the palpitations need to be controlled with drugs.

- **Faulty conduction**: A relatively common fault is a break in the wiring between the atria and the ventricles. This results in electrical activity failing to reach the ventricles, which causes them to beat at their own slow, intrinsic rate. This is called heart block. In many cases the cause is unknown. It is thought to be fibrosis of the wiring (which can be likened to a corroded electrical wire). This block can be bypassed by fitting an artificial pacemaker that stimulates the muscle of the ventricles to beat at a normal rate.

ULTRASOUND SCANS

An ultrasound scan shows the heart and its valves moving, as well as indicating the size of the four heart chambers. It shows the muscle of the heart contracting and how strong (normal or abnormal) this is, and so it is very useful in diagnosing heart muscle problems such as dilated cardiomyopathy (pages 96 and 97). Doppler ultrasound additionally permits the speed of blood flow through the heart to be measured and checked for abnormalities such as murmurs. Doppler ultrasound is of great benefit in diagnosing congenital murmurs, which are difficult to diagnose by other tests.

BLOOD TESTS

Bloods tests are needed to investigate medical or metabolic causes of collapse in dogs (see box below). When treating heart disease, they are useful for monitoring kidney function, protein levels, or electrolyte balance. When the heart fails, it struggles to maintain a good blood supply to the other organs, such as the kidneys. In addition, the kidney and liver need to metabolise the drugs used in treatment of heart disease and to maintain a balance of electrolytes. To check the body's ability to process and adapt to treatment, it is useful to take a blood sample at appropriate intervals for testing.

CONGESTIVE HEART FAILURE (CHF)

CHF is a common consequence of many forms of heart disease. The symptoms of CHF are similar, although the causes vary. There are two basic forms of CHF: left-sided CHF and right-sided CHF. There are a number of diseases that can cause either type.

Each of the four valves in the heart should act as non-return valves, permitting blood flow in one direction (forwards) only. This maintains a normal, flowing circulation. CHF occurs when the heart valves fail to work properly and allow blood to leak back into the heart. Blood dams up behind the faulty valve in the same way a dam in a river causes the water levels to increase behind the dam.

LEFT-SIDED CHF

When the valves on the left side fail, the blood builds up in the left side of the heart; the pulmonary veins (the veins that return blood to the heart) also become congested. This can then lead to the lungs becoming flooded, termed pulmonary/lung congestion. The name 'congestive heart disease' is derived from this effect of congestion.

There are three common symptoms of left-sided CHF:

- **Breathlessness**: As a result of pulmonary congestion, the lungs struggle to exchange oxygen with carbon dioxide. The dog will increase his breathing rate to try to compensate for this. In a healthy dog, the rested breathing rate (number of breaths per minute after rest and not panting) is less than 20 per minute. Dogs with pulmonary congestion can have rates in excess of 40 breaths per minute.
- **Exercise intolerance**: A dog with left-sided CHF is likely to show fatigue when exercised, due to the heart's reduced pumping ability. The heart is unable to supply the muscles used in exercise with an adequate supply of well-oxygenated blood.
- **Coughing**: When the heart becomes enlarged, because of the back flow of blood, it may press on the windpipe (trachea), causing the dog to cough.

MITRAL VALVE DISEASE

Mitral valve disease (valvular endocardiosis) is the most common cause of left-sided CHF in adult dogs. It is more common in older dogs and in smaller breeds. Some breeds are particularly predisposed to the disease, e.g. the Cavalier King Charles Spaniel.

When mitral valve disease occurs in ageing dogs, the valves become faulty, so that when the valve

COLLAPSE

Collapsing in dogs is not uncommon and heart disease can certainly be one possible cause. When a dog has collapsed and is presented to the veterinarian as fully recovered and normal, he presents a diagnostic challenge. The dog's owner can be of great assistance by observing their dog when he is in the collapsed state. Features such as the colour of the lips, the heart rate, the circumstances surrounding the collapse, the time of day, etc., are all useful diagnostic aids.

The first objective is to try to decide if it was a seizure (i.e. a fit), a type of faint (syncope), or a weakness.
- If, at the very beginning of the collapse, the dog was relaxed (sleep-like), and the colour of the inside of lips goes pale or white, it is usually indicative of a cardiac-related collapse.
- If the dog was acting abnormally prior to the collapse, and then, right at the beginning of the collapse, was paddling or swimming with his legs, it is more suggestive of seizures.
- If the dog's colour goes blue, it is more suggestive of a respiratory problem.

sniffing and very fast heart rate. Consequently, murmurs can be difficult to appreciate in very young puppies. It is also virtually impossible to discern the difference between puppy murmurs and murmurs due to congenital defects in puppies (see panel, below).

AORTIC AND SUBAORTIC STENOSIS

Aortic stenosis (AS) is a narrowing of the aortic valve due to malformation. Subaortic stenosis (SAS) is a narrowing of the area just below the aortic valve (the outflow tract).

These defects restrict blood flow out of the left ventricle. The squirt of blood through the narrowed valve produces a murmur. To overcome this restriction, the muscle of the left ventricle becomes thickened. The severity of the muscle-thickening is proportional to the severity of the stenosis, and, to some degree, the murmur produced is louder with a more severe stenosis. A dog with a mild stenosis (which usually produces a fairly quiet murmur) can remain asymptomatic throughout his life.

Severe stenosis can lead to heart failure or an abnormal heart rhythm (because of the grossly-thickened heart muscle), resulting in death within a few years. Unfortunately, there is no reliably successful surgical option to date, and drugs provide only variable relief of symptoms.

PULMONIC STENOSIS

Pulmonic stenosis (PS) occurs when a malformation in the pulmonic valve causes it to narrow. The defect restricts blood flow from being pumped out of the heart by the right ventricle, with the squirt of blood producing a murmur. The right ventricle consequently builds muscle. Like aortic stenosis, the severity of the disease is proportional to the dog's life expectancy.

Severe pulmonic stenosis can be treated (but not cured) with surgery, which relieves some of the severity. Like aortic stenosis, severe cases of pulmonic stenosis can lead to abnormal heart rhythms and early death; it can also lead to right-sided congestive heart failure (page 96).

PATENT DUCTUS ARTERIOSUS

While a pup is in the womb, his lungs are not being used. As there is no need for the blood to be 'refreshed' in the lungs, the foetal pup has a direct connection between the two main arteries of the heart, bypassing the lungs altogether. When the puppy is born, this connecting vessel closes as the body adapts to oxygenating the blood through the lungs. In patent ductus arteriosus (PDA), the vessel fails to close at birth.

A PDA murmur is continuous, whereas virtually all other murmurs are intermittent, occurring only during heart contraction. Quite often, the murmur is so loud that its vibration can be felt by placing the hand on the left side of the chest over the heart.

Left-sided congestive heart failure (page 95) is the usual outcome of this abnormality, with massive heart enlargement developing. Fortunately, this is one congenital defect that is curable by surgery, although surgery is not without risk. If the PDA is closed before any heart enlargement develops, the dog should live a full and normal life. Left untreated, the 50 per cent survival rate for dogs with a PDA is approximately one year.

HEART MURMURS

Each of the four valves in the heart should act as non-return valves, permitting blood flow in one direction (forwards). If a valve is no longer preventing backflow (e.g. as in mitral valve disease, page 94), blood squirts back through the valve with each heartbeat. This backward flow results in an abnormal heart sound called a heart murmur, which sounds like a 'squirting' or 'gushing' noise, discernible during each heartbeat.

If a valve is abnormally narrowed, such as occurs with congenital stenosis of the aortic or pulmonary valves (above), blood flow pumped out through the stenosed valve is pinched, resulting in a murmur. A murmur can also occur through a hole in the heart, the murmur produced as blood is squirted through the hole.

Murmurs in adult dogs are generally considered abnormal, although not all are serious. In puppies less than six months of age, there can be quite innocent murmurs, often referred to as puppy murmurs. These occur due to blood being pumped so rapidly in such a small heart. As the puppy and his heart grow and mature, the murmur gradually disappears. It is virtually impossible to discern the difference between a puppy murmur and most congenital defects. If a murmur persists beyond six months of age, it is more likely to be a congenital defect.

A murmur can also be produced when a dog is anaemic and the blood is thin. In this situation, the thinner blood results in a faster speed of flow and a consequent murmur. A similar situation can occur when a dog is ill for other reasons, such as during a fever.

VENTRICULAR SEPTAL DEFECT

Ventricular septal defect (VSD) is the 'classic' hole-in-the-heart condition. The hole is normally in the thinner portion of the heart muscle, between the right and left ventricles. It produces a murmur that is not necessarily proportional to severity. A puppy born with a small ventricular septal can sometimes make a full recovery naturally – the hole closes as the puppy grows into adulthood, and the murmur disappears. If the hole is not small enough to close, then it can lead to left-sided congestive heart failure (page 95) later in life. There is currently no reliable successful surgical treatment in dogs with this defect, although drugs can control the symptoms to some degree.

MITRAL DYSPLASIA

Mitral dysplasia is a congenital malformation of the mitral valve. It results in left-sided congestive heart failure just like mitral valve disease does in adult dogs (page 94). Depending upon the severity of the malformation, dogs may survive between a few months and several years.

TRICUSPID DYSPLASIA

Tricuspid dysplasia is a congenital malformation of the tricuspid valve. It results in right-sided congestive heart failure, much the same as the effects of tricuspid valve disease in adult dogs (page 97).

HEARTWORM DISEASE

This parasitic infection of the heart presents the following symptoms: coughing, exercise intolerance, breathlessness, and weight loss. In severe cases, the inflammation results in ascites (pages 96 and 97). The disease is best managed by prevention.

See also Chapter Two.

THE URINARY SYSTEM

As part of the life support system, dogs, like all other mammals, have two kidneys, safely protected inside the body just behind the ribs and well under the back muscles. Leading out of each kidney is a drainage tube, called a ureter, which removes the urine from the kidneys. Urine runs as constant trickles down each ureter, meeting each other when they connect to the bladder, which acts as the urine storage organ. The bladder empties its contents through the urethra. This tube is wider and shorter than the ureter, and it starts at the level of the bony pelvis.

URINARY SYSTEM

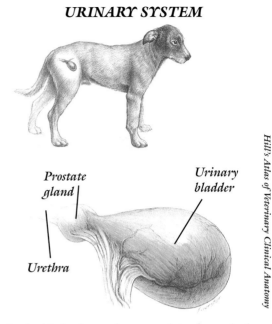

Prostate gland

Urethra

Urinary bladder

Hill's Atlas of Veterinary Clinical Anatomy

In the bitch, the urethra opens into the vaginal floor, the urine being expelled via the vulva when the bitch urinates. In the dog, the urethra is much longer, as it has to pass through the pelvic area and curve around the ischial bone (a part of the pelvis) in order to reach the penis. The urethra travels through the penis to its tip, where it is protected by folds of prepuce skin.

The difference between the male and female urinary tract systems is important when considering the reasons why urine leakage or incontinence problems are not the same in the two sexes. For example, the male dog is more likely to have an obstruction to the free flow of urine – a small stone or 'calculus' may stick anywhere in this long tube.

KIDNEY FUNCTION

The kidneys control the fluid balances of the body. They filter and remove toxic substances in the body's fluids, most of which are produced as by-products of digestion and muscle activity. The kidneys also regulate the amount of water excreted from the body as urine, so that the composition of blood can remain the same.

When blood enters the kidneys for filtration, the first filter unit it encounters are the numerous glomeruli (microscopic blood vessels). The urine formed then travels deeper into the inner part of the kidney (the medulla), where it travels through a series of tubes. Within these tubes, the urine is filtered again. Waste products and much-needed minerals are removed alike in these tubes. Any products that are needed by the blood are returned

KIDNEY STRUCTURE

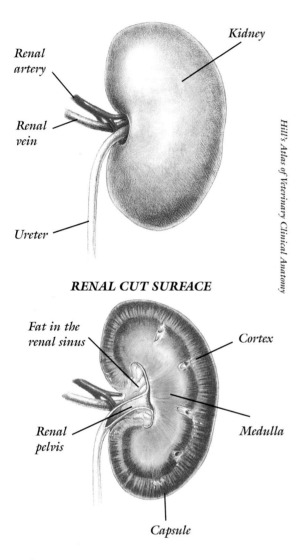

Kidney

Renal artery

Renal vein

Ureter

Hill's Atlas of Veterinary Clinical Anatomy

RENAL CUT SURFACE

Fat in the renal sinus

Cortex

Renal pelvis

Medulla

Capsule

through a process of reabsorption while the blood is in these tubes. For example, the medulla tubes remove waste products completely, while mineral salts and glucose are regulated by this process of filtration and reabsorption.

It is known that a diet too rich in salt will lead to an increase in blood pressure, but, within reason, the healthy kidney will remove enough of an excess of salt to prevent the heart being overloaded.

The kidneys are also involved in the formation of vitamin D, necessary for healthy bones and teeth. The body takes in fat-soluble vitamin D, which the kidneys convert into the more available water-soluble form.

When there are low levels of oxygen carried by the blood, the kidney responds with a greater

production of the hormone erythropoietin, which, by acting directly on the red bone marrow, stimulates the formation of more red blood cells. In the treatment of dogs with severe anaemia, as may occur in advanced kidney disease, the hormone erythropoietin may have to be injected into the dog on a regular basis.

Another kidney hormone, renin, is produced as soon as the blood level of sodium falls. Renin regulates the dog's blood pressure control. Blood plasma contains a substance called angiotensin. Renin converts the angiotensin into another substance, angiotensin II, which stimulates the adrenal cortex (the outer part of the kidney) to release the hormone aldosterone. Aldosterone increases the body's reabsorption of water and products by the outermost tube in the kidney's filtration system, so promoting the retention of sodium and chloride inside the body. Angiotensin also increases blood pressure. By constricting the fine blood vessels throughout the circulatory system, more blood is forced into the glomeruli filters in the kidney, meaning that more blood is detoxified.

RENAL DISEASES

CHRONIC KIDNEY FAILURE

Chronic kidney failure is a condition in which the kidney filtration and absorption system fails to work normally. The dog can lose up to three-quarters of his kidney function before signs of illness are noticed, and this usually starts to be seen in older dogs, from six years onwards. The other form, found in puppies, is usually seen before they reach one year of age.

A congenital kidney disease exists in several breeds, the best known being glomerulopathy and renal dysplasia, but other sorts of kidney disorder are found in litters of puppies in certain breeds. For example, Cocker Spaniels used to be affected with hereditary nephropathy, but, by means of not breeding from affected lines, the condition is now quite rare in the breed.

Signs: The signs of kidney failure include increased thirst, and the production of large quantities of dilute urine. The urine is pale in colour, and, because the kidney is filling the bladder continuously, the dog may want to go out more or exhibit a lapse in toilet-training. Left untreated, the dog may start to vomit partly-digested food, show a loss of appetite, and appear weak. When less than 25 per cent of the kidney is functioning, the breath becomes foul-smelling, mouth and stomach ulcers may develop,

CHRONIC RENAL DISEASE

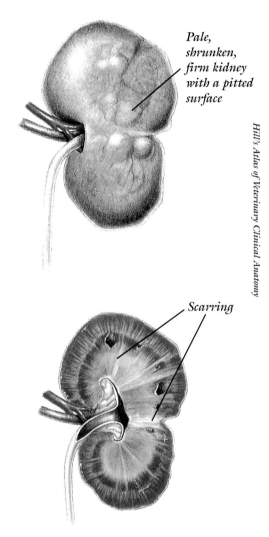

Pale, shrunken, firm kidney with a pitted surface

Scarring

Hill's Atlas of Veterinary Clinical Anatomy

and the teeth build up brown tartar much more rapidly than usual. Another sign of a failing kidney is anaemia. At a more advanced stage, there may be muscle-twitching or convulsions, due to the retained waste products affecting the brain. In the final stages, dehydration and collapse show there has been acute kidney failure.

More unusual signs are due to a lack of available vitamin D and retention of phosphates in the bloodstream. When vitamin D is supplied at inadequate levels, the dog may develop 'rubber jaw'. Mainly seen in younger dogs with an inherited renal disease, this condition makes the lower jaw feel fibrous rather than bony. The effects will be obvious on examination.

Phosphate retention leads to hyperphosphataemia

with the parathyroid glands becoming involved. The blood content of phosphate is raised due to an inability to excrete phosphate. This leads to bone-softening and calcium deposits in the kidneys.
Treatment: A low-phosphate prescription diet usually helps (see Chapter Three), but it may be necessary to add aluminium antacids to absorb excess phosphate in the gastrointestinal tract.

CYSTITIS

Causes: Inflammation of the bladder lining usually occurs when bacteria enters the body via the urinary tract. Viruses are less likely to cause cystitis. A catheter increases the chance of the dog developing cystitis, as it provides a route for the bacteria to travel. A bitch on heat is more susceptible to cystitis than at any other time in her oestrous cycle.

Bacteria may also enter the bladder through the bloodstream. The bacteria commonly found to cause throat inflammation may further invade the body and settle on the heart valves or the glomeruli filter units of the kidneys. They then travel through the circulatory system until they reach the bladder, where a stagnant pool of urine encourages multiplication and consequent urinary tract infection.

Dogs spend a significant time indoors, with the result that their opportunities to urinate are limited. Bladder distension creates favourable conditions for bacteria. It also reduces the blood supply to the bladder, so there is less defence against invading bacteria.

Prostate enlargement and 'slipped discs' predispose dogs to urinary tract infections. These complaints result in difficulty passing urine, as well as failure to empty the bladder fully with each attempt. Cystitis may also arise from bladder 'stones' or calculi (see box on page 102).
Signs: A dog will want to urinate more frequently, and, after passing urine, will remain in the same position, trying to void a few remaining drops – as if he has the feeling that the bladder has not been fully emptied. Blood may be seen in the urine, either as streaks or as a more uniform, pale-pink staining.
Treatment: Urinary tract infections are best treated after urine culture and analysis tests have been performed, as these may affect the choice of treatment. Usually, antibiotics are used, varying between a single high dose and a five- to ten-day course. The antibiotic is best given late at night, after the dog has emptied his bladder. This is because urine stored overnight will have a high concentration of the medication. Antimicrobials may

Dogs produce highly-concentrated urine, containing a number of salts and crystals.

In a healthy dog, the crystals are passed out of the body in the urine.

However, if a dog does not pass urine often enough, the crystals can act as nuclei, with bigger, sharper-edged crystals forming around them. Eventually, these may develop into bladder 'stones', causing significant bladder irritation and difficulty in passing urine.

CAUSES

Crystals in the urine are associated with dietary imbalances, limited opportunity to drink and to urinate, breed disposition, and bacterial infection. A dog suffering with bladder stones will display the symptoms of cystitis (page 101), particularly during the early stages of stone formation.

TREATMENT

Providing ample water and toileting opportunities is one of the best preventative measures.

Modification of the diet, to reduce the amount of high-quality protein, magnesium and phosphorus, will also help to prevent crystal formation, and may prove effective in dissolving pre-existing stones.

Where calculi are large, drug therapy and surgery may be required. Urine specimens, collected monthly and examined while very fresh, can be used to check for the return of crystals.

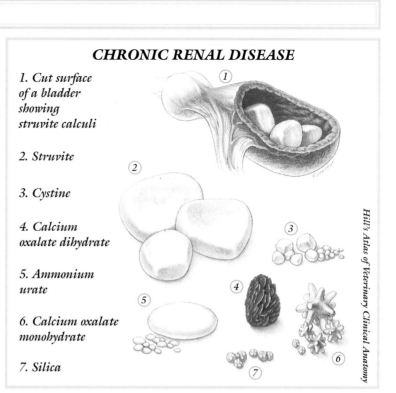

CHRONIC RENAL DISEASE

1. Cut surface of a bladder showing struvite calculi

2. Struvite

3. Cystine

4. Calcium oxalate dihydrate

5. Ammonium urate

6. Calcium oxalate monohydrate

7. Silica

Hill's Atlas of Veterinary Clinical Anatomy

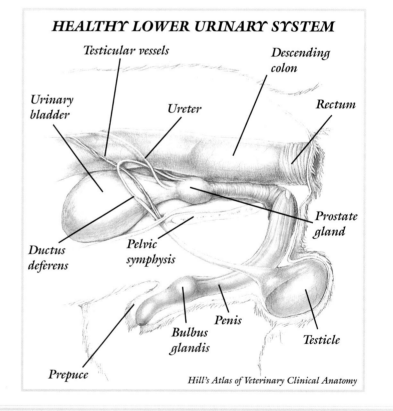

HEALTHY LOWER URINARY SYSTEM

Testicular vessels

Descending colon

Urinary bladder

Ureter

Rectum

Ductus deferens

Pelvic symphysis

Prostate gland

Bulbus glandis

Penis

Testicle

Prepuce

Hill's Atlas of Veterinary Clinical Anatomy

be used for 10 to 14 days and some products need only a single dose every 24 hours.

Evidence suggests that dietary modification and increased fluid intake may be as effective as using repeated courses of antibiotics for cystitis. Prescription diets may help to relieve the symptoms of cystitis, while increased fluid intake causes the dog to pass urine more often, helping to disperse any bacteria that may be present.

In the past, urinary antiseptics (e.g. mandelate) were used, but today, these are prescribed only in non-responsive cases that return rapidly. In resistant cases, the best results are obtained by changing the antibiotic, based on culture and sensitivity tests. A low dose of a broad-spectrum antibiotic, used at bedtime, may also be tried.

DIABETES

Diabetes is an example of a disease where too much urine is produced. However, the kidney is affected differently depending on which form of diabetes the dog has.

In diabetes mellitus, increased amounts of urine are produced as a side effect of the kidney's attempts to remove harmful, excess blood sugar. In diabetes insipidus, however, the kidney produces copious amounts of watery, heavily diluted urine in response to a malfunction in the pituitary gland of the brain – this gland releases hormones that tell the body how much urine to produce.

Some dogs seem to gain satisfaction from swallowing liquids. A dog that has the signs of diabetes insipidus may be otherwise healthy, being simply a 'naturally thirsty' dog. This condition is known as psychogenic diabetes insipidus. The kidneys have to work overtime to remove the large quantities of water that the dog has drunk, and, after the fluid has been absorbed through the stomach and intestinal walls, it dilutes the blood. Psychogenic diabetes insipidus is found more commonly in some breeds than in others (e.g. Boxers, which like splashing the water around in their mouths).

In the summer, dogs need to drink more to cool the body, but conversely, in very cold weather, some dogs also drink to excess. Stress may also play a role. Guide dogs and other assistance dogs, if things are not going right in their work, sometimes drink more water than would be needed just to satisfy normal thirst requirements.

GLOMERULONEPHRITIS

This special type of kidney disease is one where the glomeruli become clogged up with protein-like substances deposited from the dog's own antibody system. Eventually, the affected glomeruli shut down, and, as more of these filter units are affected and forced to shut down, kidney failure occurs.

Causes: Some puppies are predisposed to the disease because of hereditary factors. Other causes may be infectious. For example, glomerulonephritis has been known to follow pyometra (page 165), pancreatitis, viral infections, heartworm (page 29) and Lyme disease (page 30).

Signs: The first signs of this condition are similar to those of any other kidney disorders – increased thirst

and urination. Other symptoms include possible swelling in the dog's legs (due to retained fluid) and an enlargement of the abdomen (due to ascites). Affected dogs are likely to become noticeably thin with a protruding backbone, caused by loss of protein. This will seem doubly strange because the dog is likely to have an increased appetite. The veterinarian will be able to diagnose glomerulonephritis by measuring the quantity of protein in the urine.

Treatment: The medication used will depend on which type of disorder has been diagnosed. Antibiotics, anabolic steroids and anaemia treatment may form the basis of therapy. In nearly every case, a change in diet will help the kidney disease by lowering the blood pressure, taking the workload off the kidney (so it has fewer waste products to process), and replacing substances the dog may have become short of. Prescription diets obtained from veterinary practices are popular, and they have allowed dogs to live for additional years as the disease becomes better understood.

NEPHRITIS

This general term nephritis indicates an inflammation of the kidneys. However, the term is commonly used to describe a condition in which older dogs show an increased thirst and a larger urine output. The examination of both blood and urine specimens will give information that leads to a more definite diagnosis, and, hopefully, treatment to help the dog to lead a normal life.

PROSTATE DISEASE

Causes: The prostate becomes enlarged when the ratio of male hormone to female hormone becomes unbalanced, normally in male dogs, six years and older. The infrequency of entire dogs having opportunities for mating is quoted as a possible cause, but the biggest problem seems to be when a stud dog retires and has no more opportunities to rid himself of the prostate fluid created during the 'tie' (see Chapter Nine).

The most common prostate disease is prostatitis. Cancer of the prostate is quite rare, but the benign hyperplasia seen in the middle-aged male is unlikely in any dog that has been castrated. The only reason why a prostate will be found to be enlarged in the older, castrated dog is due to cancer, as bacteria rarely lodge in a shrunken prostate of the neutered dog. Prostate cancer may metastisise, spreading to the pelvic bone, the sublumbar lymph nodes and the lungs.

NORMAL PROSTATE GLAND

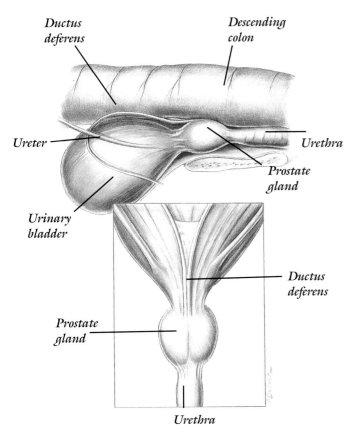

Ductus deferens

Descending colon

Ureter

Urethra

Prostate gland

Urinary bladder

Ductus deferens

Prostate gland

Urethra

BENIGN PROSTATIC HYPERPLASIA

The enlarged prostate gland may impinge on the rectum

Diffuse enlargement of the prostate gland due to epithelial or glandular hyperplasia

Hill's Atlas of Veterinary Clinical Anatomy

Prostate cysts originate from a tiny structure known as the uterus masculinis. It may be compared with the human appendix – something that has lost any real function but which can cause a major illness.

Signs: An early sign is apparent constipation, as the dog strains more than normal. The enlarged prostate bulges up towards the exit tube of the rectum, causing difficulty in passing faeces. Sometimes, there will be a discharge from the penis, often seen as blood in the urine. If there is a prostate abscess or cancer, abdominal pain and discomfort will be noticed, while any pressure near the tail will make the dog flinch.

Treatment: The veterinarian can confirm diagnosis using X-ray or ultrasound examination. Treatment may involve antibiotics, with or without anti-male-hormone injections. Radiotherapy and prostatectomy are less successful when treating cancer of the prostate, as urinary incontinence often results. This, combined with survival rates of less than a year and the painful nature of the disease, suggests that euthanasia is the only practical course once diagnosis is certain.

Castration at an early age helps to prevent prostate disease.

URETHRITIS

Causes: Bacterial infections are the most common cause of this inflammation of the urethra's exit point. In the female, the urethra tube vents into the vagina, a place where bacteria can invade quite easily. The herpes virus has been suggested as a cause of urethritis, which the veterinarian can confirm or eliminate by checking for small blisters at the opening to the vulva or at the base of the penis.

Signs: In the bitch, undue washing between the legs and licking at the vulva may indicate internal irritation. There may be no visible discharge due to fervent cleaning of the area. Male symptoms include an increased tendency to pass urine with corresponding leg-raising (if he is entire), although this is less noticeable in the castrated animal.

Treatment: This depends on the underlying cause of the urethritis. In atrophic vaginitis, which occurs in older, spayed females, low-dosage oestrogens may be used. Antibiotics are another choice. Alternatively, a diluted, live-yoghurt suspension, syringed into the vagina, is thought to help any irritation suffered by the bitch. The yoghurt is given to recolonise the interior of the vagina/urethra exit point with healthy organisms as an attempt to prevent the return of disease bacteria from the outside.

6 THE RESPIRATORY SYSTEM

The canine respiratory system is an airway system running from the nostrils to the depth of the lungs. It encompasses the nose, tongue, trachea and the lungs, all of which are essential for the dog's respiratory process. The purpose of the respiratory system is to exchange gases in the dog's lungs, so that the blood receives an adequate supply of oxygen necessary for the body's metabolism. Carbon dioxide is removed when the dog breathes out.

Dogs also use their respiratory system in another important way, which can be seen in any dog on a hot day or after he has exercised. Panting is an essential way of cooling the body. Hyperthermia (where there is a build-up of heat inside the body) can be a fatal condition unless drastic steps are taken to allow rapid cooling. The hot dog must be able to pant and have access to water – this why some dogs die quickly when left in cars in the sun.

The dog's nostrils and nasal cavities have a dual purpose. Not only are they used for breathing, but they also play a role in the dog's hunting activities. The nostrils channel various scents to scrolls of bone in the forepart of the skull. These bony scrolls are covered with a sensitive mucous membrane that helps to differentiate between various smells.

AIR COMPOSITION
Respiration is the process of gas exchange between a living organism and the environment. For every breath that the dog takes, he inhales:
- 21 per cent oxygen
- 79 per cent nitrogen
- Trace of carbon dioxide
- Traces of other gases
- Some moisture and any particulate matter that happens to be in the locality. The hunting dog will be glad of the moisture as this helps to hold a

scent close to the ground, where the nose picks it up. On a hot, dry day, the dog has more difficulty distinguishing scents.

The town dog, and especially assistance dogs waiting at the roadside to cross, will pick up more than a fair share of diesel/petrol fumes from road vehicles, while cigarette smoke in the home may cause chronic bronchitis in dogs.

To keep the air reaching the lungs as pure as possible, there is a filtering mechanism that tries to remove harmful substances. When air is inhaled, it is warmed as it passes up through the nasal chambers, mucus helps to trap particles, and fine wands (cilia) waft these particles out towards the nostrils. The trachea or major airway from throat to lungs is also

UPPER AIRWAY

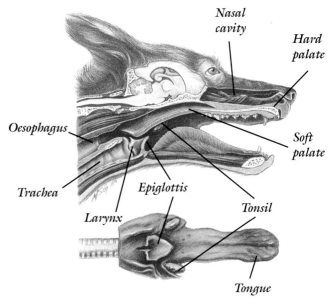

Nasal cavity

Hard palate

Oesophagus

Soft palate

Trachea

Epiglottis

Tonsil

Larynx

Tongue

THE THORAX

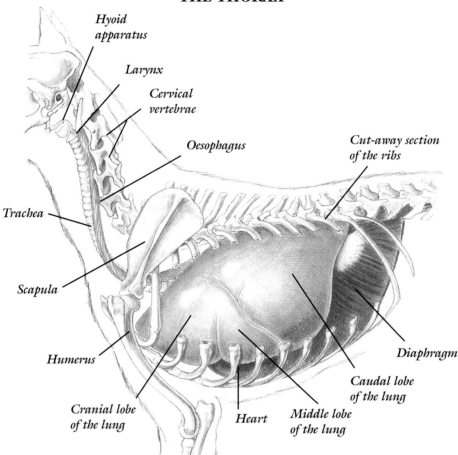

Hyoid apparatus

Larynx

Cervical vertebrae

Oesophagus

Cut-away section of the ribs

Trachea

Scapula

Humerus

Diaphragm

Cranial lobe of the lung

Heart

Middle lobe of the lung

Caudal lobe of the lung

lined with these cilia. Any foreign bodies (e.g. pollen grains) trapped by the tracheal cilia are coated in mucus and pushed outwards to the mouth, often aided by a cough so that any mucus blobs can be expelled.

BREATHING MECHANISM

The main muscles used for breathing are those situated between the ribs (intercostals), and the large muscle sheet that separates the chest from the abdomen (the diaphragm). When the ribs are arched out and the diaphragm is flattened, air is sucked into the chest.

This muscle action increases the length of the thoracic cavity and widens it – the lungs themselves do not have any muscles. The lungs are elastic, and it is this quality that allows them to inflate to fill the enlarged chest cavity created by the flattened diaphragm.

Once the lungs have expanded, gas exchange takes place, and the 'used' air is then expelled. The diaphragm relaxes, the ribs return to their resting state, and the elastic of the lungs recoils, forcing out the air. A distended abdomen, often seen after a large meal or in the pregnant bitch, will reduce the ability of the diaphragm to help with respiration.

THE LUNGS

When oxygen reaches the lung from the trachea, it travels into tubes (bronchi) within the lung. The bronchi connect to smaller, more numerous tubes (bronchioles), which in turn connect to the alveoli. The alveoli are tiny, air-filled sacs, only a single cell thick.

Deep within the lung, inside the alveoli, carbon dioxide is exchanged with oxygen. Oxygen passes through the single-celled layer into the bloodstream, where it finds the haemoglobin and binds to it. As this happens, the carbon dioxide that the blood was carrying before is released and it travels back through the alveoli wall.

The newly-oxygenated blood then circulates throughout the body, while the carbon dioxide is expelled when the lungs deflate.

PATH TO THE LUNGS

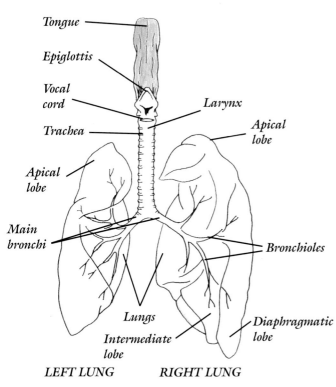

Tongue

Epiglottis

Vocal cord

Larynx

Trachea

Apical lobe

Apical lobe

Main bronchi

Bronchioles

Lungs

Diaphragmatic lobe

Intermediate lobe

LEFT LUNG   **RIGHT LUNG**

The lung is a finely-balanced, delicate structure that is susceptible to repeated damage and poor gas exchange. The single-cell layer in the alveoli also makes the absorption of harmful substances a hazard if contaminated air is inhaled. Any long-term scarring of the lungs reduces their elasticity, so that the dog is unable to take deep enough breaths. Any over-inflation of the lungs, as with some forms of anaesthesia, would depress the breathing mechanism further.

A dog will pant when he has a circulatory disease that results in the heart being unable to pump all the blood through the lungs. The veins within the lung overfill and apply pressure on the alveoli. The alveoli may collapse, resulting in inadequate gas exchange. The dog responds by panting, even when he is lying down, and when he is made to walk he becomes even more breathless.

NERVE CONTROL

The brain is responsible for controlling the breathing mechanism. The respiratory centre is situated in the hindbrain, responding to signals received from the lungs and from the gas content of the circulating blood. Stretch receptors in the lungs send information to the brain about the air content in the bronchial tubes, while specialised nerve centres in the arteries (the carotid body and the aortic body)

send signals to the brain about how much oxygen is in the blood.

The carbon dioxide content of the blood is also very important. As carbon dioxide dissolves in the blood, it increases the blood's acidity, creating carbonic acid. To some extent, the blood is buffered to stop this acidity, but the brain also plays a regulatory role by adjusting the breathing rate – breaths are made deeper and the breathing rate is made faster until the carbon dioxide is removed. Carbon dioxide can be used in small quantities to stimulate breathing, but high concentrations will lead to coma and death.

The forebrain has an overriding mechanism so that an animal can start panting in anticipation of a chase or an escape. Fear and pain also increase the breathing rate and a dog will be seen to be breathing rapidly after a road accident, even when there is no blood loss.

EXERCISE

The dog is adapted for short bursts of energetic running (e.g. Greyhound racing) or for sustained exercise over a longer time period (e.g. sled dogs). Selective breeding has shortened the legs and altered the shape of the head, the chest and the nose in some breeds, making sustained exercise more difficult, but most dogs require daily exercise in some form. Even dogs confined in kennels for long periods will voluntarily exercise themselves by pacing round and jumping, even if toys and other dogs are absent.

Owners should encourage some form of daily exercise, the length of each exercise period dependent on the dog's age and breed.

During exercise, the dog's muscles require increased amounts of oxygen. The muscles use up the oxygen released from the haemoglobin in the red blood cells at a faster rate. Oxygen has to be supplied at the same rate it is being used or blood oxygen levels will fall. The brain attempts to maintain the oxygen level and to remove the waste carbon dioxide by increasing the rate and depth of breathing. Unless the dog can breathe quickly enough to rid himself of the extra carbon dioxide, the body enters an oxygen-debt state and lactic acid builds up in the muscles, possibly leading to cramp.

After exercise, a healthy dog will pant for a short time. This is because the muscles require an increased amount of oxygen for a little time after exercise has finished.

Once the body has restored itself to its normal rate of oxygen and carbon dioxide exchange, panting ceases.

Respiratory distress manifests in marked contrast to normal, healthy panting. The mouth will be open and the tongue will hang out of the mouth. The tongue may show a purplish-blue colour. Fatigue on exercise is seen with congestive heart failure (page 94), heartworm disease (pages 29 and 99), and the muscle disorder known as myasthenia gravis. The congenital form of myasthenia gravis is seen first in puppies between three and eight weeks of age. The disorder has been found in Springer Spaniels, Jack Russell Terriers and Smooth-haired Fox Terriers.

Hereditary Labrador myopathy is another cause of exercise intolerance. You should inform your veterinarian if your dog displays signs of respiratory distress after exercising for more than five to ten minutes.

RESPIRATORY DISORDERS

ASPERGILLOSIS
A rare condition caused by the inhalation of fungal spores. Low immunity means it is more common in very young or older dogs, and there is a special problem in the German Shepherd where it may also spread to the lungs or even the bones. Nasal aspergillosis is a mycotic disease with signs of a persisting nasal discharge and sometimes extensive nose-bleeding due to erosion of the bone inside the nose. Treatment with fungicidal drugs is possible; these may have to be administered by tubes threaded into the frontal sinuses of the dog's nose.

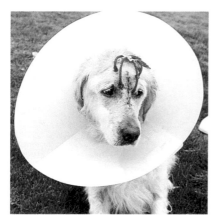

Treatment following aspergillosis, an infection of the nasal sinuses.

BRONCHITIS
Bronchitis frequently develops as the result of breathing in an allergen, e.g. pollens, moulds, and bacteria. Parasites, too, are a very common cause. Migrating worm parasites cause a type of hypersensitivity if they move through the body. In puppies, ascarid larvae pass through the lungs as part of the worms' normal development, sometimes leading to a lung disorder known as eosinophilic pneumonia. Other parasites that may be responsible for bronchitis include:
- **Oslerus osleri**: In the trachea
- **Angiostrongylus vasorum**: In the pulmonary artery
- **Dirofilaria immitis**: In the heart.

Bronchitis may also persist after infection with 'kennel cough' (page 109), an infection experienced by many dogs.

Small breeds, with their noses close to the ground, seem subject to bronchitis coughs. The older West Highland White Terrier is typically a dog that coughs at intervals (known as 'the crackling Westie'), and the cough indicates a lower airway disease. Radiographs show a dense lung structure, which is not an oedema (page 113) of the lungs but an interstitial fibrosis (scarring). The scars on the lung tissue are permanent so that the cough will never be fully eliminated, in spite of treatment.

Signs: Coughing and rapid breathing (tachypnoea) are the most obvious symptoms. The dog will be unable to walk far without needing to stop or to cough. After any form of mild exertion, the dog may exhibit signs of acute respiratory distress. There may not be a fever nor accompanying depression, and the dog may seem otherwise alert. There may be a watery discharge from the nose, and, occasionally, from the eyes as well. Atopic dermatitis may also be present, with pink or itchy skin indicating this is an allergic disease.

Treatment: Regular worming is one of the most effective preventative measures. Your veterinarian may want to take samples to identify any unusual parasites. If an allergic reaction is the cause of the disease, the dog will need to avoid the allergens responsible. Your veterinarian may take blood samples in order to identify the allergens (known as TLC screening). It is worth bearing in mind that puppies are especially at risk of developing allergies if they are kept in extremely clean conditions and then exposed to large amounts of dust or pollen.

If the allergen cannot be avoided, your veterinarian will prescribe medication to try to control the allergic response. Left untreated, bronchitis can lead to pulmonary oedema (page 113).

LARYNGEAL OBSTRUCTION
One of the reasons for wheezing and shortness of breath is a narrowing or obstruction in the airway between the nose and the lungs. The larynx is one of

Dogs can contract an infectious respiratory disease popularly called 'kennel cough'. Since kennel cough is actually part of a more complex respiratory disease, 'Canine infectious respiratory disease (CIRD)' is now considered to be a more appropriate term for this highly contagious condition.

CAUSES AND DEVELOPMENT OF DISEASE

The lungs are continually under assault by potentially damaging (pathogenic) organisms and substances which are inhaled during respiration. Fortunately, the dog has a number of highly efficient defence mechanisms that normally prevent, limit, and repair damage to the respiratory tract. To cause disease, pathogenic organisms (usually spread via discharges e.g. coughs or sneezes) have to colonise and proliferate in the respiratory tract and cause damage.

Various factors can lower a dog's resistance and/or facilitate colonisation by pathogenic organisms including:
• Close contact between diseased and healthy dogs, allowing spread of overwhelming numbers of organisms.
• Other illnesses.
• Stresses: Undernutrition, 'mechanical irritation' (e.g. persistent barking), and environmental stresses (e.g. extremes of temperature, poor air quality and overcrowding).
   Once infection is established and starts to overwhelm the defence mechanisms of the respiratory tract, the damage to the airway progresses, setting up a vicious circle of irritation and inflammation caused by coughing.

Infectious respiratory disease is mainly a problem for kennelled dogs, though it may become a domestic problem when a recently kennelled animal is re-homed with other pets. Occasionally, one or more of the infectious organisms starts to circulate in areas of heavy dog density (e.g. urban parks), where the naturally gregarious nature of dogs helps their spread.

INFECTIOUS ORGANISMS

There are two main classes of infectious organisms involved: viruses and bacteria. Generally, viruses colonise first and, by causing cell damage, promote subsequent establishment (secondary infection) by bacteria. Most of the organisms discussed below would cause a mild respiratory disease on their own, but usually combinations of organisms exacerbate the disease.

VIRUSES

CANINE PARAINFLUENZA
Causes mild upper respiratory tract disease alone, but is often involved in disease caused by other organisms.

CANINE ADENOVIRUS TYPE 2 (CAV-2)
Sometimes isolated from more severe cases of respiratory disease, this virus is closely related to Canine Adenovirus type 1 (CAV-1), which causes Infectious Canine Hepatitis (page 23). Unlike CAV-1, CAV-2 only affects the respiratory tract, causing conjunctivitis, tonsillitis, pharyngitis and, rarely, bronchopneumonia.

CANINE DISTEMPER VIRUS (CDV)
CDV causes many clinical signs (page 23), but is often associated with respiratory disease, especially in younger dogs. The disease varies from relatively mild in dogs in good condition, to very severe and sometimes fatal.
   The dry cough of the early stages is usually accompanied by listlessness and fever, with thick, yellow discharges from the nose and eyes.

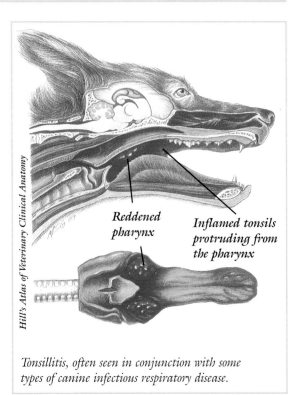

Hill's Atlas of Veterinary Clinical Anatomy

Reddened pharynx

Inflamed tonsils protruding from the pharynx

Tonsillitis, often seen in conjunction with some types of canine infectious respiratory disease.

Other signs of distemper may also be seen (vomiting, diarrhoea and nervous signs).

CANINE HERPES VIRUS (CHV-1)
CHV-1 is typically associated with 'Fading Puppy syndrome' (page 171). In adult dogs, however, CHV-1 is associated with respiratory disease.

OTHER
Other viruses (e.g. reovirus and influenza virus) have been implicated in canine infectious respiratory disease; their role in disease development is, as yet, unclear.

BACTERIA

BORDETELLA BRONCHISEPTICA: B. bronchiseptica is popularly known as 'the kennel cough bacterium' and it is often isolated from dogs which have upper respiratory tract disease. Characteristically, there is a harsh, dry cough, which is aggravated by activity or excitement, and is often followed by retching or gagging. Some dogs develop a thick nasal discharge.

MYCOPLASMAS: These are normal inhabitants of the respiratory tract, and in healthy dogs the bacteria remain in the upper respiratory tract without causing disease. However, mycoplasmas are isolated from the lower tract in dogs with bronchopneumonia.

BETA (ß) HAEMOLYTIC STREPTOCOCCI: Fortunately, this organism is less commonly involved in canine respiratory disease, since secondary infection with ß-haemolytic streptococci causes a dramatic disease, copious blood-tinged fluid is coughed up, followed by rapid decline and death.

LESIONS AND CLINICAL SIGNS: The time between exposure to infectious organism(s) and the first clinical signs (the incubation period) is between three and ten days. The morbidity rate (the number of dogs to which the disease will spread) can be very high among susceptible dogs, but fortunately death (mortality) is uncommon. Some signs specific to particular organisms are discussed above; a more general description of the clinical signs of CIRD follows.

MILD CASES: In mild or short-term disease, damage is restricted to the upper parts of the respiratory tract, and includes mild inflammation in the nose (rhinitis), throat (laryngitis, tonsillitis), and upper airways (tracheitis, tracheobronchitis). In these cases, local defences are often able to limit the damage, though dry coughing can prolong the irritation. The most common sign of mild CIRD is a persistent dry or "honking" cough, sometimes followed by retching, and the dog appears as if he is trying to vomit, or has something caught in his throat. There may be a mild or moderate nasal discharge. Appetite is near normal and the dog remains alert and active. The illness should run its course within one to three weeks, with the dog making a full recovery.

MODERATE/SEVERE CASES: In more serious cases, damage is more extensive since organisms spread from the upper respiratory tract to the lower airways and lungs (bronchopneumonia). The dog's defence mechanisms are overwhelmed, and secretions produced by the lungs, initially as an attempt to wash out organisms and debris, accumulate and become part of the disease process. Signs in more severe cases may include depression, fever, loss of appetite and thirst. A dry cough, with or without nasal or ocular discharge, may progress to a deep, productive, painful cough and breathing will be laboured. The tonsils become inflamed which contributes to the cough and inappetence. Very severe cases can be fatal.

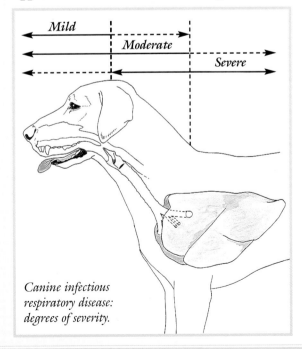

Canine infectious respiratory disease: degrees of severity.

DIAGNOSIS

Veterinary advice should be sought in all cases of persistent coughing or respiratory disease. The veterinarian will base diagnosis on one or more of the following:
- History: e.g. recent boarding.
- Physical examination.
- Elimination of other causes of coughs or respiratory distress (e.g. inhalation of dust; damage to the ribs; heart disease; parasites; etc.).
- Tracheal or lung washes: to look for the presence of white blood cells (which indicate inflammation).
- Identification of infectious agent(s) in swabs, secretions, lung washes or blood samples.
- Blood tests: to measure antibodies to specific infectious organisms.

TREATMENT

Treatment options depend upon the severity of the disease. Your veterinarian is best placed to decide which form of treatment is most appropriate for your particular dog.

MILD CASES: Many mild cases of CIRD resolve without the need for medical intervention, although veterinary advice should always be sought. Cough suppressants may be prescribed to limit further damage and to make the dog comfortable. Antibiotics may be given to limit secondary infections. For general nursing measures, see the ancillary treatments discussed below.

MODERATE/SEVERE CASES: These cases need to be treated properly and promptly. Your veterinarian may decide to use any of the following:
- **Antibiotics**
- **Cough suppressants**
- **Bronchodilators** (to open up the airways)
- **Mucolytics** (to make discharges easier to expel).

ANCILLARY TREATMENTS/NURSING
- Isolate dogs with suspected or confirmed signs of respiratory disease to limit spread of infection. Note that since infectious organisms may be shed before onset of clinical signs, close observation, or even precautionary isolation, of any dogs with which a diseased dog has had contact during the last 14 days, where practical, is a good idea.
- Allow affected dogs to rest and avoid stress factors (see Causes and Development, page 109).
- Ventilation should be adequate (see below), though sick dogs should be kept out of draughts. A humidifier may help the dog breathe more easily.
- Disinfect and evacuate dogs from the kennel, if practical.
- Hygiene: discharges from infected dogs may contaminate the environment and inanimate objects and can be spread by air currents. Personnel should be careful not to carry infectious material between isolation areas and unaffected dogs.

PREVENTION AND CONTROL

ENVIRONMENTAL CONTROLS
- Avoidance of the stresses and conditions likely to predispose dogs to infection and disease (see Causes and Development, page 109).
- Recommended indoor kennel ventilation rate is 15 to 20 air changes per hour.
- Maintenance of kennel hygiene.
- See ancillary treatments above for control measures during an outbreak.

VACCINATION: Some of the infectious organisms implicated in CIRD are covered by the standard canine vaccination programmes (page 23), so regular boosters are an important part of disease control. In addition, there are intra-nasal vaccines against B. bronchiseptica and PIV. Your veterinarian will help you plan a vaccination programme. Most vaccines require at least five days before protection is achieved, so if your dog requires a booster before a risk period (e.g. kennelling), do not leave the vaccinations to the last minute. Rarely, mild signs of respiratory disease follow vaccination; these usually resolve without treatment but consult your vet if concerned.

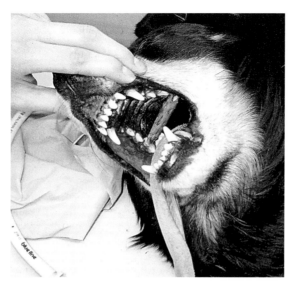

*Airway obstruction: a piece of stick
caught in the back of the throat.*

the narrowest parts of the airway and any restriction
in this space will cause severe breathing problems.

A laryngeal obstruction may be caused by a
foreign body, a tumour, an abscess or a thickening
known as a granuloma. If your veterinarian thinks
there is an obstruction in your dog's larynx, he may
use radiographs. However, the best method of
examination is by a laryngoscope or a flexible
endoscope that can be passed all the way down to
the lungs.

Obstructive laryngitis is a non-infectious,
inflammatory condition where the lining of the
larynx becomes swollen. It is similar in appearance
to tumours in the larynx and it is often only after
biopsy specimens are taken that the cause can be
diagnosed accurately.

Signs: Noisy breathing, a hard, 'honking' cough,
and an altered bark may be the first signs of an
obstruction. The tongue may become a purple-blue
colour, and may droop forwards out of the mouth.
There may also be complete collapse if the
obstruction is a large one.

Treatment: A foreign body must be removed,
although light, general anaesthesia may be required
for this. As the dog is already short of air, great care
is needed in applying anaesthesia, and an oxygen
supply should be at hand. Tumours require biopsy,
and then, if appropriate, removal.

In laryngeal paralysis, tying down the cartilage on
one side will improve breathing and food will not
get into the lungs if the surgeon works carefully.

Steroids can be used for some of the inflammatory
conditions that narrow the larynx.

LARYNGEAL PARALYSIS

Laryngeal paralysis cannot be seen on radiographs,
but it becomes very obvious when a light source
directed on the larynx shows the larynx open and
shut as air passes in and out. As air is breathed in,
the larynx cartilage and vocal folds should be drawn
open on both sides; whereas on breathing out, the
cartilages and folds should almost close the glottis.

Laryngeal paralysis usually affects both sides. On
breathing in, the cartilages are not opened widely
enough, while on breathing out, the cartilages are
passively forced outwards. Such paralysis may occur
after damage to the nerve supply, although older
dogs can develop it as an idiopathic condition. It is
especially common in the ageing Labrador Retriever,
and there is a congenital form affecting the Bouvier
des Flandres and the Siberian Husky.

NASAL DISCHARGE/RHINITIS

Nasal discharges and rhinitis (inflammation of the
nasal cavity lining) may be due to allergies, nasal
polyps, bacterial and fungal infections, and foreign
bodies. A viral infection, similar to the common
cold, may be due to a rhino-tonsillitis virus or other
viruses, but this will usually clear up after a few
weeks. The presence of polyps in the nose may cause
repeated sneezing and a watery or blood-tinged
discharge. Tumours will need to be examined
following biopsy.

Signs: Nasal discharge and repeated sneezing are
the usual signs of an infection or allergy affecting the
lining of the nasal cavity.

Treatment: Benign tumours can be dealt with
surgically, while malignant tumours might be treated
with radiation therapy. A mucopurlent (thick)
discharge from the nose suggests a bacterial rhinitis
(a secondary infection to some other injury to the
nasal cavity lining), which will respond to
appropriate antibiotic treatment. However, the signs
may return unless the underlying cause is diagnosed
and treated.

PLEURISY

Pleural membranes cover the lungs, separating them
from the other organs and forming a fluid-layered
chest cavity. Pleurisy is a condition in which these
membranes become inflamed. When this happens,
the pleura may exude fluid, so that the lungs are
unable to expand to their full size when breathing in.
Pleurisy is sometimes used to describe more severe
forms of pneumonia.

Signs: A dog suffering with pleurisy will have
exaggerated movement of the diaphragm every time

he inhales. His breathing will be distressed, with laboured inhalations, followed by short exhalations of air without effort. It is the easy exhalation that distinguishes pleurisy from a blockage of the nose or larynx. The dog may also have a raised temperature and a loss of appetite.

Treatment: Antibiotics are the mainstay for treating the bacteria cause behind pleurisy. The dog will also need plenty of quiet recuperation time, a good supply of high-quality air, and adequate food and drink supplies.

PNEUMONIA

Several viruses, including canine distemper and 'kennel cough' (page 109), can attack the lower respiratory tract causing pneumonia. Bacterial pneumonia is more common as a cause of lung damage in dogs.

Pneumonia sometimes follows an attack of bronchitis, because the bronchitis bacteria can work their way deep into the lungs, into the peribronchial tissue. If the bacteria reach the lungs via the bloodstream, the pneumonia is likely to be found in the caudal lung lobes.

Occasionally, pneumonia is caused by mould (when it is known as mycotic pneumonia), or by migrating worm parasites (roundworms, or, in North America, *Capillaria* and *Paragonimus*).

Signs: A dog with pneumonia may have shortness of breath, a reduced ability to walk, and he may become tired very quickly. If he has a cough, it may be dry and frequently repeated as a tickly irritation. Usually the body temperature is raised and the dog feels 'feverish'. The natural pink colour of the tongue and gums may also assume a purple-coloured tinge.

Treatment: Caught early, pneumonia can be treated with great success by the use of antibiotics. Even with viral and parasitic pneumonia, antibiotics may be used because they help to prevent secondary bacterial infection of damaged lung substance.

While the dog is recovering from pneumonia, he will require nursing care. He may need to be tempted to eat, with hand-feeding or a diet of soft, easily swallowed foods. If he is overweight, a nutritious but calorie-controlled diet to help weight loss will help him overcome any sort of airway obstruction and chronic cough.

Warmth and a well-ventilated room help the dog to cope with the reduced oxygen exchange in his lungs. Humidification of the air, the old-fashioned 'steam kettle' vapour, still has a place in nursing. Clean, smoke- and dust-free air is essential if the dog is to make a full recovery.

PNEUMOTHORAX

The healthy dog has an almost imperceptible space between his lungs and his ribs. The space is a vacuum, lined with pleural membranes, which moisten the area, allowing the lungs to expand and contract noiselessly.

If the rib cage is punctured (e.g. after a dog fight or a road accident) air is sucked into the pleural space, giving less room to the lungs, which can partially or fully collapse. This causes a breathing crisis, as any movement adds more air to the pleural vacuum, causing the lung to shrink further.

Pneumothorax can also arise if air escapes from the lungs into the pleural cavity. This can arise from blunt injuries to the chest or from the bursting of air cavities in weakened lungs.

Signs: If the dog has been involved in an accident, there may be an obvious chest injury. Otherwise, there will be acute respiratory distress, which is likely to get worse as the lungs collapse further. The dog will breathe forcefully to try to draw air into the reduced lungs. The blue colour of cyanosis (when the blood deoxygenates) will then develop.

Treatment: Radiographs will confirm the increased width in the space between the lungs and the rib cage. Dogs with a confirmed diagnosis should be caged up and forced to rest, with further radiographs taken, at intervals during recuperation, to measure the dog's progress.

If pneumothorax is acute, air will need to be removed from the pleural cavity by suction. In an emergency this can be done with a large syringe, but a chest aspiration kit, using a vacuum source and a water seal, is safer.

In spontaneous pneumothorax, where the air leak is internal, suction is usually effective but a thoracotomy may also be needed. This is an exploratory operation that examines the lungs to find the point from which air is leaking.

PULMONARY OEDEMA

Pulmonary oedema occurs when fluid accumulates in the lungs and fills up the air sacs of the alveoli. This is a severe condition and, unless diagnosed and treated quickly, it can lead to collapse and death.

There are many possible causes of the fluid accumulation but heart failure is the most common. Other causes include toxic substances (e.g. paraquat poisoning, tumours, and smoke inhalation).

It is important to remember that, while a fire may seem not to have caused much harm to the dog at the time, three days later he may present with severe breathlessness and coughing. If your dog is involved in a fire, always take him to your veterinarian for a check-up – even if he seems unhurt.

Lung tumours often will result in oedema as the growth increases in size. Kidney disease (e.g. glomerulonephritis, page 103) will cause oedema, and a similar effect will be found with some forms of liver disease.

Signs: A dog with pulmonary oedema will have signs of respiratory distress and his breathing patterns will be irregular.

The signs will vary according to how much lung space is available for gas exchange, ranging from an inability to walk far without sitting down and panting, to any form of unusual exertion causing collapse and even sudden death.

The dog may also excrete a frothy fluid through the nose or mouth, which, in severe conditions, may be pink or blood-tinged.

If the lungs are so badly affected that the blood deoxygenates (cyanosis), the tongue and any other visible membranes may assume a purple colour. As the dog's condition deteriorates, this may develop into an inky-black colour.

If the dog is suffering from cyanosis, handling him may cause him to gasp and throw back his head in extreme distress. Death may follow.

Treatments: Radiographs and ultrasounds will confirm if the dog is suffering from pulmonary oedema. Once the diagnosis is made, treatment concentrates on improving the air supply to the dog's lungs. Windows should be opened, and the dog supplied with oxygen, if it is available. If the dog is in shock, he will need corticosteroids.

The fluid that has accumulated in the alveoli is removed using diuretic medication and heart stimulants.

If the oedema has been caused by poison, antidotes will be administered, although there is little effective treatment for paraquat poisoning.

The dog will also be put on a course of antibiotics to protect against infection developing in the stagnant lung fluid.

NASAL OBSTRUCTIONS

Narrowing of the nostrils may be considered almost a normal state for some breeds, but in hot weather or in stress, the inability to flare open the nostrils may cause distress or even collapse.

Any discharge that coats over one or both nostrils must be removed, and growths (such as polyps) should also be attended to.

Occasionally, a length of grass or a barley awn may go up into the nasal cavity and cause an obstruction.

The brachycephalic (short-nosed) breeds are notorious for airway obstruction but any corrective surgery may be discouraged in show dogs.

Removal of the V-shaped wedge of skin is not difficult, and the surgeon may resect part of an elongated soft palate, or even remove the laryngeal ventricles.

TRACHEAL COLLAPSE

A normal, healthy trachea is supported by rings of cartilage and is circular on cross-section. The cartilage rings are not complete, there being a muscle and connective-tissue membrane making up the part nearest the vertebrae.

Tracheal collapse means the rings become flattened, narrowing the air tube. Collapse at the

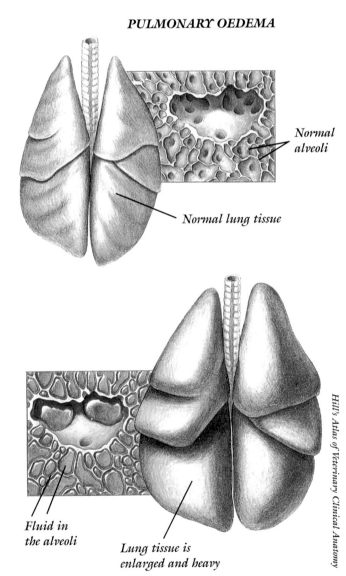

PULMONARY OEDEMA

Normal alveoli

Normal lung tissue

Fluid in the alveoli

Lung tissue is enlarged and heavy

Hill's Atlas of Veterinary Clinical Anatomy

114

opening to the chest is most common and it may extend into the main bronchi of the lung.

Signs: As with most respiratory disorders, tracheal collapse will result in the dog displaying obvious signs of respiratory distress. Noisy breathing will be even more prominent in middle-aged dogs and toy breeds.

The most common sign of tracheal collapse is a non-productive cough, described as a 'goose honk'. The cough becomes worse when the dog is excited, or if his collar is pressing on his windpipe.

Treatments: Surgical strengthening of the trachea may be needed to improve the air supply to the dog's lungs.

Alternatively, the nostrils can be surgically enlarged to allow more air down the trachea without requiring so much effort.

Medical treatment, combined with dieting and the use of a harness in place of a collar, will help to alleviate the symptoms in many dogs.

Dogs should not be left on their own to become overexcited, nor should they be left in a hot car, as collapse occurs very easily.

COLLAPSED TRACHEA

Hill's Atlas of Veterinary Clinical Anatomy

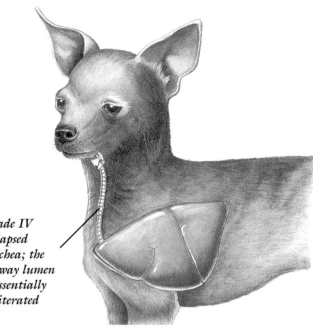

Grade IV collapsed trachea; the airway lumen is essentially obliterated

7 THE DOG'S WORLD

THE SENSES

The dog must be aware of his own environment for survival, and, by using his many senses and mental powers, he can respond to any change in the situation of the world around him.

All the senses are important, but it is easy to overlook their presence. Touch is one of these. The dog has sensory nerves all over his body that connect with the brain. The pads of the feet and the nose are used by the dog to sense his position. Equally, the dog that is patted for performing well will respond immediately to his body being touched, just as he would to a harsh choke collar being tightened.

The dog also has 'special' sense organs, where nerve endings are specifically concentrated to receive information to pass to the brain for processing. These organs deal with smell, sight, hearing and taste.

SMELL
Smell is one of the most strongly-developed senses in dogs, said to be 1,000 times more sensitive than that of a human being. The dog has many nerve cells in the lining of the nose, particularly at the back of the nose where they lie in the mucous membrane covering the ethmo-turbinate bones. These scroll-like bones increase surface area for reception so that even the weakest scent can be detected by the nerve cells. These cells transmit information, via the olfactory nerve, to the dog's brain, which has a well-developed olfactory lobe. This allows the dog to recognise a scent and follow a trail.

SIGHT
Sight is the result of a complicated process in which the eye receives light rays, and specific cells convert the light into a series of nerve impulses which are conducted to the brain. Here the impulses are converted into images, allowing the dog to be aware of his environment.

In the eye, light travels through the transparent front wall of eye (the cornea), and hits the light-sensitive tissue at the back of the eye (the retina). When the light rays are directed to the retina, they pass through the lens and a transparent gel (the vitreous). Too much light can be blinding, whereas too little will give an unclear picture. Like a camera, the eye overcomes this problem by modifying the amount of light that hits the retina. Movement of the eyelids, combined with a widening or narrowing of the pupil, adjusts the amount of light entering the eye, and the lens focuses the light upon the retina.

The retina lines an opaque container (the sclera). It is composed of two types of light-sensitive

STRUCTURE OF THE EYE

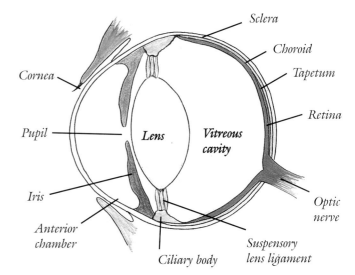

116

receptor cells (rods and cones), which are supplied with a myriad of nerve endings. The dog's retina has lots of rods, which enable vision in low levels of illumination. In comparison with humans, the cone concentration of the retina is low and, as such, definition is lost and the human colour range (particularly red and green) cannot be seen. A mirror-like layer of cells (the tapetum), is built into a tissue (the choroid) behind the retina. This mirror allows the dog to use reflected light that has already passed through the retina. This is particularly helpful when illumination is poor, but it detracts from sharp image production.

The dog's eyesight is a product of millennia of evolution, geared towards the need to be aware at all times of the environment, possible food, and any predators or competitors. However, a dog relies far less on his sight than he does on his hearing and smell. Anyone who has lived with a blind dog must marvel at the way he knows where his food is, who has come into the room, and his ability to chart his way to his favourite places in the garden. Nevertheless, a visually-impaired dog will have difficulties, particularly if his hearing is also deficient.

DISORDERS OF THE EYE

Eye diseases can result from accidents, infections or tumours. Pedigree dogs may suffer from inherited eye disease, either as a defect present from birth, or as a condition that develops throughout life.

Eye tissues can respond dramatically to the presence of disease, with the result that the diseased eye can appear very different from the normal one. Red eyes indicate inflammation and congestion of the surface blood vessels, while a dark appearance usually means the presence of pigment in the cornea. A bluish colour normally indicates fluid within the cornea, while a mature cataract will colour the pupil white.

If the dog is experiencing discomfort or pain, he may blink excessively, holding the eye closed and possibly trying to rub it. There may also be considerable tear production. Conversely, sight impairment may not be noticed until there is considerable loss or even total blindness. Many dogs with one blind eye will cope so well with the defect that the owner is unaware of the problem.

Sight disorders are not necessarily a consequence of a problem with the eye. Remember, the images that the dog sees are made in the brain although it is the eye that receives the original data. Consequently,

sight problems can be due to a problem in the brain and the connecting nerve pathways to the eye, as well as in the eye itself. A veterinarian's evaluation of sight is, therefore, somewhat limited by the fact that only the eye can be examined.

ACQUIRED DISEASES

These are normally caused by trauma or inflammation, and most can be treated effectively. Adequate first-aid measures for such diseases are almost non-existent and it is most important that veterinary assistance is sought immediately, as irreversible tissue changes can render the eye blind very quickly. The following are the most common acquired problems.

EYELID WOUNDS

Signs: A history of trauma, pain, and the presence of bleeding and distortion.
Treatment: Suture repair, together with the possible use of antibiotics.

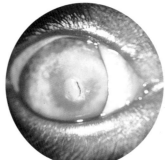

A corneal wound, the result of an accident.

CORNEAL WOUNDS

Signs: A history of trauma, combined with pain, blinking and excessive tear production. Haemorrhage is possible if the interior of the eye also has been damaged. There is also a real risk of the eye contents becoming infected.
Treatment: The cornea should be repaired by sutures, and both antibiotic and/or anti-inflammatory therapies may be required to reduce the chances of infection and control inflammation of the iris and the ciliary body.

CONJUNCTIVITIS

Signs: Redness of the conjunctiva (the membrane which covers the sclera in part and lines the eyelids), possible pain or discomfort, blinking, excessive tear production, and the presence of a discharge.
Treatment: Treatment varies depending on whether the disease is of allergic or infectious origin. Antibiotic and anti-inflammatory therapies may be used according to the cause.

CORNEAL ULCERATION

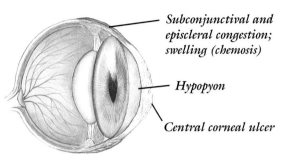

Subconjunctival and episcleral congestion; swelling (chemosis)

Hypopyon

Central corneal ulcer

Hill's Atlas of Veterinary Clinical Anatomy

CORNEAL ULCERATION

Signs: Acute ulceration is very painful, but signs of pain and discomfort may be reduced with chronicity. Tear production, discharge, blinking and eyelid closure may all be present, and the cornea is usually hazy around the ulcer site.
Treatment: Corneal rupture, with potential loss of the eye, is a possibility with all ulcers. Antibiotics are essential and various forms of surgery can be involved to effect repair. This condition is a real veterinary emergency.

CORNEAL INFLAMMATION

Signs: Keratitis may be due to trauma, infection or autoimmunity. The clinical signs vary from mild discomfort to considerable pain. Tears and discharge may be present. The cornea may appear hazy due to the presence of fluid, and blood vessels may be seen.
Treatment: This will vary with the cause, but both antibiotics and anti-inflammatory agents may be used. Dry eye, in which there is an absence of tears, will require special consideration.

INFLAMMATION OF THE IRIS

Signs: This is called anterior uveitis and it is normally extremely painful. Excessive tear production, discharge, blinking and eyelid closure may all be present. The cornea may be opaque, and if the pupil can be seen, it is usually constricted.
Treatment: Anti-inflammatory drugs and antibiotic therapy are employed, together with pain relief.

LENS OPACITY

Signs: A cataract may be as small as a pinhead or as large as the entire lens (which will severely impair sight or cause blindness). The signs are a white or hazy appearance to the pupil, and possible associated sight defects.
Treatment: Dogs cope well with small, non-progressive and unilateral cataracts, but the presence of bilateral, large or total cataracts warrants lens removal. This is normally completed using a phacoemulsification technique, in which the whole lens is broken up inside the eye and then removed by suction. A dog's vision following cataract surgery can be very good, despite the fact that the image is very blurred.

RETINAL DEGENERATION

Signs: Retinal degeneration may follow inflammatory disease elsewhere in the eye, so the signs may, initially, be those of the primary disease. The degeneration causes blindness, but only where there is extensive involvement will the dog demonstrate sight impairment. Quite a lot of severe retinal degeneration is inherited in certain breeds of dog and it is referred to as Progressive Retinal Atrophy (PRA). Nutritional deficiency and age may also be responsible for retinal blindness.
Treatment: There is no treatment for established retinal degeneration. Prevention is possible if the primary defect is treatable and is treated early enough.

CATARACT/LENS OPACITY

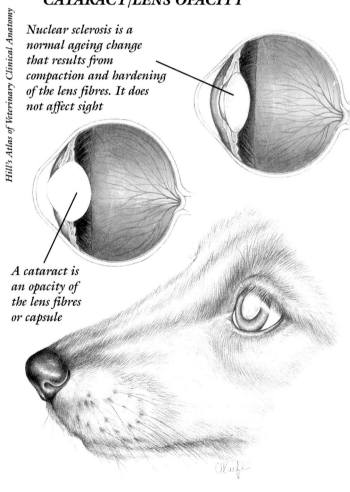

Nuclear sclerosis is a normal ageing change that results from compaction and hardening of the lens fibres. It does not affect sight

Hill's Atlas of Veterinary Clinical Anatomy

A cataract is an opacity of the lens fibres or capsule

GLAUCOMA

Caused by an increase in fluid pressure inside the eye, glaucoma destroys the retina and optic nerve. It is usually seen as a secondary complication to severe trauma, inflammation or tumour formation, but it can also be inherited.

Signs: Glaucoma can lead to destruction of the whole eyeball. The signs are the same as those seen in the original complaint, together with an increase in the size of the eyeball. Pain may be a dominant feature in acute glaucoma.

Treatment: Effective glaucoma therapy is often not possible, and the dog will usually lose his sight. The enlarged eye can be a cause of discomfort and its removal is often required. New hope for glaucoma patients is based on the possible success of surgery to drain fluid from the eye to restore normal pressure.

TUMOURS

Tumours are more frequent in older dogs, and usually develop in the eyelids and eyeball.

Signs: Vary with the site and the degree of progression.

Treatment: Most eyelid tumours are benign, but mechanical problems are best prevented by early removal. Intraocular tumours are not commonplace, but, in addition to the development of glaucoma, metastasis (when tumours spread to another part of the body) may occur, so removal of the eye may be warranted.

INHERITED DISEASES

Inherited eye disease is relatively commonplace among pedigree dogs and it is wise to check with both the breeder and your veterinarian that all possible measures have been taken to ensure that any puppy you buy will remain free from such disease. Some eye problems show a clear breed predisposition, and these diseases are well known (see below). For example, a Cocker Spaniel should come from parents that are clear for both retinal degeneration and glaucoma, both severe problems that result in blindness. With many inherited diseases, treatment is not possible, but the avoidance of these problems is achieved where care is exercised in breeding programmes. The following are some of the major inherited diseases, but the list is not exhaustive – new diseases appear with regularity.

- **Entropion**: An inward rotation of eyelid tissue, causing irritation and possible ulceration of the eye.

- **Ectropion**: An outward rotation of the eyelid that causes conjunctivitis.

Entropion in a German Shorthaired Pointer. Note the inflamed third eyelid, and the inward-turning lower lid, which is causing the facial hair to rub against the cornea.

Ectropion in a Cavalier King Charles Spaniel puppy. The lower lids are everted.

- **Distichiasis**: Hairs arise from the edges of the eyelids to irritate the cornea. Ulceration may occur.

- **Corneal dystrophy (CD)**: The accumulation of fatty material in the cornea; although dramatic in appearance, is not usually associated with sight loss.

- **Keratoconjunctivitis sicca (KCS)**: Inflammation of the cornea and conjunctiva. It is caused by a deficiency of tears as the result of an autoimmune destruction of the tear glands.

- **Pannus**: An autoimmune inflammation of the cornea, which, if untreated, will affect vision.

- **Persistent pupillary membrane (PPM)**: Remnant embryonic blood vessels and undifferentiated tissue, which may cause corneal and anterior lens opacities.

- **Persistent hyperplastic primary vitreous (PHPV)**: Remnant embryonic blood vessels that can cause a cataract.

119

DEAFNESS IN DOGS

Humans can detect sounds in the frequency range 20-20,000 Hz, whereas dogs can hear sounds up to 47,000 Hz – two octaves higher than us. Humans benefit from dogs' finely-tuned hearing to great advantage e.g. police dogs (which warn their handlers of impending danger), and hearing dogs (which alert their deaf owners to everyday sounds, such as the telephone).

PREVALENCE
At least 1 in 3,000 puppies is born deaf. More than 50 breeds are affected, and those with the highest incidence include the Dalmatian, English Setter, Border Collie, Australian Cattle Dog and Bull Terrier. Dogs with blue eyes are also more likely to be deaf.

CAUSES
Deafness can be classified into conductive or sensori-neural deafness, depending on the site of the disorder. The outer ear and the middle ear are responsible for conducting the sound signal to the inner ear. Conductive deafness therefore relates to disorders affecting these sites, e.g. infection or tumours of the ear canal or middle ear. Sensori-neural deafness relates to disorders of the cochlea, usually the hair cells. These may be absent (as in inherited deafness), or may die over time due to old age, toxic drugs, viral infections, excess noise, or lack of oxygen. Deafness may also be classified as congenital (present at birth), acquired (occurring later in life), or inherited.

The most commonly occurring causes of congenital deafness in young dogs is inherited sensori-neural deafness. Acquired sensori-neural deafness is most often due to old age, while acquired conductive hearing loss is mainly due to chronic ear infections.

SIGNS
A dog's hearing cannot be assessed until the ear canals open at around two weeks of age. Bilaterally deaf dogs (i.e. deaf in both ears) do not respond to loud noises, are difficult to arouse from sleep, may be more aggressive, and often have a higher-pitched cry. Unaware owners may not recognise this condition initially, because the affected puppies often follow their littermates closely. Dogs with unilateral deafness or partial hearing loss are hard to train and have difficulty localising sound.

TREATMENT
Dogs with conductive hearing disorders may be treated successfully using medication. In some cases, surgery may help to restore their hearing. Generally, sensori-neural hearing loss is not reversible, and management regimes are required.

BRAINSTEM AUDITORY EVOKED RESPONSE (BAER) TEST

BEHAVIOURAL TESTING
It is not possible to look at a dog and diagnose a hearing loss. For many years, behavioural tests have been used to diagnose deafness. A positive response consists of a turn of the head in response to an acoustic signal. Although cheap and quick to perform, there are a number of reasons why the results may be inaccurate. For instance, if not performed carefully, the animal may respond to visual or tactile cues instead of auditory signals. The interpretation of the results may be biased because the tester knows when the signal is present and is expecting a response. In addition, the dog may become bored and stop responding. Although the test can probably identify a profoundly deaf dog, it gives no information about which ear is affected, or the degree or site of the impairment.

BAER TESTING
The brainstem auditory evoked response (BAER) is an accurate, objective, repeatable and non-invasive test, which determines which ear is affected and the severity of the disorder. In combination with other tests (e.g.

A Bull Terrier puppy being hearing tested, using the BAER test.

radiography), the site of the disorder can be determined, and the possible outcome predicted.

The test records electrical activity generated in response to an auditory stimulus. This activity is detected using fine needle electrodes attached to the skin of the dog's head. The sound stimulus is delivered as a series of clicks of known loudness through a set of headphones/ear inserts held next to, or placed just inside, the dog's ear canal. This signal passes from the outer ear, through the middle ear to the inner ear. It is here that the electrical signals are generated which then travel to the lower part of the brain.

The results are recorded on a sophisticated computer and appear as a waveform consisting of a series of peaks. The test may be performed on puppies from four weeks of age onwards, and patient co-operation is not required. Young pups are often tested while held in their owners' arms. Older dogs may need light sedation to relax them, and the test result is unaffected by this.

BREEDERS
The test allows breeders to identify potential breeding stock from dogs that have passed the BAER test in both ears, and reject those with a negative BAER test in one or both ears. A DNA blood test will eventually be developed to identify the gene causing inherited deafness, but it is still several years away.

TRAINERS
It is more time- and cost-effective to ensure that working dogs have 'normal' hearing prior to training.

PET OWNERS
Deaf dogs are harder to train and require more patience and time. Dogs born with unilateral deafness can make good pets, but it is advisable to sterilise dogs with inherited deafness, so that the condition is not passed on to their offspring.

Pet owners who take on a deaf dog will need to adopt a special training regime (e.g. using exaggerated body language, sign signals, etc.).

Dogs that develop hearing loss due to old age normally cope much better than congenitally deaf dogs because they are already familiar with the daily household routine. Re-training, keeping them with a hearing dog, and using vibrating collars or hearing aids are all possible options. It is also useful to assess the degree of improvement or deterioration over time, using BAER tests.

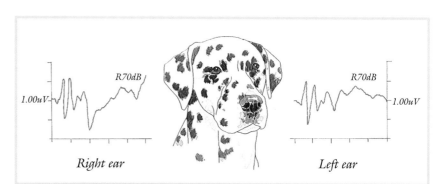

This dog passed his BAER test with both ears.

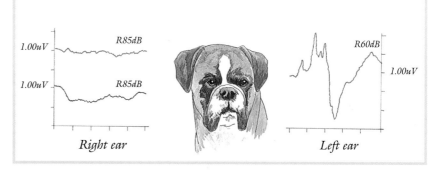

This dog failed his BAER test in his right ear, but passed with his left ear.

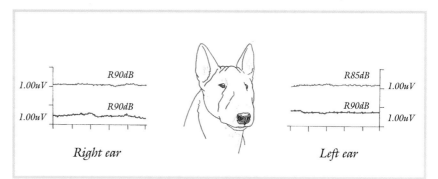

This dog failed the BAER test and has no hearing in either ear.

With the exception of Collie eye anomaly, the incidence of these diseases tends to be low. Sadly, however, the mechanism of inheritance for many diseases remains unknown. The UK has a scheme for the control of inherited eye disease, which is run jointly by the British Veterinary Association, the Kennel Club and the International Sheepdog Society. It is purely voluntary and there is no registration requirement for pedigree dogs to be certified clear for the disease problem or problems that affect their breed. Wholesale subscription to the scheme, which is based upon regular eye examinations from six weeks to nine years of age, would allow accurate incidence figures to be published and help to describe inheritance patterns, as well as facilitating disease control.

The British scheme differs slightly from the North American and European schemes, in terms of the detail and extent of the examination involved, and there are variations in breed predisposition between countries and continents. As a rule, the breeder from whom you buy your puppy should be aware of the inherited disease or diseases that affect the breed. Your veterinarian should also be helpful in this respect.

HEARING AND BALANCE

The ear is divided into three main parts: the external ear, the middle ear, and the inner ear. The outer part of the ear (pinna) acts as a trumpet, receiving sounds. Some breeds have very mobile ears, to capture any sound of possible interest. Other dogs have earflaps that hang down. These ears would appear to be less sensitive to distant sounds, although the working Springer Spaniel seems no slower to find birds than a prick-eared breed.

The sounds picked up by the pinna reach the eardrum as vibrations, which pass through the eardrum and enter the middle ear. The vibrations are then transmitted via three tiny moving bones to reach the 'oval (vestibular) window' and the 'round (cochlear) window'. These windows are membrane-covered, narrow entrances to the inner ear. When the soundwaves reach the membranes, they cause the membranes to vibrate, which disturbs the lymph fluid on the other side of the membranes, in the inner ear. The sound is then carried in fluid form.

As well as carrying sound, the inner ear has three semi-circular canals that are responsible for the position of the head and the body, allowing both to

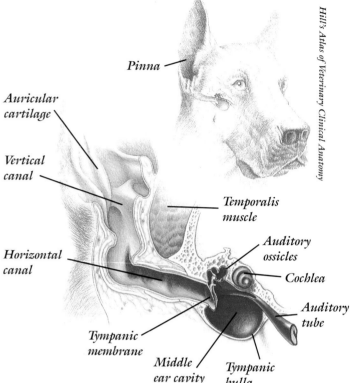

NORMAL HEARING APPARATUS

Pinna

Auricular cartilage

Vertical canal

Temporalis muscle

Horizontal canal

Auditory ossicles

Cochlea

Auditory tube

Tympanic membrane

Middle ear cavity

Tympanic bulla

Hill's Atlas of Veterinary Clinical Anatomy

move, while keeping the head at the same level, so that the dog can maintain his balance and achieve maximum sight and smell processing. The ear canals are lined with fine hairs, and the lymph fluid moving through the ear canals disturbs these hairs. The hairs register all the movements and transmit messages about them, via the auditory nerve, to the brain.

EAR INFECTIONS AND INJURIES
Ear infections and injuries can severely affect a dog's balance, even if his hearing is unimpaired. For example, a dog with vestibular disease will have difficulty in walking and balancing. He may also hang his head lower on one side and may oscillate his eyes constantly. This illness is commonly referred to as a 'stroke', but it is caused by vestibular ear problems, as opposed to a 'true' stroke, when a blood clot travels to the brain, causing tissue death.

For details of ear inflammation and disease, see Chapter Eight.

THE BRAIN AND NERVE CONTROL

The dog's nervous system consists of the central nervous system (the brain and the spinal cord), and the peripheral nervous system (the nerve trunks found all over the body). Together, these elements work in harmony, controlling the dog's responses to external stimuli. Hormones, too, can affect a dog's response – fear, pain and stress being capable of altering a dog's characteristic behaviour.

The brain is the centre of the nervous system. Its nerve cells process information constantly, receiving messages from nerve fibres in the sensory organs, such as the ears, skin and eyes. The brain processes the incoming information, responds by sending out messages to the muscles or blood vessels, and the dog is then able to react to each situation. Voluntary actions occur after decisions are made in the brain. For example, a dog may choose to chase a rabbit because his memory tells him that it is a fun thing to do, and not because he needs to eat a rabbit to satisfy his hunger.

Most reactions take the form of a physical response, involving the body's muscles. The muscles are supplied with 'motor nerves' and the brain sends messages to these nerves via the spinal cord. Some physical responses are automatic or involuntary (e.g. withdrawing the foot when a toe is pinched) and do not involve the brain directly. However, while the brain may not be involved in formulating a response to external stimuli, it will be kept informed about reflex actions unless there has been a major accident. This can be seen in a dog with a paralysed back, who can still reflexly respond to a pinprick by snatching his leg away, even if he is unable to do anything else.

The brain and spinal cord are well protected in the body. The brain is surrounded by the skull, and the spinal cord is safeguarded by the vertebrae of the spine. A tough covering, known as the dura mater, provides a further insulating layer around the brain and spinal cord. Beneath the dura mater are the more delicate arachnoid mater and pia. All three protective layers are collectively referred to as the meninges, inflammation of which produces meningitis (page 129).

The central nervous system regulates many bodily functions. The male dog thinks ahead – the bladder can be emptied when an appropriate lamppost is reached. The bitch with a false pregnancy reacts with a number of muscle activities and behavioural changes, influenced by progesterone and oestrogen hormones. External factors can also alter the nervous system's response. The heart rate can be increased, or food may be vomited if the stomach is over-distended or if a food toxin has been absorbed. There is no end to external factors that affect behaviour and movement.

HOW THE SYSTEM WORKS

The brain contains many nerve cells (neurons), each possessing a very long extension (axon) to carry nerve impulses (messages to and from the brain). Neurons interconnect with many other cells in the body, the nerve fibres of the axon spreading over large areas. At the end of each axon is a nerve ending. Where an axon connects with another nerve cell, the nerve fibres join together (synapse), and chemicals are released to transmit the message from one nerve ending to the next. The chemical is known as a neurotransmitter and a lack of it can produce a trembling disease such as myasthenia (muscle weakness disease). Neurons can have more than one axon, so that messages can be received and transmitted in different directions. In addition, cell connections allow for the exchange of information to reach many more cells at the same time. Muscles receive messages in the same way that nerve endings exchange messages – the nerve fibre transmits its message to the muscle fibre by releasing the neurotransmitter chemical.

Neurons are supported by many other cells in the nervous system. These cells provide insulation and nourishment to maintain the nervous system's rapid responses. Although nerve impulses may have to travel several different axons, as well as making the leap from nerve fibre to muscle fibre, the system generally works well – nerve transmission can be at speeds equivalent to 100 miles per hour.

DISORDERS OF THE NERVOUS SYSTEM

SPINAL INJURIES/PARALYSIS

Paralysis can take the form of tetraplegia (affecting all four limbs), hemiplegia (affecting one side of the body), or paraplegia (affecting the rear half of the body). Tetraplegia may be caused by a neck injury, while hemiplegia normally arises as the result of a brain injury. Paraplegia is probably the most common form of paralysis.

Signs: Injuries such as a road accident, a dog fight, a heavy object falling across the dog's back, or extremes of exercise. Externally-caused spinal injuries may have tell-tale wounds, but internally-caused trauma has no such indication and an apparently healthy dog may suddenly become paralysed or barely able to crawl.

In chondrodystrophic breeds (e.g. Dachshunds), paralysis is likely to be due to **disc disease**, which can develop by itself or as the result of a spinal injury. Longer-backed dogs are at increased risk of displaced ('slipped') intervertebral discs. When a disc slips, the

125

Paraplegia, where the dog's rear half is paralysed.

dog becomes progressively paralysed as blood leaks into the spaces around the spine. Paralysis may be sudden, or, more often, the dog begins with a grumbling backache and difficulty in using his hindlegs, which becomes steadily worse.

Among larger breeds, there is a predisposition to **fibrocartilagenous embolism** (although not common), a condition in which the nerve tracks are put under pressure. Even healthy guide dogs have been known to develop a sudden fibrocartilagenous embolism, and although the dog may regain some control of his hindquarters, his walking may be so disturbed that he can never work again.

Atlanto-axial subluxation, found mainly in small breeds, is caused by instability of the first two neck bones, so that pressure is put on the nerves of the spine as they leave or enter the brain. As the condition worsens, and more pressure is applied, the dog's mobility becomes further restricted.

Wobbler syndrome is found in breeds such as the Great Dane and in the older Dobermann. The disease is due to a narrowing of the vertebral canal in the bones of the neck, which applies pressure to the nerves of the spine.

Signs: These vary according to the severity of the injury/paralysis, and the underlying cause. A tetraplegic dog will be unable to move any of his limbs. A dog with hemiplegia may adapt well, if both hindlegs work to some degree. Severe paraplegia will result in a complete loss of feeling in the hindlegs, which lie forwards in a state of flaccid paralysis. A dog may learn to propel himself using his front legs, dragging his hindlegs and tail behind him, but his hind feet will become raw and bleeding as he drags his feet.

With partial paralysis, the front of the nails may be worn down because the dog cannot pick up his hind toes. Nerve reflexes can be tested to assess the level

NORMAL VERTEBRAE/SPINAL CORD

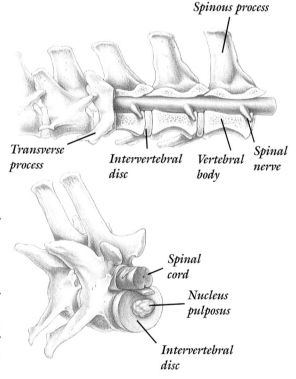

Spinous process

Transverse process

Intervertebral disc

Vertebral body

Spinal nerve

Spinal cord

Nucleus pulposus

Intervertebral disc

INTERVERTEBRAL DISC DISEASE

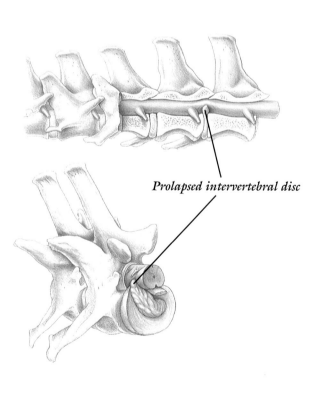

Prolapsed intervertebral disc

of damage, since the dog may appear able to move his body, but he actually possesses no control.

If the autonomic system is damaged, as with a lower-spine injury, the bladder can be in spasm, so that urine can only be passed with difficulty and catheterisation is necessary to get a free outflow. Likewise, bowel control will be non-existent. Prognosis is not good in such situations.

A dog with Wobbler syndrome may display no symptoms during the first few months of life, or in the case of the Dobermann, until he reaches an advanced age. The first signs are an unusual gait, and accompanying neck pain. As the disease progresses, the front legs become stiff and the hindlegs appear weak or wobbly. Eventually, paralysis may develop.

Atlanto-axial subluxation usually begins with a slow-developing neck pain in dogs under a year of age. The dog is likely to hang his head. Paralysis may develop and spread to all four legs if the neck is mishandled. If the neck ligaments are torn, a small bone (the dens) is driven into the spine, causing respiratory paralysis and rapid death, so great care is needed when handling the dog.

Treatment: If a dog displays any symptoms of paralysis, veterinary treatment must be immediate, and may include non-steroidal anti-inflammatory drugs, to reduce the amount of nerve damage and to relieve pain. Nursing care and bladder emptying may be required.

Where a displaced disc is the cause of paralysis, operating to remove the pressure on the spine may be advised.

Wobbler syndrome can be treated by operating on the neck, to stabilise the vertebrae. Atlanto-axial subluxation is best treated by surgical implantation of screws and wire to stabilise the joint. In skilled hands, this can be very successful.

FITS AND SEIZURES

There are various names used to describe the symptoms of central neurological diseases that occur in the fore brain (cerebrum) and the brain stem (diencephalon). These include: fits, epilepsy, ictus, convulsions, and status epilepticus.

It is said that 1 in 100 dogs may suffer from a fit at some point in life. These may be of the idiopathic type, where no cause can be seen, or due to an illness or injury that can be more easily diagnosed. Some breeds are more affected than others, so there may be a hereditary component.

During an attack of epilepsy, electrical impulses in the brain's neurons become erratic, and the brain is

Epilepsy in a Yorkshire Terrier.

no longer able to function normally. The fore brain or the brain stem may be where the neurons discharge first. If other brain cells block the spread of electrical activity, a fit may be stopped altogether, or a focal seizure may occur, in which disturbance occurs in one part of the brain only. More commonly, the erratic electrical impulses cause the brain cells to depolarise (short-circuit) and the whole of the brain is affected. In such cases, the whole body of the dog is affected – the classic 'fit'.

Old dogs can develop encephalitis where the causes of epileptic fits are not known, but it is likely to be part of the degenerative process. Encephalitis caused by the canine distemper virus was the most common cause of fits 50 years ago, but, fortunately, the use of effective vaccines has almost abolished distemper as an illness in young dogs.

Rabies is another virus that can cause fits. When the virus reaches the brain from the peripheral nerves, it may bring about epileptic behavioural changes, followed by 'rage', with salivation and drooling.

Where there has been an injury to the skull (e.g. after a blow or a road accident), the external trauma may cause an immediate fit, or, often after a delay of months, fits may develop – perhaps because of a healing skull fracture pressing on the brain surface. A brain tumour growing inside the skull is another possible (but rare) cause of epilepsy. As well as injury, some body conditions (e.g. liver failure and kidney disease) may cause fits because toxic substances (e.g. amino acids) are carried to the brain in the bloodstream.

Signs: Salivation and chewing may be the first signs. Owners often report a strange awareness of the dog before the fit commences, which is called the prodromal time. The dog will begin to breathe rapidly and may arch his back. If a full fit develops, the dog will lose consciousness for a few seconds or for as long as five minutes. Incontinence may result. All four feet may show rigidity as the dog falls over, and he may show violent paddling movements.

In its most severe form, a fit may last for 20 minutes or more, with symptoms including salivation, biting, leg thrashing, and eyes that will not focus. Known as status epilepticus, there may be a series of repeated fits or one major brain disturbance. Death often results unless urgent veterinary treatment is given.

Mild attacks are far less distressing. Head nodding, stiffness of the limbs and an inability to walk for a few minutes may be all that develop. In the mildest form of epilepsy, the dog does no more than try to bite his own tail or frantically wash his feet or flanks; these are signs of 'focal' seizures.

Treatment: Investigation, using blood tests, X-rays, MRI and CT scans may be required. Treatment with sedative drugs can be very successful in controlling the severity and regularity of epilepsy. The usual drugs used include barbiturates, phenytoin and bromide. Sometimes, it is possible to reduce the dosage once control is obtained, although, if more fits return, the dose will have to be adjusted once again.

Where a dog is known to have severe fits, the sedative diazepam is normally used during or just after the fit.

The owners of epileptic dogs can limit the occurrence and severity of fits by feeding a diet low in protein (20 per cent or less) to reduce the risk of harmful amino acids reaching the brain. Another helpful tip: when the dog appears to be about to have a seizure, wake the dog and take him for a walk. In some cases, this may prevent an attack.

DISTEMPER, FITS AND CHOREA

Causes: Canine distemper is caused by an infectious virus. Until a vaccine was created, the virus was one of the biggest causes of nervous system disorders. The virus still exists, but the high percentage of vaccinated dogs today means it is a rarity.

Likewise, today's dog owner is unlikely to encounter a dog suffering from chorea, which is caused by a loss of myelin and damage around the neurons.

Signs: Constant chattering of the teeth and severe muscle spasms, which would spread across the face and neck. One or more legs might have muscle twitching, more noticeable as the dog tries to sleep.

A more severe form would cause epileptic fits, developing after several weeks from the time when the dog initially became unwell. Permanent paralysis of the hind legs was another form of nerve damage.

Constant muscle twitching is the main symptom of a dog suffering from chorea.

Treatment: Although distemper is no longer as feared, the need for vaccination should never be forgotten. The use of anticonvulsant drugs used for fits may help the chorea. Vitamin B supplements and cortisone drugs have also been thought to help.

CDRM

Causes: Chronic degenerative radiculomyelopathy is a disease of the central nervous system that often does not appear until middle-age. It is typically seen in the German Shepherd, but can be found in the Old English Sheepdog, Collie, Labrador and English Mastiff, albeit rarely. It is a degenerative nerve disease (myelopathy), probably with an immune (rather than hereditary) origin. The disease causes the loss of an insulating substance (myelin) from the conducting axons at the spine level in the thorax, eventually causing the nerve supply to both hind legs to fail.

Signs: The affected dog will begin to drag his hind toes, no longer being able to pick them up fully. Eventually, complete hindleg loss of function develops, accompanied by bowel incontinence and bleeding from the rubbed-through skin of the dragged hindquarters.

Treatment: CDRM is not easily diagnosed until the disease has made some progression. Many affected dogs come from breeds where there is a history of hip dysplasia, so there is often confusion about whether the symptoms are due to osteoarthritis.

Once diagnosed, CDRM can be treated with high doses of vitamin E, which can slow its progression. High doses of prednisolone may also be prescribed for the same purpose. Some dogs can survive for up

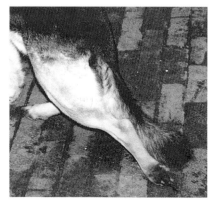

Toe-dragging associated with chronic degenerative radiculomyelopathy (CDRM).

to four years, although euthanasia may become necessary in the long term.

MENINGITIS

Causes: Meningitis is caused by bacteria or a virus. One of the most common causes of bacterial invasion is from an endocarditis of the heart valves. A throat infection may be the first point of entry for the bacteria to gain access to the inside of the body. Viruses can reach the brain/spinal cord protective meninges easily.

Signs: The first signs may be a high temperature, hypersensitivity, and loss of appetite. The dog moves carefully, as if to avoid any jarring pain, and neck rigidity is characteristic. The dog will walk stiffly, and will give an overall impression of being very unwell.

Treatment: Immediate antibiotic treatment is needed.

HORMONE CONTROL

Hormones, as chemical messagers, are produced by the endocrine glands. The effects of hormones are similar to those of the nervous system's control mechanism but are long-lasting. Disorders of hormone production can affect behaviour and activity, and cause ill health that may be so severe as to cause death.

DISORDERS OF THE ENDOCRINE SYSTEM

HYPERADRENOCORTICISM (CUSHING'S DISEASE)

Canine hyperadrenocorticism (Cushing's disease) is most common in dogs of six years of age or more, with the Poodle, Dachshund, Beagle, German Shepherd, and Labrador among those breeds most commonly affected.

Causes: This disorder is caused by excessive secretion of the cortisol hormone by the adrenal gland. Cortisol has many important actions in the endocrine system, including increasing the sugar content of the blood. A tumour in the pituitary gland (located in the brain) can release excessive amounts of a hormone called ACTH (adrenocorticotropic hormone), which then stimulates the adrenal gland to release extra cortisol. A tumour in the adrenal gland itself will directly excrete increased levels of cortisol. Other causes include the excessive administration of

Yorkshire Terrier suffering from Cushing's disease.

glucocorticoids (steroids), commonly used to treat allergic conditions in dogs (e.g. chronic skin or respiratory problems).

Signs: Dogs are likely to eat, drink, and urinate more. This leads to an enlarged liver and an increased stomach size, causing a pot-bellied appearance. The dog may also become weak and lethargic.

Hair loss, skin lesions and bruising may become apparent. In addition, the dog may show signs of respiratory distress (e.g. excessive panting), and nervous disorders (e.g. circling, wandering, staggering, and behavioural alterations).

Treatment: Chemotherapy. A drug called Mitotane selectively destroys the adrenal gland, forcing cortisol secretion to approach normal levels. The therapy is more successful in dogs with the pituitary type of the disease.

The average life span of dogs suffering with Cushing's disease is three years from diagnosis. Younger dogs, however, may live longer.

See also Chapter Eight.

HYPOADRENOCORTICISM (ADDISON'S DISEASE)

Addison's disease develops when underactivity in the adrenal gland cortex leads to a deficiency in cortisol (a steroid hormone), and aldosterone (a hormone that regulates water loss and retention).

Causes: Addison's disease may be caused by a congenital defect, an adrenal gland tumour, or an infection of, or inflammation in, the adrenal cortex. Destructive lesions (inflammation or tumour) in the pituitary gland may lead to secondary adrenal insufficiency, lowering levels of cortisol and aldosterone.

Addison's disease. The healthy, unaffected dog is on the left.

Other causes include auto-immune disease (when the body attacks itself), and a sudden withdrawal of steroids after prolonged therapy (e.g. for skin allergies). Over-treatment of Cushing's disease with Mitotane may also result in Addison's disease.

Signs: Most common in middle-aged, female dogs of large breeds, signs include:
• Anorexia
• Weakness
• Lethargy and depression
• Weight loss
• Vomiting and diarrhoea
• Slow heart rate.

Treatment: Replacement therapy involves administering cortisol and aldosterone hormones in tablet form.

HYPOTHYROIDISM

The thyroid glands are located near the top of the trachea and larynx in the dog's neck. They release an important hormone called thyroxine, which controls the metabolic rate of the body. For example, if an animal is exposed to cold, thyroxine is released to increase the rate of metabolism in order to raise the animal's body temperature. Thyroxine is also essential for growth and development of the body. Thyroxine release is controlled by the hypothalamus and the pituitary gland, both of which are situated in the brain.

There are two types of hypothyroidism exhibited in dogs – primary and secondary – both of which are characterised by low blood levels of thyroxine.

Causes: Primary hypothyroidism is caused when the thyroid gland is directly affected by a tumour, inflammation, or tissue wasting. Primary causes of hypothyroidism result in destruction of the thyroid tissue, leading to decreased thyroid hormone levels in the blood.

Secondary hypothyroidism arises as the result of an indirect effect on the thyroid gland, such as inflammation or a tumour in the brain. The brain produces specific hormones that act on the thyroid gland to stimulate a release of thyroxine, so a brain disorder will indirectly cause hypothyroidism by reducing these stimulating hormones.

Although incidences are now rare, iodine deficiency (caused by feeding all-meat diets) can result in hypothyroidism, as iodine is important for the production of thyroxine. Rare, congenital abnormalities may also lead to defective thyroid development.

Signs: It is usually seen in young to middle-aged dogs of larger breeds, such as the Boxer, Golden Retriever, and Irish Setter. Signs include:
• Lethargy
• Exercise intolerance
• Cold intolerance/low body temperature
• Muscle weakness
• Weight gain
• Slow heart rate
• Hair loss (especially around the tail)
• Dry, scaly skin and coat
• Skin thickening
• Skin infections
• Failure to grow hair after clipping
• Puffy-faced 'tragic expression' (Myxoedema).
• Diarrhoea or constipation
• Nervous signs (circling, head tilt, dragging of front feet)
• Reproductive abnormalities
• Eye abnormalities
• Dwarfism (abnormal growth of puppies).

Diagnosis: Specialised blood tests can detect low levels of thyroxine.

Treatment: Standard treatment is a course of a synthetic version of the thyroxine hormone, which can be given in tablet form. Within one to two weeks, the dog's energy levels should increase, and the hair should begin to grow back within one to three months.

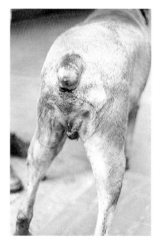

Hair loss, particularly around the tail, is one of the signs associated with hypothyroidism.

DIABETES MELLITUS

The pancreas plays an important role in digestion and in the endocrine system. It produces pancreatic juices to aid the digestion and absorption of food, and also manufactures the hormone insulin, which is important for controlling the amount of glucose (sugar) in the bloodstream.

When a dog has diabetes, the pancreas fails to produce enough insulin, causing excessive levels of blood glucose (chronic hyperglycaemia). The glucose settles in the blood because glucose can no longer be stored in body tissues due to a lack of insulin. The kidneys attempt to remove the excess blood glucose, resulting in an increased amount of urine characterised by its glucose concentrate (diabetes mellitus means 'sweet urine').

Diabetes mellitus is twice as common among bitches as among dogs, and normally develops in the middle-aged or older animal. Small breeds are more prone to the condition (e.g. Poodle, Dachshund, Miniature Schnauzer, Beagle). Entire bitches are commonly affected when they are just coming out of season.

Causes: Often obscure, with many agents acting in combination. However, several factors may predispose a dog towards the destruction of pancreatic tissue and a resulting reduction in insulin levels.

- Genetic predisposition
- Infection/inflammation of pancreatic tissue (pancreatitis)
- Obesity
- Chemical toxins and drugs (e.g. steroids, hormones used to control the bitch's season)
- Auto-immune disease (when the body attacks its own supply of insulin)
- Hyperadrenocorticism (steroids can exhaust the supply of insulin)
- Pregnancy and bitches in season (the hormone progesterone can reduce insulin levels).

Signs:

- Increased thirst
- Increased urine output
- Ravenous appetite
- Weight loss
- Cataracts (leading to sudden blindness)
- Recurrent urinary tract infections (characterised by an increased urination and apparent straining)
- Enlarged liver (only apparent on clinical examination).

Diagnosis: A blood test will show excessive levels of blood glucose, even after a 12-hour fast. A urine sample can also be tested for high glucose levels.

A Jack Russell suffering from diabetes.

Treatment: A daily injection of insulin for the rest of the dog's life. Dietary attention, exercise, and careful management of any concurrent illnesses are also important. Owner awareness of the clinical signs that follow accidental insulin overdose at home is vital, as the resulting hypoglycaemia (fall in blood sugar levels) can be fatal.

Usually, your veterinarian will hospitalise your dog until he is stabilised. Daily injections of insulin will be administered until the correct dosage has been established and the dog's blood glucose levels are under control. There are several types of insulin, including one that lasts 24 hours, so that only one injection per day is required. Your veterinarian will show you how to administer the insulin correctly. The insulin injection is usually given in the morning and it should be given at the same time each day. It is best to feed the dog a snack at the time of the injection and then to feed the main meal two hours before the insulin reaches its peak effect (usually 8 to 10 hours later).

It is beneficial to monitor your dog's urine glucose levels, using a home kit. This should be done every morning before the insulin injection. Your veterinarian will advise you how to adjust the dose of insulin according to the urine glucose levels. It is also helpful to maintain a daily diary about insulin dose, appetite and water consumption.

Regular daily exercise will help to stabilise the dog, as well as preventing obesity. Maintenance of a normal body weight is essential, as obesity can exacerbate diabetes mellitus. Your veterinarian will discuss the most appropriate diet for your dog.

Once entire females have been stabilised, it is recommended that they are spayed to prevent wide fluctuations in insulin requirements around the time of their season.

Finally, it is important to observe your dog closely for signs of hypoglycaemia, which may occur if too much insulin has been administered, normally during the time of peak insulin action. If you notice any sign of weakness or collapse, give oral glucose or syrup (e.g. a spoonful of honey) and seek veterinary advice immediately.

DIABETES INSIPIDUS

This is an uncommon condition characterised by the excessive production of watery urine. Unlike diabetes mellitus, the urine does not contain high levels of glucose.

Causes: May be caused by the pituitary gland failing to produce adequate levels of ADH, an anti-diuretic hormone that reduces the amount of urine production when the body becomes dehydrated. The pituitary gland can be damaged by trauma, inflammation, or the growth of a tumour.

Alternatively, the kidneys can develop a malfunction that leads to diabetes insipidus. Kidney disease can result in the kidneys' failure to recognise ADH.

Signs: The main sign is a marked increase in urine production, manifested as apparent incontinence, or a need to urinate during the night. As a consequence, the dog may also develop an increased thirst.

Treatment: Medicated eye drops, which need to be given once or twice daily. This treatment is expensive and may need to be continued on a long-term basis.

LEARNING AND MEMORY

The way in which dogs learn and remember is not dissimilar from the way in which humans learn. In both species, positive and negative associations form the basis of each type of behaviour. Internal motivational drives (e.g. hunger, fear or pleasure) interact with external environmental influences (e.g. food, fire and free running).

To some extent, a dog's behavioural characteristics and temperament are the result of his genetic make-up. This can aid learning and it is the reason why certain breeds are so adept at playing certain roles, e.g. retrieving or herding. However, early environmental exposure and experiences also play a crucial role in shaping a dog's character. Pet ownership should be a partnership, where the owner understands the dog's motivation and learns to communicate effectively with their dog. This allows the owner to shape and to develop pleasurable associations in the dog's mind, so that training is made easier and the dog develops behaviour that complements both him and his owner.

SOCIALISATION PERIOD

Primary social skills are learnt between the third and twelfth week of a dog's life – a period known as the socialisation period. During this time, a dog should develop 'good manners', communication skills, and learn to be at ease interacting with a wide variety of people and other pets. Exposing your dog to as many friendly situations as possible at this early age significantly reduces the probability of his developing aggressive or antisocial behaviour later on.

During his first three months of life, the dog is highly susceptible to learning about individual signals within his environment, known as stimuli. From a biological standpoint, survival is paramount and it is essential that dogs very quickly learn to determine which stimuli are important and which can be ignored. As the dog becomes familiar with non-dangerous stimuli, he learns to ignore them – a process known as habituation. Stimuli that pose a threat to him, however, he becomes highly sensitive towards (sensitisation), so that he can escape at the first available opportunity.

Increased sensitivity also develops when the dog learns that reacting to certain stimuli brings about a pleasurable response. For example, if the dog learns that chasing a rabbit is great fun and results in a good meal, his body will attune itself to make chase as soon as his eyes spot a rabbit.

Socialisation to a wide range of experiences is essential for all puppies.

FACTORS AFFECTING HABITUATION AND SENSITISATION			
PROCESS	STIMULI	RESPONSE	OUTCOME
Sensitisation	Highly relevant/ arousal/aversive (e.g. loud bang)	Fearful	Fright/flight (fear response activated)
Sensitisation	Highly relevant/ arousal appetitive (e.g. sound of leash)	Pleasurable	Non-fearful, stimulating response
Habituation	Irrelevant/low-value (e.g. sound of washing machine)	With exposure, ignores stimuli	Response decreases

The dog owner can use these processes of sensitisation and habituation as a training aid. A dog that becomes habituated to something will cease to be afraid of it. For example, the sound of a washing machine may alert the dog the first time it is heard. However, as it has no real value or biological significance, the dog eventually learns to ignore it.

Conversely, a dog can become sensitised to something. One example, known to dog owners everywhere, is the dog's reaction to his owner taking up a leash, which the dog has learnt to associate with being taken for a walk.

Dogs also learn to 'discriminate' or 'generalise' appropriately, between similar stimuli, which may or may not be of value in other contexts. These processes, known as stimulus discrimination and stimulus generalisation, explain why a dog may react differently to an owner's approach to the door, as compared with a stranger's approach.

PRIMARY/SECONDARY ASSOCIATIONS

Dogs learn to develop complex associations between events. These are divided into primary and secondary associations. Primary associations highlight stimuli or signals, which are related to food, reproduction or survival, and are usually of greater significance. Secondary associations relate to other stimuli and are generally less important.

CLASSICAL CONDITIONING

Classical conditioning refers to the dog's ability to learn that a signal or cue of little/no apparent significance is followed by an event/stimulus of value. As the dog repeats the experience, he learns to make an association between the two stimuli. For example, a wild dog that had experienced a stampede would learn to take refuge at the sound of an approaching wild herd. By learning this natural

signal, he increases his chance of survival. Similarly, a household dog soon learns the sound of his food being prepared and responds accordingly.

OPERANT CONDITIONING

Operant conditioning, or trial-and-error learning, is dependent upon the feedback that the dog receives when he carries out a particular action. A dog rewarded for returning to the handler when called is more likely to repeat this action in similar circumstances.

Positive reinforcement can also result in undesirable associations being formed. Owners will often stroke their dogs to give reassurance if, for example, fearful behaviour is displayed during a thunderstorm. Such feedback from the owner will often have inadvertent results – owner reaction to displays of fear is the basis of many phobias becoming established.

NEGATIVE REINFORCEMENT

Negative reinforcement occurs if a dog performs an action to avoid an unpleasant response. A dog that has been previously injured by a car will learn to avoid contact with moving vehicles.

Similarly, owners who admonish or punish their dogs for not returning immediately when called may inadvertently encourage their dogs to keep their distance. In this scenario, it is better to ignore the undesirable response and to work on encouraging the dog's immediate return through the use of positive reinforcers, such as food and praise.

PUNISHMENT

Punishment is identified as an aversive stimulus, applied immediately after an action in order to decrease the probability of such behaviour being repeated. Training methods reliant upon the regular application of punishment aim to dominate the dog through a regime of fear. Such methods induce stress and anxiety, are likely to prove counterproductive to training, and should be avoided.

Training methods that rely on positive reinforcement rather than punishment are generally more successful, reliable, and more enjoyable to both the dog and his owner.

GOOD TIMING

Giving praise or reinforcement at the right time during training is crucial. A desirable response should be immediately reinforced with a positive signal or reward to encourage repetitive behaviour. If more than a few seconds elapse, you may actually reward a less desirable response. Once an action or training response is established, then intermittent or random reward should be used to strengthen or shape a more precise response, and to encourage repeat behaviour.

LEARNING PROCESSES

When training a complex action, such as a retrieve, one should generally break down the learning task into smaller, more easily achievable stages. Each stage is then shaped, reinforced, and linked to the next part of the task. This shaping process, known as successive approximation, continues until all the stages are successfully linked together and the retrieve exercise is taught in full.

Dogs also learn through the observation and copying of their peers or other dogs. This process, identified as social learning, is utilised by trainers to teach a young dog to herd sheep. It is also responsible for dogs learning inappropriate or undesirable behaviour, such as barking and chasing.

Despite numerous studies carried out in relation to learning processes and the dog's mind, there remain many questions still unanswered.

- Does the dog have an ability to 'think' or give forethought?
- Can he really make decisions, or is his behaviour simply a result of conditioning?
- What is the dog's degree of consciousness?

It will be many years before these questions can be answered, during which time the responsibility remains with us to communicate, train and monitor the welfare of our companions.

THE VALUE OF REINFORCERS IN LEARNING AND BEHAVIOUR MODIFICATION

STIMULUS	GIVE	TAKE AWAY
Pleasant stimuli	Positive reinforcer: increases the probability of the behaviour. This may include the giving of any resource of value (e.g. praise, food, touch, play, attention, chewing, or a toy) in return for a desirable behaviour.	Negative punisher: decreases the probability of the behaviour. This may include the withdrawal of any valuable resource if the animal performs an undesirable action.
Unpleasant stimuli	Positive punisher: decreases the probability of the behaviour. May include the giving of physical punishment or mental punishment (i.e. confinement, flooding techniques). N.B. Such forms of punishment should not be used on dogs suffering from anxiety-related disorders.	Negative reinforcer: increases the probability of the behaviour. Encourages certain behaviour, which will prevent the occurrence of undesirable stimuli (i.e. the use of Halti/Gentle Leader encourages the dog to walk by your side).

Clicker training can be used with puppies to instil good behaviour and obedience.

It can also be used with adult dogs to treat obsessive-compulsive disorders, such as tail spinning.

LEARNING DISORDERS

OBSESSIVE-COMPULSIVE DISORDERS (OCD)

Most obsessive-compulsive disorders derive from stress and anxiety. They have neurological and physiological components which contribute to the development and reinforcement of such undesirable behaviours.

The conditions associated with OCD often require a combination of counter-conditioning, desensitisation and pharmacological intervention. Urgent referral to a veterinarian or behavioural consellor is recommended.

TAIL/KENNEL SPINNING

This describes the repetitive locomotor activity of chasing the trajectory of the tail in excess of any activity required for grooming. Such behaviour requires a conditioned interruption (sound of a clicker or doorbell) to stop this behaviour, preferably before it becomes obsessive.

SELF-MUTILATION

This generally relates to the removal of the coat, abrasion of the skin, or greater mutilation, using the teeth, claws or an external substrate (i.e. rubbing against a wall). Such behaviours are in the absence of dermatological or physiological conditions.

These behaviours often have an environmental derivative, such as lack of physical or mental stimulation. Once self-mutilation commences, it requires immediate treatment.

Physiological associations, which develop as a result of pains, pruritis (itching), and anxiety, will strengthen rapidly, making the treatment of this condition difficult.

Treatment will generally incorporate environmental modification and interruptions, with pharmacological intervention.

COGNITIVE DYSFUNCTION

This term is used to describe behavioural changes related to ageing, which are not directly caused by the primary failure of any organ system. Such behaviours may be associated with degeneration of the brain, similar to Alzheimer's-like senile dementia or lesions.

General behaviour modification techniques may be used to re-establish desirable responses. Pharmacological intervention may aid in certain cases.

TRAUMA/INJURY

If a dog sustains a severe physical injury, there may be widespread effects beyond the site of the injury. If these interfere with the blood supply to vital organs, severe mental or physical damage may occur, including shock, and head injuries/bleeding into the brain.

Dogs under stress, or those that have received ineffective training or socialisation, may produce deviant behaviour patterns. Once these become habitual, they can be very difficult to break.

There are many reasons why deviant behaviour starts, and, although these vary in detail, the main causes fall into three main categories: anxiety, aggression, and dominance. These problems are complex, and it is advisable to seek the help of a qualified behaviourist.

ANXIETY
An anxious dog, with little or no self-confidence, will panic if he is left to cope with life on his own. He will follow his owner from room to room, and will probably nudge repeatedly for attention. If the over-anxious dog is left alone, his behaviour may become more extreme. Instead of waiting calmly for the return of his human pack leader, the dog may bark excessively, soil the room he is left in, or become destructive.

WHAT CAN YOU DO?
It is all too easy for the over-anxious dog to 'win' the battle. You rush back to stop him barking, or you make a great fuss when you return home to find he has chewed something. As far as the dog is concerned, his attention-seeking behaviour has paid off handsomely.

The over-anxious dog cannot cope with being left on his own.

A crate may help in the short term.

SHORT-TERM SOLUTIONS
Accustom your dog to going in a crate. Most dogs see a crate as their own special den, where they feel safe and secure. Make sure the crate has comfortable bedding, and provide some safe toys. The great advantage of a crate is that the dog does not have access to anything he can destroy, and he is less likely to soil his own sleeping quarters.

LONG-TERM SOLUTIONS
The aim is to cure the dog's anxiety, and you can only do this step by step, proving that nothing terrible happens if he is left alone.
• When you are at home, put a small barrier (e.g. a stair gate) between two rooms. Leave your dog in one room while you spend a short period in the adjoining room. Your dog will be able to see you, but he is learning to cope without close physical contact. Build up the amount of time your dog is left in this way.
• When you leave your dog alone in the house, do not make a fuss saying goodbye or when you return. Try to create a calm atmosphere, with no heightened emotions. To begin with, leave your dog for a short period, and gradually build up the amount of time you spend away.
• It may help if you can leave your dog with a boredom-busting toy, such as a cube with a small amount of food squeezed inside. With any luck, your dog will be so busy trying to get the treat, he will scarcely realise you have gone.
• Obviously, no dog should be left alone for long periods, as this will bring its own problems of boredom and frustration. The aim is to have a dog that is happy to be left alone for a reasonable period, without showing undue distress.

A boredom-busting toy will keep the dog occupied during your absence.

In the majority of cases, aggressive behaviour is directed towards other dogs. Rarely, but more seriously, it may be focused on people.

An aggressive dog may have a strong desire to fight, but it is equally likely that fear is the root cause. If a dog has no self-confidence, and fears encounters with other canines, he may begin growling and snarling to appear bigger and braver than he is.

It is important to find out what is triggering the behaviour. Close observation of the dog in a variety of situations will usually supply the necessary information. However, unless you are a very experienced handler, you will need to enlist the help of an animal behaviourist to interpret what is going on, and to attempt to reshape the behaviour.

An aggressive dog is a menace.

WHAT CAN YOU DO?
Some breeds are more likely to be aggressive than others. A breed that has been developed specifically for guarding (e.g. Rottweiler or German Shepherd) will have strong protective instincts in their make-up. They are bold and loyal, and if they perceive a threat to themselves, or to their owners, they are likely to react aggressively. It is essential that these breeds are kept only by experienced handlers, who are prepared to provide a comprehensive programme of socialisation and training. In this way, inherent guarding instincts are correctly channelled and kept under control.

Initially, the aggressive dog should be muzzled in public places.

SHORT-TERM SOLUTIONS
If your dog shows signs of aggressive behaviour, you must ensure that he is muzzled and kept on a lead in public places. It helps to inhibit aggression, and, if you know your dog cannot do any harm, your handling will be more positive.

LONG-TERM SOLUTIONS
- Seek the advice of an experienced dog trainer/behaviourist, and start work on a comprehensive programme of socialisation and training.
- Create a controlled environment and allow your dog to meet another dog that has a steady, equable temperament. Make sure your dog is on the lead and muzzled, and be swift to reprimand any sign of aggression. Gradually increase the amount of time spent this way, moving on to extending your dog's circle of acquaintances.
- When a dog shows aggression or becomes suspicious of people, it is usually directed toward a particular category – for example, a dog may develop a sudden dislike of men. Again, the best plan is to create a controlled environment, and recruit someone who is confident with dogs. Arm them with lots of treats, and stage a supervised introduction. Given time, most dogs will learn to overcome their suspicion, and, in gradual stages, you can expose your dog to a variety of different situations.
- Sometimes, aggressive behaviour is allied to dominance, and this will need to be tackled in a different way (see page 138).
- In all cases, aggressive behaviour must not be tolerated, and it is essential to seek expert advice when dealing with this problem.

Supervise an introduction to a dog of sound temperament.

A dominant dog has decided that he is the leader of the pack, and he will, therefore, refuse to accept commands from his human owners. This may take the form of wilful disobedience, which makes the dog a trial to live with, or, worse still, the dog may become aggressive, growling at his owner if he is asked to move off the sofa or give up a favourite toy.

Although all dogs may go through a period of 'trying it on', particularly during adolescence, the dominant dog will show behaviour that has become completely out of hand.

The dominant dog may become possessive over his food, or over a toy.

WHAT CAN YOU DO?

Although it is difficult, you must try to turn the clock back and re-educate your dog. It may be necessary to seek the help of a dog trainer/behaviourist to help map out a programme.

SHORT-TERM SOLUTIONS

- Keep your dog on the lead, and muzzled if necessary, in all public places.
- At times of conflict, use diversion techniques, such as distracting your dog with a toy or a treat.
- Aversion techniques can be used. These include squirting the dog with a water pistol, or using training discs (where sound interrupts, and then prevents, the unwanted behaviour).
- If your dog has become possessive about a particular area (e.g. the sofa), use a stair gate to prevent your dog's access to it.

LONG-TERM SOLUTIONS

A comprehensive programme of training is needed to reshape the dog's behaviour. Starting with basic training exercises, the dog must learn to accept that his status is inferior.

- Groom your dog, so that he accepts your right to handle him.
- Make sure you always go through doors before your dog.
- Do not let the dog lay claim to furniture, such as the sofa or a bed.
- Feed your dog after the rest of the family.
- When playing with your dog, make sure you always 'win' the toy at the end of the game.
- When you have visitors, do not allow your dog to rush to the door and be the first to greet them.
- In the car, make sure your dog stays in his designated area. When you arrive at your destination, do not allow him to get out of the car until you give the command.
- Sit your dog next to you, and place a treat or a toy just in front of him. Do not allow him to take the treat/toy until you give the command.

A dog must learn to accept handling and grooming.

The dog is asked to "Wait" at every doorway, so the owner can go through first.

Make sure you always 'win' the game.

8 THE SKIN

The skin is the largest organ in the body and the only one we can see. Skin diseases are extremely common, and, in this chapter, we will look at the structure and function of the skin and how to manage common skin complaints.

STRUCTURE AND FUNCTION OF THE SKIN

The skin consists of three layers:
- **The subcutis**: This fatty layer insulates and shapes the body.
- **The dermis**: This is a tough, flexible and elastic layer. It contains blood vessels and nerves to the skin. Cells within the dermis play an important role in inflammation, repair, pigmentation, glands, and hair follicles.
- **The epidermis**: The outer layer of the skin forms a tough, waterproof barrier. Cells at the base of the epidermis continually divide, migrate outwards and are shed from the surface.

HAIR FOLLICLES
Hair follicles are found everywhere in the skin, except for on the nose and on the footpads. In dogs, hair is denser along the back, and sparser on the underside, of the body. There are three types of coat:
- **Basic coat type**: This has coarse, primary or guard hairs, and a dense undercoat of fine, secondary hairs (e.g. German Shepherd Dog).
- **Short coat type**: Short coats can consist of primary hairs (e.g. Rottweiler) or secondary hairs (e.g. short-coated Dachshund).
- **Long coat type**: Long coats usually consist of fine (e.g. Cocker Spaniel), or woolly (e.g. Poodle), secondary hairs.

COAT COLOUR
Pigments or melanins occur in two colours:
- Black/brown
- Yellow-red.

The final colour depends on their relative abundance and distribution. For example, blue coats and fawn coats are dilutions of black and red respectively. White skin and hair lacks pigment. The genetic control of colour is very complex and many colours do not breed consistently from generation to generation.

SEBACEOUS GLANDS
Sebaceous glands secrete sebum, which moisturises the skin, supplies nutrients and protects against infection. Sweat glands in dogs are not used to regulate temperature as in humans. Instead, sweat forms part of the sebum.

CROSS-SECTION OF SKIN

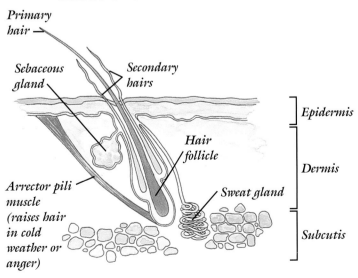

Primary hair

Sebaceous gland

Secondary hairs

Hair follicle

Epidermis

Dermis

Sweat gland

Arrector pili muscle (raises hair in cold weather or anger)

Subcutis

- **Forms a tough, outer barrier**
- **Protects against infection and injury**
- **Insulation**
- **Protects against UV radiation**
- **Provides shape and form to the body**
- **Produces vitamin D**
- **Responsible for sensations of touch, pressure, itching, pain and heat**
- **Eliminates waste products**
- **Stores fat and vitamins**
- **Retains water and essential salts.**

DISORDERS OF THE SKIN

This section deals with skin disorders according to the symptoms they present:
- Changes in coloration
- Ear infections
- Anal sac problems
- Erosions and ulcers
- Hair loss
- Itching
- Lumps and bumps
- Nail diseases

It is important to eliminate malignant melanoma, clusters of black tumours.

CHANGES IN COLORATION

COLOUR LOSS
Greying around the muzzle is a common sign of ageing. Permanent or seasonal loss of pigment from the nose and elsewhere is also common. This may be hereditary or secondary to immune-mediated diseases, deep infections or injuries.

Albinos have red eyes and white skin and hair because of a hereditary lack of melanin. There is no treatment, and affected dogs should be kept out of strong sunlight as the lack of melanin makes them susceptible to skin damage and to UV radiation.

Vitiligo is a rare condition associated with destruction of cells that produce melanin. Colour is lost from small patches of skin and hair. These may wax and wane or coalesce into large areas.

The skin itself is otherwise normal. There is no effective treatment, but affected areas need protection from sunlight.

COLOUR CHANGE
A diffuse pattern of dark skin is commonly seen with allergies, skin infections, *Demodex* mites, and hormonal diseases. Focal patches of dark skin can also be caused by benign accumulations of pigment or melanomas. It is important to eliminate malignant melanoma, particularly if the patch is raised or if it appears suddenly.

PROTECTION FROM THE SUN
- Exposure to strong sunlight can cause sunburn and skin cancers in dogs with sparse coats, light-coloured skin, or scars.
- Keep dogs indoors when the sun is strongest.
- Hats, T-shirts, shorts and goggles can be customised to protect dogs. Commercial bodysuits are also available.
- Use a black marker pen to protect small areas of skin. Tattooing is not helpful as the dye penetrates underneath the skin.
- Sun block is useful, but dogs tend to lick it off – use waterproof sun block and re-apply frequently.

EAR INFECTIONS

EAR STRUCTURE
The ear consists of three parts:
- **The external ear:** This comprises the earflap or 'pinna', and the ear canal. Made of cartilage lined by skin, these form an L-shaped tube leading to the eardrum. The earflap can be pendulous (e.g. Bloodhound), semi-erect (e.g. Labrador), or erect (e.g. German Shepherd Dog).
- **The middle ear:** This is a bony cavity within the skull. The tiny bones of the middle ear convey sound to the inner ear.
- **The inner ear:** This is a part of the brain that controls hearing and balance.

See pages 124 and 142 for more detail about the ear.

EARS AND SWIMMING
For most dogs, swimming is a great form of exercise, but can trigger ear infections in dogs with narrow or hairy ears, or with other skin problems. Dogs at risk should avoid water.

Most healthy dogs do not need baths. Regular grooming removes dead skin and hairs, stimulating the production of healthy skin and the distribution of sebum. However, show dogs, some longhaired breeds, and older dogs may require bathing.

- Use a mild veterinary shampoo – human shampoos are too harsh.
- Medicated veterinary shampoos are useful for treating infection, some parasites, dry or greasy scaling, and inflamed or itchy skin.
- Whirlpool baths are excellent, but good results can be obtained using shower attachments. Some veterinary practices offer regular bathing clinics. Garden hoses are distressing for all concerned.

Longhaired breeds will benefit from bathing.

HOW TO BATH YOUR DOG

- Make sure the coat is free from debris, as this can inactivate the shampoo or prevent its contact with the skin. Clip long coats if necessary.
- Wet the coat with lukewarm water for 5 to 10 minutes, to allow the shampoo to make proper contact with the skin. Avoid over-wetting, which macerates the skin.
- Massage the shampoo into affected areas. Use a sponge or cloth for delicate (e.g. eyes, ears and mouth) or difficult (e.g. feet) areas. Doing the head last minimises shaking and struggling.
- Most shampoos need 10 minutes of contact time.
- Rinse thoroughly with water or use emollients. Gently towel and allow to dry naturally – blow-driers can over-dry and burn the skin.
- Do not use ointments or earplugs – water in the ears is swiftly removed by shaking, and anything splashed into the eyes should be rinsed away immediately.

HOW OFTEN?

- Dogs with skin problems should be bathed two to three times a week.
- Once the skin problem is under control, the frequency or product can be changed, following consultation with your veterinarian.
- Dogs with long-term skin problems will generally need bathing once every two to three weeks, although this may vary depending on the dog's response to treatment.
- You should cease treatment and seek veterinary advice if your dog develops new skin lesions or experiences irritation.

HAIRLESS DOGS

There are a number of genes that can cause hairlessness. Some breeds are deliberately bred this way, whereas it is a serious problem in other breeds. Hair loss can also be caused by a variety of skin diseases (see Hair Loss, page 145). The skin of hairless breeds is often thickened, oily and scaly.

- Vigorous massaging loosens scale, removes excess skin, and promotes healthy blood flow.
- Use a degreasing shampoo to counter the oiliness. Depending on your dog's skin type, you may need to use a moisturiser afterwards.
- Hairless dogs need protection from cold weather and strong sunlight.

Badly ulcerated lips and feet may be painful.
Antibiotics will clear up the infection, but infections
will recur unless the folds are kept clean and dry.
Cosmetic surgery is the only long-term cure.

IMMUNE-MEDIATED DISEASES

A number of immune-mediated diseases occur when
the immune system malfunctions and begins
attacking the body.

Most occur spontaneously, but causes include
infections, drugs, vaccines, UV light and cancers.
Some breeds, including German Shepherd Dogs,
Jack Russell Terriers, arctic breeds and collies, have a
genetic susceptibility. For example, Rough Collies
and Shetland Sheepdogs suffer from an inherited
disease of the skin and muscles called
dermatomyositis. Relatives of affected dogs should
not be bred from.

Erosions and ulcers of varying severity can appear
anywhere on the body, such as in the mouth, lips,
nostrils, eyelids, anus, and prepuce or vulva, or
involve other parts of the body, including the lymph
nodes, liver, kidneys, eyes, joints and muscles.
Affected dogs can be off-colour, lame, lose weight,
and suffer anaemia or bleeding.

Diagnosis: Skin biopsies examined by specialist
veterinary pathologists are essential. Blood tests,
urine analysis, radiography, ultrasound scans, and
biopsies from internal organs and joints will show if
other organs are affected. Food trials can diagnose
allergic reactions to food additives, although this is
rare.

Treatment: Aims to suppress the immune system
so that it does not produce the inappropriate
reaction. Some drugs are better for certain diseases
than others, so an accurate diagnosis is essential.
Unless an inciting cause is found and eliminated,
life-long treatment is necessary.

In milder cases, treatment may consist of creams
or lotions that are applied locally to the skin.
Combinations of essential fatty acids and vitamin E,
or nicotinamide and tetracycline antibiotics, can also
prove effective and are relatively free of side effects.
Avoiding strong sunlight may also help.

In more serious cases, steroids and chemotherapy
are normally used. Most dogs tolerate these drugs
well. More-potent drugs are used to put the disease
in remission, with less-potent drugs (with fewer side
effects) used to keep the disease under control.
Potential side effects of chemotherapy include liver
and kidney problems, bleeding disorders, anaemia
and secondary infections. Blood and urine tests
should be performed every two weeks at the start of

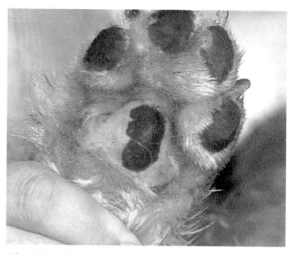

Sloughing of the footpads, caused by an antibiotic reaction.

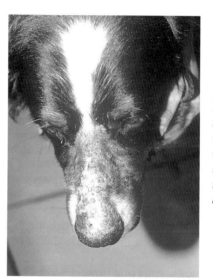

*Nasal erosions
and crusting,
which are the
result of an
immune-
mediated
disease.*

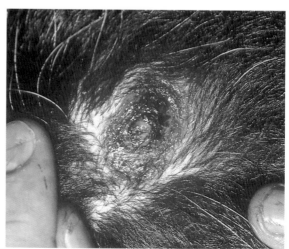

*Deep ulcer around a nipple, caused by
a severe immune-mediated disease.*

treatment and every three to six months thereafter to detect any side effects.

HAIR LOSS

Each hair follicle goes through a growing, a transition, and finally a resting phase. New growing hairs eventually push out resting hairs. Most dogs moult and grow a new coat each season. Exceptions to this are breeds (such as Poodles), who have continually-growing hair and need haircuts, and arctic breeds (e.g. Siberian Husky) who retain hair for long periods. However, dogs exposed to artificial light indoors shed hairs all year.

Shed hairs can be annoying, but hair loss is only significant if it leaves bare skin. The commonest cause is scratching, so your veterinarian will investigate any itching first.

DEMODEX MITES
Demodex mites are normal inhabitants of the hair follicle. However, in large numbers, they can cause patchy hair loss and scaling, usually in adolescent dogs. Most cases will heal spontaneously. More severe infections can cause widespread hair loss, scaling, crusting, and secondary bacterial infections, which can be fatal. Some dogs have an inherited susceptibility to *Demodex* infections and should not be bred from. Other causes include hormonal and metabolic diseases, cancers, steroids or chemotherapy.
Diagnosis: Mites are found on skin scrapes or biopsies.
Treatment: Underlying causes and secondary infections should be treated first. Shampoos, dips and oral drugs are used to eliminate the mites. Treatment may last several months and can be life-long in some dogs.

RINGWORM
Ringworm (or dermatophytosis) is a fungal infection caught from dogs, cats, and wild animals, which can be passed to humans. Spores remain viable for months or years. Infection is commonest in young dogs, causing patchy hair loss, scaling, crusting, and secondary bacterial infections. Older dogs often have underlying conditions, such as hormonal and metabolic diseases, cancers, steroids, or chemotherapy.
Diagnosis: Your veterinarian will take some hair samples from the edge of the affected area, which will then be tested in a fungal culture. If fungus grows, the diagnosis of ringworm is confirmed.

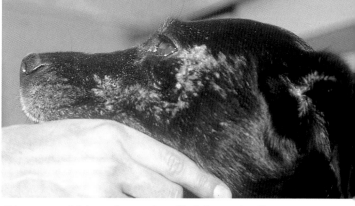

Ringworm with irregular patches of hair loss and scaling.

Some types of ringworm fluoresce in ultraviolet light, and your veterinarian may examine your dog under a 'Woods' lamp to check for any fluorescence.
Treatment: Ringworm in young dogs can spontaneously resolve, but treatment is recommended because of the risk to humans. A combination of antifungal drugs and shampoos is used, and clipping longhaired dogs may help to reduce contamination. Dogs are not considered cured until three fungal culture tests are negative – stopping too soon is the most common reason for treatment failure. Collars, leads, coats, blankets, beds, etc., should be disposed of or thoroughly disinfected.

STRESS-RELATED HAIR LOSS
Widespread hair loss can occur in the days and weeks following any stress, such as pregnancy, nursing, malnutrition, shock, fever, illness or chemotherapy. Despite the hair loss, the underlying skin is usually normal. In most cases, the coat grows back quite quickly.

GENETIC HAIR LOSS
Mexican Hairless and Chinese Crested Dogs are naturally hairless. In normally-haired breeds, the same genes are a major problem. Affected dogs, siblings, and parents should not be bred from.

FOLLICULAR DYSPLASIAS
Abnormal growth and development of the hair follicles lead to a dog's coat becoming dull and brittle. Eventually, hair is lost, predominantly from the trunk. There is often scaling and secondary infection.
• **Black hair follicle dysplasia**: This affects black areas in black and white dogs.
• **Colour dilute alopecia**: This affects dilute colour coats, such as blue or fawn Dobermanns.
• **General follicular dysplasias**: Hair loss has also been reported in Irish Water Spaniels, Portuguese Water Dogs, and sporadically in other breeds.
Diagnosis: The clinical signs of follicular dysplasia, combined with the dog's breed (if his breed is predisposed to it), are highly suggestive of the condition. Confirmation can be made by examining

hair and follicle biopsies under the microscope.

Treatment: Shampoos and antibiotics are used to control scaling and bacterial infections. Some cases respond to retinoids and high-quality diets, but the prognosis is usually poor.

HORMONAL HAIR LOSS

The various hormonal diseases tend to look similar to each other. Common features include:

- Symmetrical hair loss
- Dull, dry, faded coat
- Failure to regrow the coat after clipping
- Mild to moderate scaling
- Easily bruised skin and poor wound healing
- Secondary infections.

HYPOTHYROIDISM

Hypothyroidism is caused by a lack of the thyroid hormone. Clinical signs are variable and include hair loss from the collar, nose, tail and trunk, with thickened, pigmented and cool skin. Affected dogs are often dull, lethargic and overweight, but others are bright and well.

Diagnosis: Routine blood tests and biopsy findings are suggestive, but rarely diagnostic. No single thyroid test is perfect, and test results are often combined to confirm diagnosis.

Treatment: The prognosis with thyroid hormone replacement is very good, although life-long treatment and monitoring is required.

HYPERADRENOCORTICISM/ CUSHING'S DISEASE

This is caused by an excess of steroid hormones from the adrenal glands. Overproduction may be due to a pituitary gland tumour in the brain (which controls the adrenal glands), adrenal gland tumours, or steroid treatment. Symptoms include hair loss, excessive drinking, a 'pot-bellied' appearance, calcium deposits in the skin (which may be itchy or painful), thin and wrinkled skin, muscle wasting, and sugar diabetes.

Diagnosis: Routine tests are suggestive but rarely diagnostic. No single adrenal test is perfect and results are often combined to confirm a diagnosis.

Treatment: Dogs with hyperadrenocorticism caused by steroid treatment need to be weaned on to alternative therapies. Adrenal tumours can be surgically removed. Drugs to limit adrenal output are used in other cases. Over-treatment and insufficient steroid hormone levels can cause weakness, vomiting, and collapse. Dogs are hospitalised during the initial treatment and owners are given steroid tablets for the dogs, in case of emergencies.

The prognosis is reasonable, although pituitary tumours eventually cause neurological problems.

See also Chapter Seven.

SEX HORMONE DISORDERS

These affect the hindlimbs, genitalia, flanks and neck, causing hair loss. Hormone disorders can also cause swelling of the nipples and vulva, signs of oestrus, a pendulous prepuce, swollen anus and tail glands, and black spots around the anus and genitals.

Treatment: Neutering will cure testicular and ovarian tumours or functional abnormalities. Infantile genitalia, irregular or absent oestrus, and urinary incontinence can be associated with low hormone levels, which can be treated with androgens or oestrogens, although dogs should be closely monitored in case of side effects. This rarely occurs after neutering, however.

MISCELLANEOUS CAUSES

- **Seasonal hair loss:** This common condition usually affects the hair on the back and on the flanks. The underlying skin is darker, but otherwise normal. Hair loss and regrowth can vary from year to year, and has been linked to changes

Nasal hair loss with hypothyroidism.

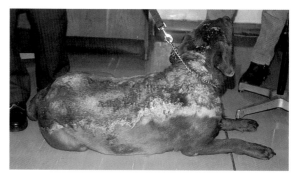

Severe hair loss and calcium deposits with hyperadrenocorticism.

Most skin diseases cannot be diagnosed with a single visit to the veterinarian, and tests are necessary to confirm the diagnosis.

COAT BRUSHINGS
- Run a fine-toothed comb through the coat, and examine the skin using a hand lens.
- Fleas are fast-moving, dark brown insects. Flea dirt is dark, shiny and leaves a reddish stain on damp paper.
- Lice are slow-moving, white insects. Look for their eggs ('nits') stuck to hairs.
- *Cheyletiella* mites can be seen as small, white specks. Their eggs are also stuck to hairs.
- Fungal spores are collected for culture using a toothbrush.

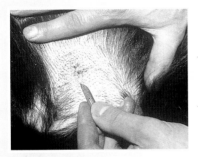

A skin scrape, usually performed to detect the presence of mites.

SKIN SCRAPES
- Skin scrapes are usually carried out when looking for mites.
- Superficial skin layers are scraped on to a glass slide using a scalpel blade.
- This leaves a graze that quickly heals. Most dogs tolerate skin scrapes very well, but excitable dogs may need sedation.

HAIR PLUCKS
- Hairs are firmly grasped by forceps, pulled out, and examined under a microscope for fungal infections, parasites, the stage of the hair cycle, and hair-shaft defects.

CYTOLOGY
- Cytology means looking at cells. Glass slides or swabs can pick up surface cells when pressed firmly against the skin. A needle and syringe can collect cells from deeper lesions.
- Cytology is very good at detecting infections, inflammation, abnormal cells and cancers.
- Dogs tolerate cytology very well.

SKIN BIOPSY
- Skin biopsies show how cells interact with each other and the rest of the skin. Biopsies are routine in inflammatory diseases, tumours and hair loss.
- A local anaesthetic is injected under the skin, a small cylinder of skin removed with a

punch, and the edges sutured together. Biopsies are normally taken from several sites.
- A general anaesthetic is given for biopsies from sensitive sites, such as the feet or face, but most dogs are just sedated to keep them still.

BLOOD SAMPLES
- Blood samples are taken from the foreleg in large dogs, and from the neck in small dogs.
- Samples can be analysed by in-house laboratories or sent to an outside laboratory.
- Routine profiles look at general health, liver and kidney function, and blood cell numbers, but other tests may be performed if particular diseases are suspected.
- Urine tests are often carried out at the same time.

HORMONE TESTS
- Hormone levels are usually measured in blood samples. However, thyroid, adrenal, and sex-hormone levels vary widely throughout the day.
- Dynamic tests, which reflect the gland's activity, are therefore preferred to single tests.
- Samples are taken before and after dosing with a drug that stimulates the gland.
- Tests are usually expensive.

BACTERIAL/FUNGAL CULTURES
- Cultures are taken to confirm infection, to discover the type of infectious agent, and to determine which antibiotics or antifungals are most effective.
- Cultures can be grown from swabs, smears, hair plucks, coat brushings or biopsies. Most bacterial cultures take a few days, but fungi and some bacteria can take several weeks.

SELLOTAPE
- A simple strip of Sellotape, pressed to the skin, can be examined under the microscope to check for yeasts and parasites.

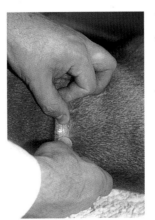

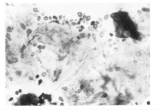

◀ *A tape strip is used to check for yeasts and parasites.*

▼ *Yeasts show up as blue-purple 'peanuts' on tape strips taken from affected skin.*

in day length, but the causes are not fully understood. Some dogs respond to melatonin (the hormone often used for jet-lag), but no treatment is consistently beneficial. The causes are unknown.

- **Pattern baldness**: This condition, seen in short-haired Dachshunds, Boston Terriers, and other short-coated breeds, results in progressive hair loss from the earflaps, head, neck, chest, and tail. The skin remains unaffected, but the hair loss is permanent.
- **Scarring**: Hairless scars can be caused by deep wounds, infections, burns, injection reactions, collars, or immune-mediated diseases.
- **Clipping**: Some dogs fail to regrow hair after clipping. This can be due to an underlying problem, but it is most common in arctic breeds, which have a long resting phase in the hair-growth cycle. Vigorous massage, and covering the affected area to keep it warm, may encourage early regrowth.

ITCHING

An itch is an unpleasant sensation causing dogs to chew, lick and scratch. The skin often becomes red and inflamed as a result. Itching is usually caused by parasites, anal sac problems or allergies.

PARASITES
Common parasites include fleas, lice and mites (e.g. *Sarcoptes, Otodectes, Demodex* and *Cheyletiella*). Fleas and mites will attack humans, but infestations can be destroyed rapidly by treating affected dogs. See also Chapter Two.

FLEAS
Fleas are a common cause of skin problems, causing inflammation and crusting, especially over the back, hindlegs, and flanks. Flea control is mandatory with all itchy dogs, as any infestation makes other skin diseases much worse.

An adult cat flea (above).

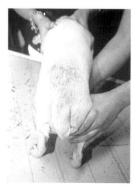

Flea-bite dermatitis, with licking and inflammation of the back and tail (right).

FLEA ALLERGY DERMATITIS

Hill's Atlas of Veterinary Clinical Anatomy

Self-inflicted trauma results in reddening, papules, pustules, crusts, and hair loss in areas where fleas feed.

Sequence of flea-allergy dermatitis

Flea punctures skin to feed.

Flea saliva sets up an antigen-antibody reaction.

Excoriation and inflammation result from self-inflicted trauma.

Acute bacterial infection results.

Diagnosis: Fleas or flea dirt can be easily found among the hairs. Flea allergies can be identified using skin or blood tests.
Treatment: Prevention is better than cure. Your vet will discuss flea control with you (see page 33).

SCABIES
Caused by the *Sarcoptes* mite, scabies is highly contagious, and can be transferred to people. Foxes may be a reservoir of infection. The mites burrow into the skin, causing intense irritation of the elbows, hocks and ears.
Diagnosis: Skin scrapes, or a response to trial therapy, normally confirm diagnosis.
Treatment: A variety of insecticidal sprays, spot-on preparations or dips are used. All affected and in-contact dogs should be treated for several weeks, so that any mites hatching from eggs are also killed. Treatment of the house is not necessary, but collars, bedding etc. should be thoroughly washed.

EAR MITES

Otodectes ear mites are most common in young dogs. They cause ear infections with a dark waxy discharge. They can also affect the head, neck, back and legs.

Diagnosis: Mites can be detected from skin scrapes, or in the ears, using an otoscope.

Treatment: A combination of eardrops and flea drops/sprays, used for three to four weeks, is necessary to kill off mites and eggs. All animals in the household should be treated, as some animals are carriers.

CHEYLETIELLA

Cheyletiella are highly contagious, although some dogs show no ill effects from carrying these parasites. Others suffer itchiness, with dry, whitish scaling, particularly over the back and flanks.

Diagnosis: The mites are relatively large, and the condition is sometimes described as 'walking dandruff', as the mites can be seen moving on dark skin or coat.

Treatment: Shampoos are used to remove scale, and longhaired dogs should be clipped to allow proper penetration of the insecticide. All animals in

Scaling caused by Cheyletiella mites.

Harvest mites: bright orange dots between the toes.

the household should be treated for at least three weeks to kill the newly hatched mites. The house should also be treated, as female mites can live in the environment for up to ten days (for flea control, see page 33).

LICE

Lice are relatively uncommon, except in young, ill, or kennelled dogs. There are two types of louse – biting and sucking – which are differentiated by their mouthparts. In large numbers, lice can be associated with irritation and poor general condition, and can also transmit infections.

Diagnosis: Lice and their eggs ('nits') are easily seen on hairs.

Treatment: Most flea products are effective against lice. All affected and in-contact dogs should be treated for at least three weeks.

HARVEST MITES/CHIGGERS

Also known as Berry Bugs or Chiggers, these mites cause intense itching. Dogs are infected by the larvae of a common mite that lives on plants. Larvae are active from July to September and readily infest dogs and their owners.

Diagnosis: The bright orange mites are easily seen between the toes, on the belly, and around the ears.

Treatment: Most insecticides kill them but reinfestation is a problem. Long-acting flea sprays can prevent new infestations, and dogs should be kept away from long grass and woods. Severely affected dogs may need steroids during the mite season.

OTHER PARASITES

Hookworms occasionally cause itchy and inflamed feet in kennelled dogs (see page 27). Reactions to other internal worms are very rare.

ALLERGIES

Skin allergies are common in dogs. There are three main causes:
• Food allergies
• Atopic dermatitis
• Contact allergies.

Food allergy and atopic dermatitis can occur together. The muzzle, ears, feet and underside of the body are usually affected. In cases of contact allergies, only skin that is in contact with the irritant becomes inflamed.

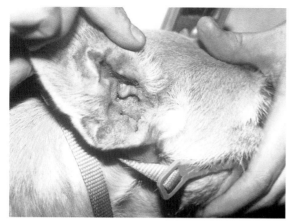

Early atopic dermatitis.

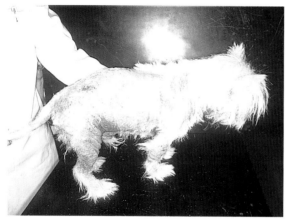

Untreated atopic dermatitis with severe and widespread hair loss, inflammation, pigmentation, and thickening of the skin.

FOOD ALLERGIES

Allergic reactions to food are uncommon. It is a misconception that dogs react only to a change of diet – reactions are just as likely after months or years on a particular diet.

Diagnosis: The only reliable way to diagnose a food allergy is to feed a novel diet for at least six weeks. This is preferably a home-cooked diet (e.g. fish and potatoes), or a special, commercial diet, supplied by your veterinarian. Standard diets are unsuitable. Improvement, followed by deterioration on returning to the original diet, is diagnostic.

Suspected foods should be added one by one to the exclusion diet. Beef, dairy products, and cereals are most commonly implicated.

Treatment: Once the offending food has been discovered, it can be avoided using special commercial diets or home-made diets supplemented with oils, vitamins and minerals.

ATOPY OR ATOPIC DERMATITIS

Atopic dogs react to environmental substances (allergens), which are harmless to normal dogs. Common allergens include house dust mites, danders, insects, pollens or moulds.

Diagnosis: Dogs are normally sedated and given a series of skin tests. A patch on the side of the chest is shaved and allergens are injected into the skin. After 20 minutes, the skin will redden at the spot where the allergens were injected.

Alternatively, blood samples can be taken. Atopic dogs will have antibodies to particular allergens present in their blood.

This is not as reliable as skin testing, but can be useful if the dog's skin is so bad that skin tests are not possible.

Treatment: The prognosis is generally good, but life-long treatment is required. Some allergens can be avoided, while exposure to others can be reduced. This can involve anti-dust-mite sprays, vacuuming, plastic dog beds, regular washing of bedding, improving ventilation, removing carpets, and keeping dogs out of bedrooms.

Various drug therapies are available:

- **Immunotherapy**: When specific allergens are identified, this is the treatment of choice. Dogs are injected with gradually increasing amounts of the allergen. This can take up to ten months to work and is effective in 60 to 70 per cent of cases. Initial injections are given at a veterinary surgery, in case of an allergic shock reaction, but side effects are rare.

- **Antihistamines**: These are generally safe but can cause drowsiness or tummy upsets. Your veterinarian will try several different drugs to find the best, but no more than 50 per cent of cases respond successfully.

- **Essential fish and plant oils**: Naturally-occurring oils, such as evening primrose, cod-liver oil or borage, are safe and can be very effective. Veterinary products are preferred to cheaper, 'over-the-counter' brands, which vary from batch to batch. The initial course is usually eight weeks, but no more than 50 per cent of cases are cured.

- **Steroids**: Although they are very effective, steroids have a lot of side effects, and dogs on steroids should have regular check-ups. A low dose, given every other day, is usually well tolerated. Long-acting injections should not be used in dogs. Concurrent immunotherapy, antihistamines, essential oils, and shampoos can reduce steroid requirements.

- **Alternative Therapies**: see Chapter Twelve.

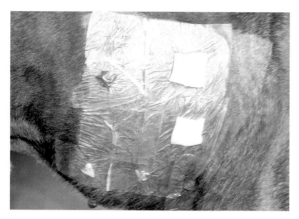

Patch tests in a Boxer with a contact allergy to carpet dyes.

CONTACT ALLERGY

Contact allergies are rare, but may occur as a reaction to dyes, cleaners, pollens, eye/ear drops, or shampoos. Irritant reactions can also occur with cement, concrete, caustic liquids, cleaners, soaps, and shampoos (especially human).

Diagnosis: Dogs are hospitalised for up to a week. If the skin improves, suspect allergens are applied to shaved skin for two to three days. The skin becomes inflamed where it has been in contact with an allergen.

Treatment: Ideally, dogs should avoid all contact with the irritant, which may involve removing carpets, etc. If this is not possible, steroids may be needed. Ointments can be used on non-hairy skin.

RARE CAUSES OF ITCHINESS

Internal diseases and certain skin cancers can cause itching, usually in older dogs. Your veterinarian may suggest biopsies or blood tests to eliminate these.

Allergies to biting insects occasionally cause hair loss and reddening on the face, ears and other sites. Insect repellents, keeping dogs indoors when insects are active (usually early morning and evening), and using steroid ointments are also useful. Bee and wasp stings can be painful and swollen, requiring antihistamines or steroids. True allergies to stings are rare, but can cause collapse that needs emergency treatment.

LUMPS AND BUMPS

INFLAMMATORY NODULES

- **Panniculitis**: This is a non-infectious or infectious inflammation of the fat beneath the skin. Most nodules appear on the trunk; in German Shepherd Dogs, the footpads are often affected. They often have a fatty discharge.
- **Bacterial/fungal infections**: These usually occur following wounds or a foreign body (e.g. grass seeds etc.) entering the skin. Many are difficult to treat and require long courses of antibiotics and surgery. Foreign bodies must be found and removed.
- **Sterile inflammatory nodules**: Sterile inflammatory nodules develop slowly and are usually firm and non-painful. They can be triggered by insect or tick bites and immune-mediated diseases, but most are spontaneous. Steroid treatment normally clears the problem, but some may require more potent drugs (see immune-mediated diseases, page 144), but infectious organisms must be ruled out before treatment.
- **Juvenile cellulitis**: Common in young puppies, this is normally seen as a sudden swelling of the muzzle, eyelids, ears or lymph nodes, accompanied by a thick discharge. Puppies are usually unwell and depressed. Juvenile cellulitis responds very well to a short course of steroids, with antibiotics to counter secondary infection, but severe scarring can occur if the condition is not treated quickly. There is no evidence that it is caused by vaccinations. Cause is unknown.

SKIN TUMOURS

Most skin tumours in dogs are benign. Benign tumours develop slowly, while malignant tumours develop quickly, ulcerate, and attach to surrounding tissues. Identifying the tumour is essential to select the best treatment. This may involve surgery, radiotherapy or chemotherapy. Blood tests, X-rays or ultrasound scans will show if a tumour has spread.

- **Viral warts**: These are common in young dogs. Most warts will regress spontaneously. Warts in older animals are actually benign sebaceous tumours, which are only removed if they become inflamed.
- **Histiocytomas**: Small, red, hairless nodules, which rapidly ulcerate, are quite common in younger dogs. Most resolve spontaneously, although they can be removed if they become itchy and inflamed.
- **Histiocytosis**: This condition is seen mostly in Bernese Mountain Dogs, with multiple nodules and ulcers appearing. Virtually all affected dogs eventually die of the disease.
- **Squamous cell carcinomas**: Caused by sunlight, these carcinomas appear as thickened, red and scaly patches of skin, which develop into ulcerated tumours.

They are slow to spread, but are malignant and require radical surgery or radiotherapy.

151

- **Perianal gland tumours**: These are common around the anus and tail in older male dogs. They are usually benign and surgery is curative. They are caused by changes in the sex hormones, so are unlikely to recur provided the dog is castrated.

CYSTS

Most cysts are benign tumours that have a porridge-like discharge. Most do not require treatment, but squeezing them can cause infection and inflammation.

- **Dermoid cysts**: These are congenital problems in Rhodesian Ridgebacks and other breeds where the skin along the back turns inwards. They are surgically removed.
- **Interdigital cysts**: These form red, painful masses between the toes that rupture and discharge. Causes include *Demodex* mites, hormonal diseases and foreign bodies, but chronic licking – due to an allergy – is most common. Treatments include antibacterial soaks, flushing, and a long course of antibiotics. The underlying cause must be identified to prevent a recurrence.

OTHER LUMPS AND BUMPS

- **Mucinosis**: Commonly seen in the Shar-Pei, mucinosis forms soft, rubbery nodules, thick skin folds, or 'bubbling' of the skin. It can also be caused by hypothyroidism. If necessary, it can be treated using steroids.
- **Urticaria**: Causing fluid to accumulate under the skin, urticaria is normally the result of an allergic reaction, although spontaneous urticaria is also

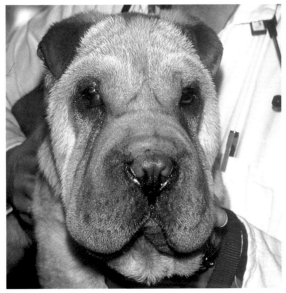

Severe mucinosis and skin-folding in a Shar-Pei.

seen. Pressing a finger on the affected skin leaves a dent. Steroids or antihistamines will calm down acute reactions.

NAIL DISEASES

Nail diseases may occur in isolation or as part of a generalised skin condition. They can be very painful and may cause severe lameness. Nail growth is slow, so resolution can take several weeks. It is far better to prevent the problem from occurring, by incorporating a regular routine of nail care into your grooming pattern (see page 69).

Causes: Scars and poor foot conformation can cause deformed nails, which can grow into the pads and cause infection. Dogs trapping their nails on escalators is another common cause – always carry your dog when using one of these.

Underlying medical problems can be responsible for nail and nail bed infections. Immune-mediated diseases, *Demodex* mites and ringworm are major culprits, with bacteria and yeasts causing secondary infections. In some cases, only the nails are affected.

Diagnosis: Samples taken from the nail or nail bed often only reveal non-specific changes and the end of the toe and the nail must be amputated for an accurate diagnosis.

Treatment: Essential fatty acids, mineral and vitamins supplements, and high-quality diets may help some dogs. Amputation of all the nails has been successfully used in intractable nail disease. Other treatments depend on the final diagnosis.

SCALING AND CRUSTING

Scaling (also called seborrhoea) is a common problem with many causes. Some breeds (e.g. Cocker Spaniel) have oily scaling, while others (e.g. Boxer) have dry scaling. Scaling can be a primary problem or secondary to an underlying disease.

PRIMARY SCALING

Caused by an accelerated turnover of skin cells, primary scaling is common in spaniels, but may be seen in other breeds. Signs first appear in young dogs. The coat is dull with local to generalised scaling, and ear and skin infections are common.

Primary scaling disorders are difficult to diagnose. The final diagnosis relies on history, clinical findings, skin biopsies, and eliminating other causes. These diseases can be inherited, so it is advisable not to breed from affected individuals.

Dry scaling in a Golden Retriever.

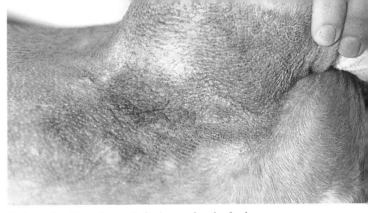

Itchy and inflamed yeast infection under the foreleg.

There is no cure for primary scaling, but most cases can be managed with appropriate treatment. Life-long therapy is usually needed.

SECONDARY SCALING

Secondary scaling is more common than primary scaling. Parasites, bacterial and fungal infections, allergies, immune-mediated diseases, some skin cancers, hormonal or metabolic diseases, follicular dysplasias and low humidity, may be responsible. Vitamin, oil and zinc deficiencies are rare with high-quality diets, but may occur in dogs on poor-quality, unbalanced diets, and Siberian Huskies. A careful examination often reveals clues to the underlying condition, but thorough investigations can be time-consuming and costly.

VITAMIN A RESPONSIVE DERMATOSIS

Commonly seen in Cocker Spaniels, with malodorous skin and thick scales stuck to the hairs. Bacterial and yeast infections are also common.

The condition responds well to vitamin A supplements. These can produce side effects, however, so dogs should be monitored.

SEBACEOUS ADENITIS

Seen in Standard Poodles, Vizslas, Akitas, Samoyeds, and, occasionally, other breeds, the symptoms of sebaceous adenitis include dry skin, thick scales stuck to the hair, hair loss, and secondary infections. Clinical signs are worse in Poodles and longhaired breeds. Several biopsies are necessary to confirm diagnosis.

ICTHYOSIS

This is a rare, congenital disorder seen mainly in terriers (but also in other breeds), with very severe scaling of the skin and footpads, skin thickening, and hair loss. Symptoms are normally present from birth. The condition is probably hereditary, so it is advisable not to breed from parents or siblings. Most dogs can live a relatively normal life with treatment.

LOCALISED SCALING

- **Ear margin scaling**: Occasionally seen in Dobermanns and other short-coated breeds, with greasy scales on the edges of the earflap. More severe cases may have hair loss and ulceration. Mild cases can be safely ignored, but severe cases require treatment.
- **Naso-digital hyperkeratosis**: This is scaling and crusting of the footpads and nose. It is particularly common in spaniels, but may also be seen in older dogs of any breed. Occasionally, cancers, and immune-mediated or metabolic diseases may be responsible for causing severe crusting. Treatment is not necessary unless the nose or pads become fissured (cracked) and painful. Supplementing the diet with zinc may further help.
- **Calluses**: Calluses develop at pressure points overlying the bone, such as the elbows, wrist, stifle, knee, hock, and pelvis. Treatment is not necessary unless the calluses become fissured or infected. Surgical removal is usually unsuccessful. Home-made elbow or kneepads and soft beds can help.

MANAGING SCALING

- Feeding a high-quality diet can result in significant improvement. Many dogs benefit from vitamin and essential oil supplements.
- Treating secondary infections promptly prevents further complications. Anti-microbial shampoos can reduce the number of bacteria and yeasts on the skin, and so help to prevent infections.
- Anti-scaling shampoos remove scales and slow the turnover of skin cells, and are very effective. Moisturising shampoos are best for dry scaling whereas de-greasing shampoos are best for greasy scaling. Propylene glycol diluted 1:1 in water is very effective at removing stubborn scale.
- Wet dressings and petroleum jelly are very good on dry, fissured skin. Ointments with salicylic acid cause thick layers of dead skin to slough away.
- Retinoids are very effective in some forms of primary scaling. Although generally well tolerated, side effects include liver and joint problems, dry eyes and dry skin, and dogs should be regularly monitored. Retinoids are very toxic to the foetus so should not be given to breeding animals or handled by women of child-bearing age.

153

9 THE NEXT GENERATION

THE REPRODUCTIVE SYSTEM

The only essential differences between the dog and the bitch are in their reproductive systems.

DOGS

The male should have two descended testes. The testes are retained in a bag of skin known as the scrotum, which hangs down from the abdominal cavity. The testicles are held outside the body because the testes require a low temperature to produce spermatozoa.

Each testicle is a mass of tubular tissue, the lining of which sheds cells constantly, some of which become spermatozoa. Each testicle contains a tube known as the epididymis, which is tightly coiled and many feet long. Sperm enter the epididymis, remaining there until they are required.

The system of tubes that sperm travels along, on its route from the testicles to ejaculation, is known as the spermatic cord. It includes all the blood vessels and lymph ducts.

The prostate gland lies in the pelvis, surrounding the neck of the bladder and the start of the urethra.

MALE REPRODUCTIVE SYSTEM

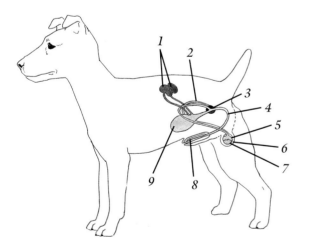

1. Kidneys
2. Vas deferens
3. Prostate
4. Urethra
5. Epididymis
6. Scrotum
7. Testicle
8. Penile bone
9. Bladder

FEMALE REPRODUCTIVE SYSTEM

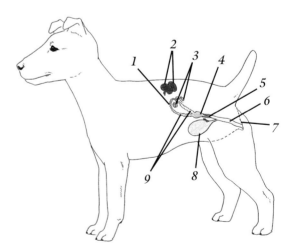

1. Fallopian tube
2. Kidneys
3. Ovaries
4. Body of uterus
5. Cervix
6. Vagina
7. Vulva
8. Bladder
9. Horns of uterus

When mating occurs and a dog is ready to ejaculate, the sperm rushes along a tube, the *ductus deferens*, to the urethra. At the same time, the prostate gives out an alkaline fluid that mixes with the sperm, and both are carried into the urethra and expelled together through the penis. If more sperm is produced than the dog ejaculates, the superfluous sperm passes out of the dog's body when he urinates.

The dog's penis tends to be long and rather pointed. The point is actually shielded by a sheath or prepuce. This is retracted when mating takes place. The penis consists of a mixture of bone (the os penis), lymph ducts, nerves and muscle. At the base of the penis, there are internal cavities. During mating, these become filled with blood, significantly expanding the size of the penis, and allowing a 'tie' to take place (see page 160).

BITCH

The main sex gland of the bitch is the ovary. As with other female mammals, bitches have two ovaries, both of which produce egg cells. The ovaries do not become fully functional until the bitch reaches sexual maturity. This can vary even within breeds but normally occurs at about eight to twelve months of age, being later in the larger breeds.

Throughout the adult bitch's life, she will come into season approximately every six months and she will not go through a menopause, unlike human females. Therefore, although her fertility will almost certainly decrease with advancing years, she will still be capable of becoming pregnant until the day she dies.

The ovaries are small, flat and oval-shaped, and contain the germ plasm that produces the eggs or ova. The ovaries are enclosed in a membranous sac (the bursa) and are situated on either side of the abdomen. During heat, fluid-filled sacs, called follicles, grow inside the ovaries. These nourish some of the ova until they are ready to be discharged into the fallopian tubes.

If a bitch has been mated, the ripe ova will meet the sperm cells in her fallopian tubes. The eggs are then fertilised and descend into the uterus. Here, they attach to the walls and begin to grow.

The uterus or womb is in the ventral (lower) part of the abdominal cavity. The top of the uterus has two 'horns', known as uterine horns, which connect it to the oviducts or fallopian tubes.

The other end of the uterus ends at the cervix. The cervix opens into the vagina, the entrance to which is via the vulva – the external element of the bitch's reproductive organs.

BREEDING

It is often fondly imagined that dog breeders make handsome profits. This is not true. Only a few, very fortunate, individuals actually make money. If you intend to breed, you should consider the costs you are likely to incur.

- **Stud fees**: A fee for a high-quality dog will be in three figures. Do not use a stud simply because he is cheap – you get what you pay for.
- **Travel costs**: You are unlikely to be fortunate enough to find a dog of sufficient quality on your doorstep. Be prepared to travel, and do not be tempted to use a stud simply because he is conveniently local.
- **Veterinary costs**: You must be prepared for worst-case scenarios, such as the need for a Caesarean section, as well as the routine veterinary care your bitch and her litter will need.
- **Feeding costs**: The dam will require an extremely high-quality diet while she is pregnant and nursing, and the puppies will require specialised diets when they are being weaned.
- **Administration fees**: Fees mount up. The cost of registering your puppies with your national kennel club, and providing insurance cover for the dam and her pups, can be expensive.

RESPONSIBILITIES

The golden rule of breeding is to make every attempt to retain the qualities already evident in the breeding pair and to improve them. In other words, you should breed only from the best examples of the breed. Be honest with yourself – if your dog/bitch does not match up, do not allow him/her to breed. Non-pedigree dogs should not be mated for any other purpose than the creation of a specific, working-type dog.

There are too many mixed-breed dogs already in rescue centres without adding more. A pedigree is certainly no guarantee of quality but it is a start. It also has the advantage of allowing the dog's ancestors to be traced, so illuminating any genetic faults that may be present.

Similarly, if you have a pedigree bitch you consider to be of good quality, make sure you are breeding from her for the right reasons. Do you want her to produce show stock or working animals? Can you honestly state that the resulting puppies will be up to the task? If you are breeding pets, are you certain the market is not already saturated? You should never breed from your bitch simply because you think it would be a kindness to let her have pups.

Neutering is the generic term for the operation that prevents dogs and bitches from breeding. The male operation is known as castration, while the female operation is referred to as spaying (ovariohysterectomy). Both operations are painless and straightforward – veterinary surgeons perform thousands every year.

Neutering is irreversible, so for dog owners who may wish to breed their dogs or exhibit them in the show ring, it is unlikely to be appropriate. However, anyone considering breeding should question whether homes are available for the subsequent litter. If they cannot guarantee to find responsible homes for all the puppies, breeding is not an option and neutering should be considered.

Neutering is most appropriate for the pet owner, who has no intention of breeding or showing their dog. Neutering prevents the pet owner from having to deal with unwanted pregnancies, and, in these times, when the dog-owning population is under intense attack, it would seem part of our duty to those around us not to produce unwanted puppies. Every year, hundreds of unwanted puppies end up at rescue shelters, a situation which neutering could have prevented.

CASTRATION

Many people mistakenly believe that neutering adversely affects a dog's temperament, but dogs do not miss what they have never had. In fact, neutering may actually improve a dog's temperament. Owners are often advised to castrate their dog if he displays overly dominant or aggressive behaviour. While castration is not a panacea – it will not cure bad behaviour resulting from inadequate training, for example – it may help to prevent a problem worsening. In cases where aggressive behaviour is due to too much testosterone, castration can have a highly beneficial effect.

The working ability of the neutered dog is unaffected by castration. He will still perform as well as his entire colleagues, and he may work better because he is not as distracted. All assistance/service dogs are neutered – with no detrimental side effects on their abilities. For example, a neutered male sniffer dog on his first mission saved several people's lives. He detected a 500-lb (226-kg) bomb primed to explode in a bus shelter.

A castrated dog is at much less risk of developing prostate disorders than an entire one. Testicular disease (page 169) can be prevented, and there is a much lower risk associated with cryptorchidism (page 169) and inguinal or scrotal hernias. His life may be saved in other ways, too. Many dogs are lost, injured or killed each year because they have caught the scent of a bitch in heat. Even a well-trained dog can lose all traffic sense and run straight across a busy road when chasing a female.

Castration should be performed when the dog is approximately 12 months of age. At this age, the dog has not developed too many male characteristics but he has had adequate time to become reasonably physically mature. Most veterinary surgeons have their

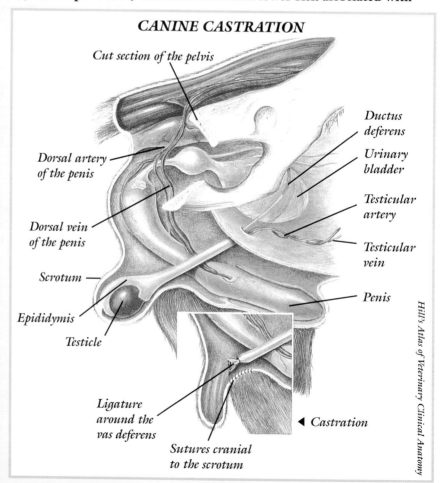

CANINE CASTRATION

Cut section of the pelvis

Dorsal artery of the penis

Dorsal vein of the penis

Scrotum

Epididymis

Testicle

Ductus deferens

Urinary bladder

Testicular artery

Testicular vein

Penis

Ligature around the vas deferens

◀ Castration

Sutures cranial to the scrotum

Hill's Atlas of Veterinary Clinical Anatomy

own guidelines about when surgery should be performed, so, if you are considering having your dog neutered, you should discuss the operation and its implications with your veterinarian beforehand.

SPAYING

An unspayed bitch will come into season approximately twice a year. During this period, she must be kept away from entire male dogs or she may become pregnant. This is often more difficult than owners think. Likewise, some unspayed bitches have a lot of bloody discharge while they are on heat, which can leave unpleasant marks all over the owner's home. Spaying solves both these problems at a stroke.

The main advantage to spaying, however, is in the long-term health implications.

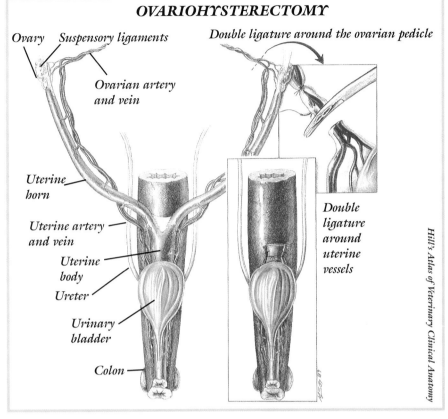

OVARIOHYSTERECTOMY

Ovary Suspensory ligaments

Double ligature around the ovarian pedicle

Ovarian artery and vein

Uterine horn

Uterine artery and vein

Uterine body

Ureter

Urinary bladder

Colon

Double ligature around uterine vessels

Hill's Atlas of Veterinary Clinical Anatomy

Older bitches can suffer from very serious, and often fatal, conditions. Pyometra is a good example (page 165). By spaying your bitch, the risks are eliminated. Spaying also reduces the risk of mammary tumours (page 166), and the unpleasantness of phantom pregnancies (page 167).

Opinion varies as to when is the best time to spay a bitch. Some veterinary surgeons argue that a bitch should have had at least one season, while others believe it is better to perform the operation before the first season.

There is evidence that bitches spayed at too young an age are more likely to suffer incontinence problems in later life. However, incontinence can just as easily occur in bitches who have never been spayed. The evidence does not really substantiate either argument, and there are plenty of examples, such as at rescue kennels, where the risk is considered so low that bitches are spayed early.

If you want your bitch spayed, you should consult your own veterinarian, who will be happy to explain the arguments and who will outline the practice in his or her surgery.

NEUTERING AND WEIGHT

It is a popular myth that neutering causes weight gain, particularly in the case of bitches. This is not true. Overfeeding, coupled with inadequate exercise, causes this to happen.

However, neutered animals require a lower calorie intake than their entire counterparts, so need a slightly modified diet. See Chapter Three for more details about calculating the energy requirements of neutered animals.

NON-SURGICAL BIRTH CONTROL

If you would like to breed from your bitch in the future (but not now), the option of hormonally suppressing oestrus is available. The hormone progesterone, when administered by injection or given in tablet form, suppresses the onset of oestrus, so rendering the bitch infertile. The main advantage to progesterone doses is that, unlike spaying, the bitch can still produce pups at a later date.

The main disadvantage to progesterone doses is that some compounds can increase the risk of the bitch developing uterine problems, e.g. pyometra. Hormonal birth control is not an easy option, and should only be used by those who are certain they want their bitch to produce puppies at a later date. If the hormone is given in tablet form, the owner will need to administer tablets daily. If the dose is administered by injection, the effects take far longer to wear off, so timing the next season can be unpredictable.

PARENTS' QUALITIES

If you have any doubts or queries about the qualities of your bitch, talk to her breeder. Any responsible breeder should give advice freely – it is in their interest that you do not make unnecessary mistakes with 'their' bloodlines.

A bitch should not be bred from until she has had at least two seasons and is fully mature. Likewise, no bitch aged more than eight years should be allowed to produce puppies. It should be noted that the UK Kennel Club does not register puppies born to any bitch eight years or over. With the American Kennel Club and the Canadian Kennel Club, dams and sires must be under 12 years of age. However, many breed groups have their own rules regarding breeding.

Both stud dog and bitch should be physically and temperamentally sound with a full pedigree and other relevant documents (e.g. hip score certificates, eye tests, etc.). You are strongly advised to check the individual breed guidelines with your national kennel club.

It is possible to breed a superb litter in terms of appearance and genetic quality, but at the expense of temperament. However, temperament, although too frequently ignored, is equally as important as physical appearance. Avoid breeding from any dog with an unsound temperament, which may be better

described as 'nervy', 'whiny', 'aggressive' or 'dominant'. It is not a certainty, but the chances of the puppies inheriting the unfortunate trait are high.

Finally, it is very important to ensure that any stud or brood bitch is physically fit. Fat, flabby studs often have great difficulty when it comes to the mating, while a healthy dam will find pregnancy, giving birth, and nursing far easier than an unfit dam. You should also remember that even a top-quality, fit bitch should not be allowed to produce more than one litter a year.

OESTRUS CYCLE

A bitch is most likely to come into season during the spring and autumn/fall of each year, but modern living conditions and changing weather patterns mean there is some variation to this. Some bitches come into season every eight months; some will even have one, almost imperceptible, heat and then show a stronger heat on a once-a-year basis.

Generally, a bitch will have her first season at approximately eight months of age. From then on, she will come on heat about every six months. Each season will last approximately 21 days.

As each season commences, the bitch's vulva will swell and there may be a bloodstained discharge. Some bitches keep themselves immaculately clean,

OESTRUS CYCLE

— Anoestrus (75 days) — Pro-oestrus (9 days) Oestrus (3-5 days) — Met-oestrus (90 days) — Anoestrus

— Approximately 6 months —

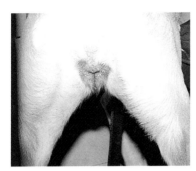

The vulva swells during the pre-oestrus stage of a bitch's cycle.

and you may not notice any discharge. Others are not so tidy. Most owners will discover spots of blood on the floor when their bitch is in heat. Other signs that your bitch has come into season include out-of-character behaviour, and a strong desire to roam.

When a bitch is on heat, she passes pheromones (scent hormones) in her urine. These act as signals to the local dog population that she will soon be ready for mating. From day one of the season, it is essential to isolate your bitch from male dogs. She is unlikely to permit any dog to mate with her this early in her cycle, but, if mating does take place, it is not impossible that she could become pregnant.

After about ten days into her cycle, the bloodstained discharge from the bitch's vulva will clear and become pale in colour. The vulva swelling changes from a stiff swelling to a softer, more widespread swelling, and the bitch may stand with her tail held to one side if approached by the male. To test her receptiveness to mating, rub the back of her spine – if she raises her tail enticingly, she is ready. This is the point when she is most likely to conceive.

Within a few days, the bitch will go off heat. The discharge may be bloodstained once again, and her attitude towards males will be indifferent, if not hostile. However, she should remain isolated from male dogs until the full 21 days of the season are over. If your bitch is accidentally mated, you will need to take steps to avoid an unwanted pregnancy (see page 167).

TESTING FOR OESTRUS

If you are uncertain about your bitch's readiness for mating, there are tests that can confirm the right time.

- **'Elisa' test for progesterone (e.g. Premate™)**: A small specimen of blood will be collected by your veterinarian, who will measure the level of the hormone progesterone. Certain levels of the hormone indicate where in her oestrus cycle the bitch currently is.
- **Vaginal cytology**: Your veterinarian will take a smear sample from the upper vagina of the bitch. This is then examined under a microscope. When about 80 per cent of the vaginal cells have no nuclei and have a very definite outline (like cornflakes) she is ready for mating.

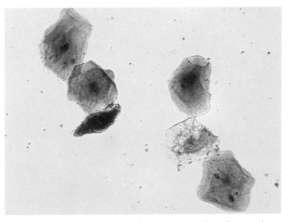

Smear cells can determine the optimum time for mating.

MATING

Feral dogs compete for the attentions of a female in heat. Normally, the higher-ranking male – the alpha male – will be the successful suitor, but others in the pack may be lucky. In nature, natural selection tries to ensure that the bitch is mated to the fittest and, in theory, the best dog in the pack.

STAGES OF THE OESTRUS CYCLE		
Stage	**Duration**	**Features**
Pro-oestrus	Approximately 9 days	This is the beginning of the cycle.
Oestrus	Approximately 3-5 days	The middle of the cycle, and the time when the bitch is most likely to conceive.
Met-oestrus	Approximately 90 days	This stage occurs in the un-mated bitch, whose heat is not affected by pregnancy hormones.
Anoestrus	Approximately 75 days	The period of sexual inactivity between cycles.

Pre-mating courtship.

The domesticated bitch meets only the one stud dog, with the mating being planned for the middle of her season – between day 11 and 14. Timing the mating is critical. If the bitch is not ready and will not accept the male, you may find you have travelled several hundred miles for nothing. Remember that any kind of 'assisted' mating will cause unnecessary distress to the bitch.

When mating takes place, the stud will mount the bitch. If all goes smoothly, a few thrusts will cause his penis to penetrate the bitch and then to ejaculate sperm. Unlike other mammals, a 'tie' may occur between the dog and bitch. This happens when the cavities in the soft tissue of the dog's penis fill with blood, and occurs when the dog has already penetrated the bitch. When the penis expands, it causes the muscles of the bitch's vagina to contract, which locks the penis inside the bitch. When this happens, the dog and bitch cannot be parted until they are ready. The dog will eventually try to step over the bitch's back so that the penis rotates and the dog and bitch are back to back. This position can last from a few seconds up to an hour or more, although 20 minutes is the average duration. It is not always necessary to have a tie for the bitch to conceive, but it is considered to increase the chances.

While the dog and bitch are tied, the dog ejaculates three different mixtures of semen. The first, which comes mainly from the prostate gland, acts as a liquid flush to get rid of urine and cell debris in the dog's urethra. It also prepares the bitch's vagina for the second, sperm-rich fraction of the ejaculation, which follows immediately. The third fraction, which is produced later in the tie, is produced by the prostate, and is clear and watery in consistency, acting as a lubricant to help the sperm pass through her cervix and into the uterus.

Eventually, the sperm will reach the fallopian tubes where fertilisation of the ova should take place.

To help increase the chances of conception, it is recommended you try a second mating around 48 hours after the first.

ARTIFICIAL INSEMINATION

Artificial Insemination (AI) is the process of placing semen into a bitch's reproductive tract without using a natural mating. It is mainly used when a bitch is to bear a litter from a dog in another country. The majority of breeders should discount AI.

AI is normally done using fresh sperm, which is, at the most, a few days old. It is possible for an expert to take semen from a dog and inseminate it directly into a bitch. This is useful in a situation when a natural mating is proving to be very difficult. An alternative is to store semen in a frozen state for long periods. Using modern technology, semen can now be stored indefinitely.

Anyone contemplating AI should investigate the legislation and kennel club regulations applicable in their country.

PREGNANCY

Pregnancy normally lasts 63 days, although there can be some variation to this, as gestation is 63 days from fertilisation. If your bitch ovulates early in her season, she will have mature eggs waiting to be fertilised when she is mated. Conversely, if she ovulates later in her season, the eggs may be fertilised several days after the mating. Thus, the normal gestation period can appear to vary from 63 to 70 days.

During the first half of the pregnancy, the bitch should be exercised and fed as normal. In the latter half, feeds can be divided into two and you should

A pregnant Boxer bitch.

ensure that your bitch receives an adequate intake of protein. The bitch should be kept as fit and healthy as possible, and any medicines, unless prescribed by a veterinary surgeon, should be avoided. Make sure your bitch has been wormed before any mating and that she has received all relevant booster inoculations. Except in an emergency, your bitch should not be X-rayed as this could damage the pups.

During pregnancy, watch out for any unusual discharges from the bitch's vulva. Do not panic if a little blood should appear, but if a green or black discharge appears, you should contact your vet immediately.

An ultrasound machine.

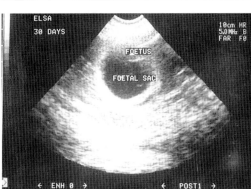

An ultrasound scan showing a puppy in the uterus.

CONFIRMING PREGNANCY

Pregnancy confirmation is most reliable if performed at 28 days after mating. Diagnosis is made in a variety of ways:

- **Manual palpation**: Your veterinarian will feel the bitch's abdomen and be able to feel the foetal pups inside the womb. However, this form of diagnosis is difficult in obese or tense bitches, when a single foetus may easily be missed. By six to seven weeks onwards, when the foetal skeleton has developed, it becomes easier, but even then a single foetus may be missed if it lies close to the pelvis.
- **Ultrasonic scanning**: Bitches can be scanned for pregnancy diagnosis, from about four weeks onwards, using a similar type of machine to that which is used in humans. An ultrasound machine can give some indication of the size of the litter. There is no evidence that it can harm the foetus or the bitch, but, as a precaution, it may be advisable to limit the number of scans.
- **X-rays**: After the foetal skeleton has developed, from approximately 49 days of gestation, it is possible to see the foetus on X-ray. This method is reserved for late pregnancy only, however, as radiation may damage the young foetus.
- **Hormone assays**: Blood samples taken from the bitch will be tested for pregnancy hormones, which, if present, confirm that the bitch is pregnant. These are not usually commercially available.

PREPARING FOR THE BIRTH

Well before your bitch is due to give birth, you need to make thorough preparations.

A uterus full of pups will put increased pressure on the bitch's bladder, so she will need to relieve herself more frequently. Her house-training may break down, but do not chastise her. Cover the floors with absorbent newspaper, or move her living quarters. If you move her, it should be to the same place you wish her to whelp. Your bitch should be allowed to accustom herself to the maternity area for at least two weeks before the expected date of birth.

The whelping area must be warm, dry, and free from draughts. Your bitch will appreciate a sense of privacy and security, so try to keep other family members and pets away from the whelping area.

The whelping box should be large enough to allow your bitch to lie on her side and to fully stretch her head and legs. It should also allow enough room for the puppies. Ideally, the box should back on to at least one wall, or, if possible, it should be surrounded on three sides. However, remember that you will probably need access and, if there are serious problems, so will your veterinarian.

The whelping box should be located near to an electrical supply. Not only will you need a source of good lighting, but you will also need somewhere to plug in a heat lamp. This is a lamp that provides heat – essential for the wellbeing of the newborn puppies. The heat lamp should be suspended above the bed. The temperature provided by the lamp should not exceed 24-27 degrees Celsius (75-80 degrees Fahrenheit). Increasing or reducing the distance between the lamp and the whelping box can adjust the temperature.

It is recommended that you hang the lamp up before introducing your bitch, and, using a thermometer, adjust the height until it is just right. Fix the lamp so that it cannot be accidentally adjusted. If it is too low, it can literally cook the pups, with fatal results.

WHELPING CHECKLIST

With careful preparation and a little luck, whelping

should pass smoothly. To maximise your chances of easy whelping, there are a number of items you should have ready to hand for the whelping.

- The 24-hour telephone number of your veterinary practice.
- A large supply of newspaper for bedding. Newspaper is warm, absorbent, and can be disposed of easily.
- Other bedding will be needed after the birth and you will need some absorbent items like fleecy, veterinary bedding.
- Accurate scales will be needed to weigh each puppy as it is born.
- Antiseptic lotion and a sponge for cleaning the bitch before and after the whelping.
- Plenty of clean towels for drying the pups.
- A clock for noting the times of births.
- A small box where you can place puppies out of harm's way, if needed. This can be used as a temporary bed for the pups if the bitch is being a little clumsy. It is a good idea to keep a hot-water bottle handy to help the pups to stay warm. However, the hot-water bottle should be at blood temperature only.
- Milk and glucose to offer to the bitch during whelping.
- A jar of petroleum jelly or another similar lubricant.
- Containers for soiled paper and towels.
- Strong, sterilised, silk or cotton thread, in case a pup's umbilical cord requires tying.
- A spare bulb for the heat lamp.
- Adequate refreshments for yourself. You should not leave the bitch for more than a couple of minutes.

WHELPING

There are three stages of whelping:
- **Labour**: The bitch has internal contractions that dilate the cervix and prepare the birth canal.
- **Birth**: The puppies are born.
- **Afterbirth**: The bitch expels the afterbirths of the puppies.

LABOUR

Whelping normally occurs with few problems. It is worth bearing in mind that bitches often prefer to whelp at the quietest time of the day, which can mean the early hours of the morning. Whenever your bitch goes into whelp, you should stay with her throughout, to check that all is well. However, try to make your presence as unobtrusive as possible.

Undue anxiety, exhibited by the owner, can unnecessarily upset the bitch. If you talk to or pet your bitch during labour, move slowly, and talk in a calm and reassuring manner.

While the bitch has contractions, she is likely to behave in a restless manner, being unwilling to remain relaxed for more than short periods. She may pant a lot or shiver. Her periods of sleep will become shorter and she may refuse food. If she is eating well, she is less likely to whelp within the next few hours.

If your bitch starts scrabbling at her bedding, it is often a sign that labour is imminent. However, not all bitches will do this. Some bitches may vomit immediately prior to whelping. There may also be an increasing amount of mucus discharged from the vulva. The vulva itself may become more swollen.

The bitch's temperature should drop from the normal 38.5 degrees Celsius (101.3 degrees Fahrenheit) to about 37 degrees Celsius (98 degrees Fahrenheit) within 12 to 24 hours before the birth. A good tip is to take her temperature twice a day for about a week before the anticipated date of birth. If you do not know how to do this, ask your veterinarian to show you – it is a simple procedure.

BIRTH

By now, your bitch should be calmer. Observe her contractions. She will appear to go tense, followed by a relaxation of her body. It will look as though she is squeezing from the ribs all the way down her body. If all is proceeding normally, panting will cease and you will see contractions lasting a few seconds.

The first thing produced during whelping is the outer birth sac or 'waters'. Each pup is enclosed in a double layer of membranes with fluid in between each layer. The fluid protects the pup while the uterine muscles contract. The waters seen before any puppies are born normally indicate that the outer sac has broken. This yellow-coloured, slimy fluid will be discharged from the vagina and is quite normal.

If your bitch continues to have strong abdominal contractions without producing a pup for more than one hour after her waters have broken, there may be a problem and you should seek veterinary attention. It helps to keep a notebook handy at the whelping box. Note the exact time of each event – this is the information your veterinarian will require if there is a problem.

Carefully observe the birth of the first puppy. The appearance of a discharge, particularly one that is blood-coloured or dark green, can indicate that the placenta has started to separate from the wall of the

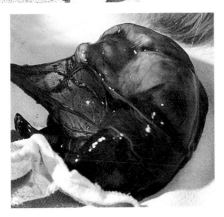

The mother will clean the puppy, and bite through the umbilical cord. Photo: B. Simon.

The arrival of the first puppy. Photo: B. Simon.

uterus. This puppy will need to be delivered quickly as he is likely to be deprived of oxygen. However, if you see a similar discharge before the birth of the remaining puppies then, surprisingly, this is probably nothing to worry about. You may see a blackish, glistening ball at the vulva. This is the foetal fluid in the unbroken sac surrounding the puppy.

The inner, amniotic, sac is filled with a dark-coloured fluid, which may burst as the pup is forced out through the vulva. The pup's head or rump will be seen emerging, then the sac will burst. This causes a gush of fluid to appear from behind the vulva, which is a good indicator that the pup is nearly out. If the amniotic sac does not break during birth, the bitch will break it with her tongue as she licks her newborn pup.

The next puppy will usually be born within 20 minutes, but may arrive quicker once the birth canal is dilated and lubricated by the previous birth. The period of time between the births of each puppy can vary from breed to breed and among individuals within those breeds. If the bitch has been straining hard for half an hour, without success, it is wise to assume that there is a problem and to seek veterinary assistance.

If your bitch had an ultrasound scan at 28 days, you will have a reasonable idea of how many pups to expect and when whelping is nearly at an end. If you are not in this position, remember that litter sizes can range from one pup to double figures.

AFTERBIRTH
Each puppy is attached by an umbilical cord to its individual placenta. After the puppy has been born, the placenta should emerge as a reddish-black mass. Often, the afterbirth will be expelled immediately before the birth of the next puppy, so whelping and afterbirth are often combined. It is a good tip to count the afterbirths, as this will tell you if any have been retained. If any afterbirth has been retained, it may well be expelled later. If it does not appear, you should seek immediate veterinary advice.

CARE OF THE NEWBORN PUPS
When the puppies are born, encourage the bitch to lick them clean. The mother may be concentrating on producing another puppy or she may not be accustomed to washing pups. Gently hand the pup to the bitch's face and encourage, but not force, her to eat the afterbirth.

Some bitches, particularly first-time mothers (maidens), may behave erratically or appear to be a little bewildered about what to do. If your bitch behaves clumsily, she may accidentally injure the newborn pups. Try to reassure and calm her, guiding her through the right actions. If all else fails, you will have to remove the pups from danger.

The bitch should chew through the umbilical cord of each puppy. Take care that she does not chew too close to the pup. If she does not break the cord, you will need to tear it yourself. Do not cut the cord with sharp instruments very close to the pup's abdomen. Hold the cord a couple of inches from the pup's tummy with one hand and pull the cord with the other hand, stretching the cord so that it lies across your thumb nail, tears, then breaks.

If your bitch appears tired or loath to lick her newborns, give each pup a vigorous rub with a clean towel, holding it firmly and close to a soft surface in case you lose your grip. Hold the puppy so the head is lower than the rear as this will help any fluid to flow, thereby clearing the airways. Snuffling noises will indicate that the pup has fluid in its airways.

Check that all the puppies are suckling.

163

NEWBORN

- Puppies are born blind and deaf, with a weak sense of smell. They have no teeth, but they have a strong instinct to suck.
- A newborn puppy can whine and yelp in pain, but he cannot bark.
- The brain and nervous system are immature – the twitching and stretching of limbs seen in very young puppies is a reflex action, which helps to develop the nervous system and the muscles.
- Puppies move around by slithering on their bellies. This takes a lot of effort so they rarely move far from the dam's side.
- The puppy coat is soft. Texture and colour will often change as the pup matures.
- The pups need the stimulation of their mother's licking in order to pass urine and faeces.

The litter 24 hours after whelping. ▲

At ten days, ▶ *the eyes of this Dalmatian puppy are beginning to open, and the spots are starting to show.*

10 TO 13 DAYS

- The puppies' eyes open. They are generally pale blue, but will darken over the next few weeks.
- It is believed that proper vision is not established until day 17.

2 WEEKS

- Hearing starts to develop from two weeks of age. By three weeks, the puppies will react to unexpected noises.
- The ability to bark seems to coincide with the development of hearing.

▲ *Hearing starts to develop at two weeks.*

2 TO 3 WEEKS

- Milk teeth emerge. Most breeders will wean the litter on to solid food at this stage.
- The sense of smell becomes increasingly developed.

▲ *By three weeks, the puppies will be mobile.*

3 WEEKS

- The puppies will be on their feet, and become more active.
- They show an increasing desire to leave the nest and to follow their mother.
- All their senses are fully developed, and they will be ready to explore their surroundings.

At four ▶ *weeks, the puppies increasingly interact with each other.*

4 WEEKS

- Interaction between littermates becomes more frequent and intense, and a social hierarchy will develop within the litter.

5 WEEKS

- If the weather is fine, the puppies can be allowed outside in a puppy run for short periods.
- They will show an interest in playing with toys and each other. Maternal discipline will be handed out if games get too rough.

◀ *These five-week-old puppies are now playing with toys.*

6 TO 7 WEEKS

- Play-learning is a vital aspect of this period, when most pups learn the basis of canine manners and communication.
- Interaction with humans is very important, and as much time as possible should be given to handling and talking to the puppies.

Between six ▶ *and seven weeks, interaction with people is all-important.*

When you are confident that all the puppies have arrived safely, and that the bitch has settled down with them, make a note of the following:
• The time of each pup's birth
• The weight, colour and sex of each pup
• The presence of dewclaws
• Any obvious abnormalities.

FEMALE REPRODUCTIVE DISORDERS

PYOMETRA

Pyometra is also known as cystic endometrial hyperplasia (CHE). It is the most serious of the reproductive problems in the non-pregnant bitch. It is usually seen in the middle-aged or mature bitch, but it can arise in an animal of any age. It is more common in bitches that have received reproductive hormone therapy. Pyometra normally develops six to eight weeks after the bitch's last season.

When a bitch develops pyometra, the glands in the lining of the uterus secrete mucus, which causes the uterus to swell. This mucus becomes infected with toxin-producing bacteria, and it is these toxins that make the bitch ill. Pyometra is life-threatening and requires immediate veterinary attention.

Signs: The bitch is usually dull, off her food and drinking excessively. She may also start to vomit intermittently. There may be a dirty or bloody vaginal discharge if the cervix is open (so-called 'open pyometra'). In the absence of a discharge ('closed pyometra', when the cervix is closed), there may be abdominal swelling.

Treatment: An ovariohysterectomy or spaying is normally required. However, in a small number of cases, it is possible to treat more conservatively. There are now drugs which, together with antibiotic supportive therapy, will allow the cervix to open, and the uterine discharges to be expelled. However, this is not always an option and your veterinary surgeon will decide the most appropriate therapy.

VULVAL HYPOPLASIA

Also referred to as an infantile vulva, a bitch suffering with vulval hypoplasia has been born with an extremely small vulva that has failed to enlarge at puberty. Often, there is no clinical problem, but occasionally, a peri-vulvar inflammation of the skin (dermatitis) can develop.

Treatment: The condition often resolves itself at the first oestrus when oestrogen levels rise. Therefore, a young bitch should be left to undergo her first season before treatment is considered. If the condition persists, the vulva can be enlarged surgically.

VULVAL HYPERPLASIA

This is often described, incorrectly, as a vaginal prolapse, and it is seen most often in Boxers, Bullmastiffs, Bulldogs and Shar-Peis.

Signs: The bitch presents either with a discrete swelling from the wall of the vagina or has a doughnut-shaped swelling around the circumference of the vagina. In both cases, the tissue protrudes from the vulval lips.

Treatment: It is usually only seen in bitches in season since raised oestrogen levels predispose her to hyperplasia. The swellings will decrease in size once the season has finished, but, if not, the swollen tissue may have to be removed by a veterinarian. This involves a small operation under general anaesthesia. Spaying the bitch will stop the condition recurring.

VESIBULO-VAGINAL STRICTURES

These are caused by inelastic fibrous rings of tissue between the vestibule and vagina. They cause a

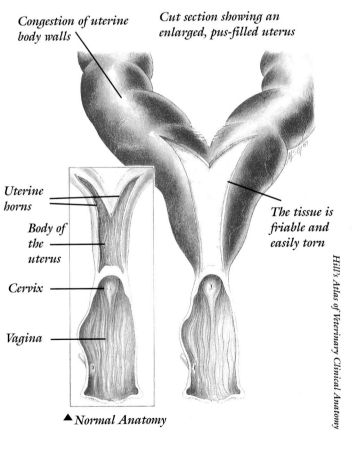

PYOMETRA

Congestion of uterine body walls

Cut section showing an enlarged, pus-filled uterus

Uterine horns

Body of the uterus

Cervix

Vagina

The tissue is friable and easily torn

▲ *Normal Anatomy*

Hill's Atlas of Veterinary Clinical Anatomy

165

narrowing within the vagina, resulting in an inability of the male dog to insert the penis. Attempted surgical correction is often unsuccessful, and, since these are congenital abnormalities and may be inherited, correction in order to allow mating is not to be recommended.

JUVENILE VAGINITIS
This is inflammation of the vagina and it is a common condition.

Signs: There may be copious amounts of white, or even purulent, vaginal discharge due to secretions from the vaginal glands that can then maintain bacterial growth. If the discharge has an odour, the bitch may be attractive to males. The bitch is otherwise fit and well but the persistent discharge may cause excessive licking of the vulva.

Treatment: The condition usually regresses spontaneously once the bitch has her first season. However, it can sometimes persist into adulthood. In general, there is no need to treat with antibiotics and indeed this can be contraindicated since overzealous use of antibiotics can lead to overgrowth of fungi, yeast and mycoplasms.

MASTITIS
This is an inflammation of the mammary gland usually due to a bacterial infection.

Signs: The affected glands will be swollen and painful, and abscesses may form. Instead of milk, squeezing the teat will produce a purulent discharge. Old lesions may become hard and solid but will not increase in size.

Treatment: The bitch requires antibiotic treatment as soon as possible. If the condition is severe, the gland may become incapable of producing milk in a subsequent pregnancy.

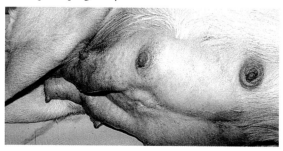

The teats should be pain-free, and clear of purulent discharge and abscesses.

MAMMARY TUMOURS
Tumours are classified as:
• **Benign**: They are discrete, slow-growing, well circumscribed, and relatively easy to remove surgically.
• **Malignant**: They are fast-growing and spread to other parts of the body, and it is difficult to ensure complete surgical removal. Malignant tumours often spread to form new tumours in the lungs and the liver. When this happens there is no cure.

Tumours most commonly occur in the mammary gland of the older, unspayed bitch. Approximately half the tumours are benign and a further 40 per cent are aggressively malignant.

Signs: Tumours first appear as lumps that are not initially painful. Benign tumours are usually slow-growing and the outlines can be distinctly identified. Malignant tumours grow quickly and often cause ulcers in the mammary gland. Their outline is difficult to define and they can spread to other organs.

Treatment: Benign tumours can be removed surgically. Malignant tumours can also be removed surgically if they are identified early enough. If treatment is delayed, it is not possible to ensure that the complete tumour is removed at surgery, and the tumour may regrow.

OESTRUS CYCLE PROBLEMS

SPLIT/SHORT OESTRUS
A split oestrus can cause confusion to owners because it appears as though the dog is having very short but frequent seasons. The cause is not known, but the occurrence can be diagnosed by monitoring progesterone levels.

Signs: The bitch shows signs of coming into season, in that she has a bloody vaginal discharge. However, instead of progressing to accept the dog, the discharge stops after four or five days and she is no longer attractive to the dog.

Treatment: Usually the bloody discharge recurs in a few weeks and this time progresses into a normal oestrus.

PROLONGED OESTRUS
Sometimes, a bitch can remain in oestrus and continue to be attractive to males for weeks or even months. This is due to a failure of ovulation and the development of cysts on the ovary. In rare instances, a persistent oestrus may be due to a tumour of the ovarian tissue.

Signs: The bitch will present her usual signs of being in heat, but the 'season' will last for much longer than normal.

Treatment: The condition can be treated with

hormones but there is a high risk that the problem will recur the next season, and the next. It is therefore best to have the bitch spayed once the season has passed.

FAILURE TO CONCEIVE

The most common problem at oestrus is that the bitch is served but fails to produce puppies. If there is good evidence that the male is fertile, the most likely reason for failure of conception is that mating has taken place at the wrong time. The timing of ovulation in the bitch can be quite difficult to identify without clinical tests (see page 158). The best breeding management is to allow the male to serve the bitch every other day while she will accept him.

PREGNANCY PROBLEMS

MISMATING

If a bitch is mated by accident, it is possible to prevent implantation of the embryo in the uterus by means of a series of oestrogen hormone injections. These injections have to be given on the 3rd, 5th and 7th day after service. Although oestrogen injections are largely successful, a small proportion of treated bitches will maintain their pregnancy and so a pregnancy diagnosis should always be carried out to confirm that the treatment has been successful.

There are some possible side effects to oestrogen injections. Approximately five per cent of bitches will develop a pseudopregnancy (see opposite column), eight per cent will develop pyometra (see page 165), while another eight per cent will develop a vaginal discharge.

REABSORPTION OF EMBRYOS

It is not uncommon for bitches to appear to be pregnant in the first few weeks after mating, but then fail to produce pups at the predicted time. This may be due to one of two reasons:
- The bitch may never have been pregnant. Sometimes, the body prepares for pregnancy, just in case. In this situation, the bitch may eat more than normal and begin to put on weight. After approximately 40 days, she will lose weight and slim down to her normal size.
- The bitch may have been pregnant but the embryos may have died and been reabsorbed. There is no vaginal discharge so an abortion is not noticed. Often, there is no obvious reason why the embryos are lost.

ABORTION

This is characterised by a bloodstained vaginal discharge. The aborted foetuses may not be seen, either because they have been reabsorbed while in the uterus, or, if expelled from the body, they may have been eaten by the bitch. Often, the cause of the abortion is unclear. Infectious abortion is not nearly so common as owners suppose. The presence of bacteria in the vagina is not necessarily an indication of an infection in the uterus. However, if there is an infection, the bitch will appear dull and off her food.

CAESAREAN SECTION

A Caesarean section is the surgical removal of the foetuses from the uterus. This is necessary when it is impossible to deliver the puppies through the birth canal in the normal way. It requires general anaesthesia. An incision is made in the midline of the abdomen, the uterus is then identified and incised, and the puppies removed. If the placentae have separated from the uterus, they are removed at the time of the operation. However, they may be left to separate spontaneously, as forceful removal can cause bleeding.

PSEUDOPREGNANCY

Often referred to as a phantom, pseudo, or false, pregnancy, the correct name for this condition is pseudocyesis. It is caused by falling levels of progesterone, combined with raised levels of prolactin – the hormone responsible for lactation. Pseudopregnancy can occur in animals of any age and usually occurs between two and three months after oestrus.
Signs: Despite the absence of pregnancy, the bitch will have enlarged mammary glands that produce milk. She may also exhibit nest-building behaviour and a mothering instinct towards soft toys.
Treatment: Pseudopregnancy can be treated by a specific, anti-prolactin drug, which is administered orally as drops. However, because pseudopregnancy may recur after the next season, it is often recommended that the animal be spayed once the condition has been resolved.

WHELPING PROBLEMS

DYSTOCIA

This is defined as difficulty at birth or the inability to expel the foetus through the birth canal. In some breeds, the incidence of dystocia is very high. Although dystocia may be caused by problems in the foetus, most cases of dystocia are due to problems in

167

The majority of pregnancies and births are problem-free but always be prepared for emergencies.

the bitch. It is possible to treat dystocia by the administration of drugs, but most often a Caesarean section is required (see page 167).

Signs: Once a bitch starts abdominal straining during whelping, a puppy will usually appear within half an hour. If nothing has happened within two hours, veterinary help should be sought. If there is a watery, greenish fluid, without any pups appearing, veterinary assistance should be sought immediately. Once the pups start to come, there should be no more than about 30 minutes between each puppy. If the bitch strains for longer than this without anything happening, then veterinary help should again be sought.

Maternal Causes: There are a number of reasons why a bitch may have dystocia.

- **Uterine inertia**: This is the most common cause of dystocia. The uterus either fails to contract at all, or it becomes exhausted after prolonged, unproductive contractions. In the former, a small litter size (e.g. a single pup) is normally responsible, whereas the latter may be a result of carrying a very large litter.
- **Narrow birth canal**: This may be due to the breed conformation (as in the Chihuahua), or it may be due to trauma (such as a road accident) that has altered the bony alignment in the pelvis. In these cases the foetus cannot be delivered through the vagina and a Caesarean section is required.
- **Obstructed birth canal**: This is normally the result of uterine torsion or rupture. It is a serious condition and the bitch quickly becomes unwell. Surgery is always required.

Foetal Causes: These are less common than maternal causes of dystocia.

- **Malpresentation**: This is when the puppies are wrongly positioned in the uterus. Those causing the most problems have a lateral or downward deviation of the head. This is seen in long-necked breeds, such as Rough Collies. Other malpresentations include backward flexion of the front legs, breech presentation (where the bottom is coming first, with the hindlegs pointing towards the head), and transverse or bi-cornual presentation (where the puppy lies across both arms of the uterine horns). If the foetus is present in the birth canal, it may be possible to correct a problem by manipulation. However, there is a danger of trauma to the vagina and a Caesarean section is often the most suitable treatment.
- **Simultaneous birth**: When two puppies are whelped simultaneously, they will jam in the birth canal.
- **Oversized puppies**: This can be associated with a small litter size since each pup will have grown to its maximum potential. However, some breed conformations require a large head relative to the hips (e.g. Boston Terrier) and this can cause problems at birth.

POST-PREGNANCY PROBLEMS

ECLAMPSIA
Low levels of calcium in the blood cause eclampsia, which is otherwise known as puerperal tetany or hypocalcaemia. It is most commonly seen in small-to medium-sized bitches in late pregnancy or early lactation.

Signs: The bitch may be restless and become increasingly stiff. She may also, in the latter stages, suffer from muscle spasms. Other symptoms include panting and increased salivation.

Treatment: Left untreated, eclampsia will kill. If the condition is suspected, the puppies should be removed to stop them suckling, and veterinary assistance should be sought immediately.

The veterinarian will administer an intravenous calcium solution. While the bitch is lactating, her diet should be further supplemented with calcium and vitamin D.

POST-PARTURIENT METRITIS
This is inflammation of the uterus and it usually develops within a few days of giving birth. It is a serious condition that is potentially life-threatening.

Signs: Clinical signs include vaginal discharge, depression, and loss of appetite.

Treatment: Unless the condition is treated quickly,

the bitch may become toxic and die. Supportive fluid therapy, together with antibiotics, is the first line of treatment, but an ovariohysterectomy may be required in extreme cases.

MALE REPRODUCTIVE DISORDERS

CRYPTORCHIDISM

Cryptorchidism is when the testes fail to descend into the scrotum from the abdomen. The testes normally descend soon after birth, although this is difficult to confirm until the puppies are five to eight weeks old. Cryptorchidism may be unilateral or bilateral, i.e. only one testicle may descend, or none may descend. If both testes are retained in the abdomen, the dog will be sterile. If only one testis is retained, the dog may be fertile, although he should not be used for breeding because the condition is believed to be hereditary.

The retained testis has an increased risk of developing a tumour, and it should be surgically removed. When a dog has one testis retained in the abdomen and one that has descended to the scrotum, it is recommended that both are removed at the same time to ensure that the dog cannot be used for breeding.

INFLAMMATION OF THE PENIS/PREPUCE

This is a common condition in male dogs. Young, pre-pubertal dogs may have a yellow-to-green discharge from the prepuce. This has no clinical significance and does not require treatment. Hormonal changes occurring in dogs of this age may be responsible.

Older dogs may have an infectious inflammation where the penis is inflamed and possibly ulcerated. This can be treated with antibiotics.

NARROW PREPUTIAL ORIFICE

This condition is usually congenital and results in the dog being unable to protrude the penis. It can be corrected surgically.

PENILE BLEEDING

Bleeding may follow fighting or trauma but in rare cases it is associated with a penile tumour. Careful examination by the veterinary surgeon will establish the exact source of the bleeding.

HYPOSPADIA

This is a congenital condition whereby the urethra opens in the perineal area instead of in the penis tip. It may be confused with intersexuality (see page 170). The condition can be repaired surgically, but reconstruction is difficult and may require penile amputation.

ORCHITIS

This is an inflammation of the testis. It can be caused by trauma, but it is usually caused by an infection. It is an acutely painful condition and the testis is often swollen. It needs to be treated with antibiotics and may result in infertility.

TESTICULAR TUMOURS

The incidence of testicular tumours is higher among cryptorchid dogs (see opposite column). There are three different types of tumours: Sertoli cell tumour, interstitial cell tumour, and seminoma. The first type of tumour secretes oestrogen, the female hormone, and so the dog may become attractive to other male dogs.

Signs: There may be a lump present in one testis with a decrease in size of the other testis. Alternatively, one or both may become enlarged and soft. The dog may also lose hair along his flanks.

Treatment: Testicular tumours are not directly life-

TESTICULAR TUMOURS

Sertoli cell tumour

Seminoma

Leydig cell tumour

Normal testis

Hill's Atlas of Veterinary Clinical Anatomy

threatening unless they spread, but there are a number of other complications, which make castration advisable, such as hormone secretion and ulceration.

PROSTATE ENLARGEMENT

Prostate enlargement is normally due to one of three factors:

- **Benign prostatic hyperplasia**: As a dog ages, the prostate tends to enlarge. This is normal, but, in some dogs over the age of five years, the enlarged prostate can cause problems by pressing against other abdominal structures. Castration (page 156) will cause the prostate to reduce in size. See Chapter Five.

- **Prostatic metaplasia**: Some testicular tumours secrete oestrogens, which cause the prostate cells to change and the gland itself to become enlarged and irregular. Castration, or removal of the source of oestrogen, will cure the problem.

- **Prostatic tumours**: These are very rare, but, unfortunately, when they occur, they spread to other parts of the body. The condition is usually not recognised until the spread has occurred, and treatment is often unsuccessful.

INTERSEXUAL REPRODUCTIVE DISORDERS

Intersexes have some of the physical characteristics of both sexes. They are usually genetic females, in that they generally appear to be female but they have an enlarged clitoris, which may surround the bone normally found in the dog's penis (the os penis). Internally, there is an underdeveloped uterus and undifferentiated gonads.

There are various complications with intersex dogs. Such cases will not be able to breed, and genetic females may need to undergo surgery on the clitoris because it becomes traumatised when the bitch sits down. Even in the absence of a grossly enlarged clitoris, the animal should be spayed to avoid the possible complication of tumours of the abdominal, undifferentiated gonads.

Urinary incontinence, because of the abnormal vaginal structure, may also occur. Less commonly, an intersexual dog may develop a urinary obstruction. This is more likely in intersexes that appear to be male.

MATING PROBLEMS

LACK OF LIBIDO

This is defined as an unwillingness to mate, and the causes can be quite complex. It may be due to pain (e.g. in the back or legs), an intimidating or aggressive female (usually because the bitch is not at the correct time in her season), illness, immaturity, or poor nutrition. It is rarely due to an inherently low hormone level.

FAILURE TO UNTIE

The bitch and dog usually remain tied at mating for approximately 30 minutes, although longer has been known. However, occasionally they become locked and the dog cannot disengage. If the dog is left erect for too long, there is a danger that the engorged penis will be damaged. Since the dog's erection is maintained due to the contraction of the bitch's vaginal sphincter, it may be necessary to enlarge the vulva surgically to allow the penis to be released.

FAILURE TO PRODUCE PUPS

If mating has been carried out at the appropriate time in the bitch's season, then a common reason for failure to produce pups is that there are abnormalities in the dog's ejaculate. This can be checked to see whether there are sufficient numbers of spermatozoa, that they can swim vigorously, and that they have the right shape to enable them to fertilise the eggs. A generalised infection, as well as a specific infection of the testis, can cause damage to the sperm, which may be temporary or permanent.

NEWBORN PUPPY COMPLAINTS

CONGENITAL DEFECTS

Congenital defects are those that are present at birth. Some are hereditary, while others are not. Sometimes, the same abnormality can be caused by either genetic or non-genetic factors.

Examples of congenital inherited abnormalities include:
- **Cardiac abnormalities**: A common example is a ventricular septal defect (hole in the heart). See Chapter Five.
- **Dermoid cyst/sinus**: This is often seen in the Rhodesian Ridgeback (page 152).
- **Eye abnormalities**: The Collie eye anomaly may be the best known (Chapter Seven).
- **Cleft palate**: This is one of the more common abnormalities seen in the newborn pup. The roof

of the mouth fails to join in the middle and consequently when the puppy tries to suckle milk, it can enter the nose or pass down into the lungs. The condition is usually due to chance accidents of development during gestation. However, in the Bulldog, there is a possibility that some cases of cleft palate are due to an autosomal recessive gene.

Non-genetic congenital defects may be caused by certain drugs (often given during pregnancy), certain dietary components and various environmental contaminants. However, frequently, the cause remains unidentified.

FADING PUPPY SYNDROME

This is an ill-defined syndrome in which the puppies fail to thrive, and they lose weight, and die between three and five days after birth.

There are a number of factors associated with the newborn that may predispose such puppies to death at this time. For example, puppies cannot control their own body temperature and are therefore susceptible to chilling.

Similarly, they are at greater risk of dehydration than the adult animal. Failure to suckle will result in a rapid depletion of energy stores, dehydration and chilling. Infectious agents, such as herpes virus, have also been implicated. Nevertheless, in about 50 per cent of cases, no cause is found.

PARASITES

- **Roundworms**: *Toxocara* spp. and *Toxocaris leonina*
- **External parasites**: Fleas, lice and ticks
- **Ear mites**
- **Mange mites**: *Demodex* or *Sarcoptes scabiei var. 3canis*

See Chapter Two for more details on these parasites.

BACTERIAL INFECTIONS

Bacterial infection of the newborn can spread rapidly in the blood. Death may occur suddenly and without clinical symptoms if the infection is overwhelming.

When symptoms occur, they include diarrhoea, difficulty with breathing, and general lack of condition. If the condition is identified quickly, it can be treated with antibiotics and supportive fluid therapy.

VIRAL INFECTIONS

Provided the puppy has obtained passive immunity from his mother's milk, viral infections are rare before the age of five to six weeks. However, canine herpes virus, which can infect the puppy in utero, will cause death within 24-48 hours.

10 THE QUESTION OF INHERITANCE

From the moment of conception, each dog develops following a genetic blueprint that determines his breed, sex, colour, and so on. This complete set of instructions for an animal's make-up is called the genome. The instructions can be found in the nuclei of each and every cell within the dog's body. Within the cell nuclei, the instructions are organised into structures known as chromosomes.

CHROMOSOMES

All breeds of dog, wolf, coyote and jackal have 78 chromosomes that are grouped together in 39 pairs. Under powerful magnification, each chromosome looks like a piece of string, with there being 39 different shapes of 'string'.

Chromosomes are numbered from the largest pair to the smallest pair. Canine chromosomes are difficult to differentiate because they show less variation than is seen in many other species.

Chromosome pairs are known as homologous chromosomes. One member of each pair is obtained from each parent. In other words, each dog is made up of 39 chromosomes from his father, and 39 chromosomes from his mother. The dog is able to inherit 39 from each parent because of a process called meiosis.

MEIOSIS AND MITOSIS

During the production of germ cells (i.e. sperm and egg cells), only one member of each chromosome pair may enter the germ cell. This results in the father's sperm cells carrying 39 chromosomes each, and the mother's egg cells carrying 39 chromosomes each. When fertilisation occurs, the single chromosomes find their partners in the other germ cell and reform into pairs. The resulting embryo then has the 39 pairs of chromosomes – the expected 78 chromosomes that make up a normal member of the canine species.

The embryo grows by duplicating its cells. This process is known as mitosis. As mitosis leads to exact duplication of the cell nuclei, this explains why, in all the millions of cells that constitute the dog, each cell holds the same, identical 78 chromosomes.

GENES

Chromosomes carry genes, the coding responsible for the make-up of every living animal. There may be about 40,000 genes in the dog and all breeds will have these genes, though not in the same sequence. Genes are made of deoxyribonucleic acid (DNA).

Each individual gene consists of four different nucleotide bases. These are known as adenine, cytosine, guanine and thymine, which are usually abbreviated to A, C, G and T. The order in which they occur in a gene determines its nature and its action. A specific gene is always found on the same chromosome and in the same place (locus) on that chromosome.

Because chromosomes are paired, a gene can only exist twice, i.e. on the same locus on the same chromosome. A dog can have the long-coat gene twice, but it cannot have it three times.

The close ancestral relationship between dogs and wolves means that the two species share many genes. As a result, matings between dogs and wolves, though not to be recommended, would be viable and fertile. The same is true for any mating between dogs and coyotes or jackals. Packs of Coydogs are not uncommon in North America and have little fear of humans. They are often seen in farmyards raiding the garbage.

ALLELES

Genes can be dominant or recessive, with the different versions being known as alleles. For example, the gene L is responsible for the normal, short coat in the dog. Its alternative l is responsible for a long coat. The use of an upper case letter illustrates a dominant allele, while a lower case letter shows a recessive allele. A dominant allele will work if it is present in only one of the two chromosomes making up a pair. A recessive allele must be present on both chromosomes if it is to function. This means that there are three genotypes (genetic combinations) for coat length: LL, Ll and ll.

LL will cause a short coat, because both alleles carry the coding for a short coat. It is known as a homozygous dominant. In the case of ll, which is known as a homozygous recessive, both alleles carry the set of instructions for a long coat, so the dog will have long hair. The heterozygote Ll will appear short-coated. Although the long-coated gene is present, it is recessive to the dominant L, so it is the L gene that determines the coat length.

Although Ll is indistinguishable from LL in terms of a dog's appearance, it will breed differently. The offspring from an LL dog will all carry the L allele. However, the offspring from an Ll dog may be a mixture of long and short coats.

Some breeders will refer to a dog as "producing lots of long coats" and to another as producing fewer. If both dogs are short-coated but produce some long-coated puppies, both sires are Ll. If one produces more long-coated progeny, it is because he was mated to more dogs that carried the l recessive. The amount of long-coated puppies a sire produces is, therefore, a reflection of the mating plan and not an ability of the dog to 'transmit' the recessive allele.

Some genes influence more than one character trait. For example, the gene responsible for producing a merle coat (M) not only gives rise to a specific coat colour but also influences the development of sight and hearing (in both cases adversely). Although all dog breeds carry the merle gene, most breeds are made up of the non-merle alternative (m). Consequently, most individuals within a breed are mm, with their offspring also being mm. The dominant merle allele is mostly seen in breeds such as Rough Collies, Shelties, Australian Shepherds and Dachshunds (where the gene is termed dapple). These dogs can be Mm (merle) or MM (white, deaf and with seriously defective sight).

POLYMORPHISM

Some genes have more than two versions or alleles.

For example, the gene responsible for causing spots in coat colour can have four versions, though not all are present in every breed. The versions are:
• S (solid colour)
• s^i (irish spotting)
• s^P (piebald spotting)
• s^w (extreme white).

A dog can have any two of these four alleles – either two the same or two different ones – but he cannot have three or four because there are only two chromosomes on which they can occur. The allele S gives solid colour, though minus modifiers (minor genes which modify the main effect) can sometimes give a splash of white on the chest. The si allele gives rise to a dog with a white blaze – white collar and white chest, usually with white feet, and a white tip to the tail. In some breeds, e.g. the Boxer, selection for a full collar has taken place but in the Berner Sennenhund there has been selection to avoid white around the neck. This has been brought about by breeding programmes that have concentrated on mating dogs with modifying genes to influence the expression of the s^i allele. The s^P allele causes white patches over the body as in Landseer Newfoundlands, and s^w leads to a white dog with, say, a black eye patch, as in Bull Terriers.

SEX DETERMINATION

Among the 39 pairs of chromosomes, females have a pair that is larger than the others. Instead of a same-sized pair, males have one large chromosome and one very small chromosome. The large chromosome is termed an X and the small one a Y and these are called the sex chromosomes because their presence determines the sex of the dog. Females are XX and males are XY. Female ova carry only the X along with the other 38 chromosomes, whereas male sperm carry either an X or a Y with the other 38 chromosomes. The sex of the progeny will depend upon which type of sperm fertilises the ovum, so sex is determined by the sire and not the dam of a litter. Generally, more male sperm fertilise the ova than female. At birth, there are approximately 104-106 males for every 100 females. This can vary with certain sires, but in broad terms, slightly more males than females are born.

At times, dogs can be born with abnormal sex chromosome numbers. Thus we see animals that have only one X and they are termed XO. Such females are infertile. Similarly, one can have females that are XXX and even males that are XXY or sometimes XX in certain cells and XY in others. Such chromosomal anomalies are rare and stem from faulty meiosis but they can be seen more often in certain breeds like the Cocker Spaniel or the Weimaraner, though even within these breeds they are still rare. Mostly, such animals are infertile.

SEX LINKAGE

Any gene carried on the sex chromosomes will be passed on with that chromosome. Few, if any, genes are carried on the Y chromosome but that is not true of the X. On the X chromosome, a number of genes can be carried, including the genes for haemophilia A, haemophilia B and a kind of Duchenne Muscular Dystrophy (a specific type of muscle-wasting disease).

Haemophilia A is a recessive trait so a female will only be a haemophiliac if she carries the recessive allele on both of her X chromosomes. However, a male with a defective X will present haemophilia because his Y chromosome is largely inactive and cannot countermand the haemophilia allele. If we designate the haemophilia allele as X^h and the normal, healthy state as X^H, there are three kinds of female but only two kinds of male. These are:

	Male	Female
Normal	$X^H Y$	$X^H X^H$
Carrier		$X^H X^h$
Affected	$X^h Y$	$X^h X^h$

PHENOTYPE (COLOUR)	GENOTYPE (GENE COMBINATION)
Black	BBEE, BBEe, BbEE, BbEe
Chocolate	bbEe, bbEE
Yellow (black nose)	Bbee, BBee
Yellow (brown nose)	bbee

There is no such thing as a carrier male. Most haemophiliacs arise when a carrier female is mated to a normal male. This mating gives females that are either normal or carriers and males that are either normal or affected. If an affected male is mated to a normal female, he will not produce any affected progeny. However, while all his sons will be normal, all his daughters will be carriers. In this way, the problem can arise generation after generation.

EPISTASIS

Some genes act in isolation whereas others are influenced by genes at another point on the DNA strand. The gene that acts to influence a gene at another locus is termed an epistatic one. This is illustrated by coat colour in Labrador Retrievers. This breed is black, chocolate, or yellow. Black is caused by the allele B and chocolate by the recessive bb combination. The bb combination also affects nose colour, so that chocolate dogs have a light-coloured nose.

LABRADOR 'COLOUR GENES'

Some people imagine that, to get a black Labrador, at least one of the parents must be black. This illustration shows this is not true. A BBee and bbEE mating (regardless of which parent is which) will produce all black progeny.

A BbEe and Bbee mating. Obviously, all the colours may not occur in one litter, but large numbers of matings will follow this ratio.

The black and chocolate colours of a Labrador are made up not only of the B or bb allele, but also of the E allele. A Labrador need only carry one E allele to be born black or chocolate-coated. However, if he carries both recessive alleles (ee), he will be born with a yellow coat and a black nose (dilute black) or a yellow coat with a brown nose (dilute chocolate).

There are four phenotypes of Labrador, but nine genotypes. Black dogs can be one of four types, only one of which – BBEE – will produce solely black offspring. BbEe can produce any of the four colours depending upon the type of Labrador he mates with.

SELECTION FOR SIMPLE TRAITS

Selecting for a single trait is simple. If the number of genes being studied is increased, however, the pattern becomes more complex. An example can be seen in the coat colour of the Newfoundland.

The Newfoundland breed can be black, brown, or black and white (called Landseer – after the Victorian painter). Black is caused by the allele B, and brown by the combination bb. S causes solid colour, while sᴾsᴾ is responsible for Landseer colouring (piebald spotting).

If a brown dog of type bbSS is mated with a Landseer bitch of type BBsᴾsᴾ, all the progeny will be BbSsᴾ, or black. This is because the brown dog will produce sperm that are all bS, while the bitch

GENE COMINATIONS IN NEWFOUNDLAND COAT COLOUR			
		Brown sire	
		bS	bsᴾ
Landseer dam	BsᴾP	BbSsᴾ (black)	BbsᴾsᴾP (Landseer)
	bsᴾP	bbSsᴾ (brown)	bbsᴾsᴾP (brown and white)

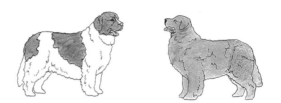

A mating between a brown dam (bbSS) and a landseer sire (BBsᴾsᴾ) mating. The results apply even if the sexes of the parents are reversed.

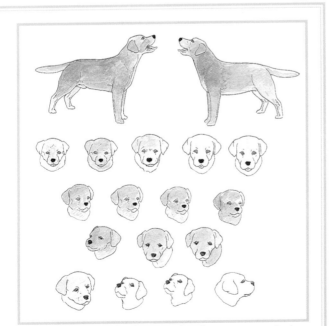

Two black Labradors can give rise to many variations, depending on the genotype of the dogs involved. The above is just one example, using a BbEe and a BbEe.

A mating between the same coloured dogs as above, but with very different results, due to the genotypes involved (bbSsᴾ and Bbsᴾsᴾ). As before, the results apply even if the sexes of the parents are reversed.

175

will produce ova that are all Bsp. The alleles for the colour black in solid form are dominant over the alleles for brown and the Landseer pattern.

If a brown dog of type bbSsᴾ is mated with a Landseer that is Bbsᴾsᴾ, the result is different. This mating, although with two animals of the same phenotype as the previous mating, produces four different colours in equal proportions (assuming a large litter), one of which (brown and white) is not an acceptable colour in the breed.

Although this may seem complex, given numbers of progeny and pedigree information, it is possible to work out the genetic patterns governing colours in many dogs.

GENE MAPPING

In recent years there have been significant developments in the techniques of identifying and mapping genes.

Most research has been related to farm livestock and to humans (from which most of the research money has been derived), although there has been some canine mapping.

By using a sample of blood or hair (or other tissue), the DNA pattern can be assessed by using an electric field and supporting gel. The net result is rather like a bar code, but it allows gene identification to be made.

GENETIC DEFECTS IN THE DOG

DEFECT	MODE OF INHERITANCE	AGE AT ONSET (approximately)
Cataracts	Mostly Mendelian	<2 years
Cerebellar degeneration	Autosomal recessive	4 months
Cleft palate	Polygenic	Birth
Craniomandibular osteopathy	Autosomal recessive	6 months
Cryptorchidism	Polygenic	6 months
Cyclic neutropenia	Autosomal recessive	Birth
Deafness	Mendelian	2 months
Deep pyoderma	Polygenic	5 years
Degenerative myelopathy	Unclear	2 years
Disc disease	Unclear	12 months
Ectopic ureter	Unclear	Birth
Elbow dysplasia	Polygenic	4 months
Epilepsy	Polygenic	18-42 months
Fucosidosis	Autosomal recessive	12 months
Glaucoma	Various	3 years
Haemophilia A and B	Sex-linked recessive	Birth
Hemeralopia	Autosomal recessive	12 months
Hermaphrodite	Chromosomal anomaly	3 months
Hip dysplasia	Polygenic	>2 months
Histiocytosis	Polygenic	>3 years
Hydrocephalus	Polygenic	2 months
Laryngeal paralysis	Autosomal dominant	12 months
Legg-Calvé-Perthes Disease	Polygenic	12 months
Lens luxation	Autosomal recessive	12 months
Missing teeth	Unclear	9 months
Mitral valve problem	Unclear	12 months
Myopathy	Sex-linked recessive	12 months
Panosteitis	Polygenic	4 months
Patellar luxation	Polygenic	12 months
Patent ductus arteriosus	Polygenic	Birth
Pituitary dwarfism	Autosomal recessive	2 months
Progressive retinal atrophy	Autosomal recessive	2 years
Pyruvate kinase deficiency	Autosomal recessive	>2 years (most breeds)
Renal disease	Various	6 months
Subaortic stenosis	Polygenic	3 months
Torsion	Unclear	5 years
Megaoesophagus	Unclear	2 months
Umbilical hernia	Polygenic	Birth
Von Willebrand's disease	Mendelian (various types)	12 months
Wobbler syndrome	Polygenic	12 months

KNOWN GENETIC DEFECTS

There are about 300 to 400 known canine problems that may be of genetic origin. Some of the more common ones are listed.

The defects listed vary in both their incidence and the breeds they affect. Some, such as hip dysplasia, are fairly widespread across all breeds, while others, such as craniomandibular osteopathy, are found in a small number of breeds only. The mode of inheritance is the most likely cause for these discrepancies, but this may be subject to change as more knowledge is accumulated. Very often, the mode of inheritance is unclear because breed clubs have not collected suitable data to permit genetic analysis of the results. Scientists are dependent on breeders for data, and, if this is not available, the mode of inheritance may remain undiscovered.

AUTOSOMAL INHERITANCE

Progressive Retinal Atrophy (PRA) is a serious eye disease found in many breeds, notably gundogs. PRA is a simple autosomal recessive, i.e. it is a recessive allele carried on an autosome (an autosome being any chromosome, apart from the two sex chromosomes).

There are three versions of the basic gene:
• PP (normal)
• Pp (carrier)
• pp (affected).

The disease is late in onset in most breeds but DNA testing can identify an animal as one of the above three types. This means that pp and even Pp cases can be discarded from the breeding pool, and the genetic defect reduced in incidence quickly and effectively, without long and laborious test-mating. Although PRA exists in many breeds, it manifests differently in the genes of different breeds. Consequently, although DNA mapping for the Irish Setter has been achieved, it has not yet been done for most other breeds.

To date, approximately 20 genes have been located in the same way as with PRA, either directly or via a marker (a gene, already identified, which is known to mark the area where the defective gene is to be found). Given more DNA testing, more genes will be isolated, and breeders will benefit from the ability to assess accurately which dogs are free from defects, and which are not.

POLYGENIC INHERITANCE

Depending on the breed, dogs are normally bred for conformation, behavioural characteristics, and for working potential. Most of the traits sought by breeders are not inherited in a simple fashion, such as those described above. Instead, they are the result of a number of genes, each one having a small effect, but, when combined with the others, having a significant impact. Each specific gene may be inherited in a dominant, recessive, or epistatic fashion, but, collectively, they influence a trait in specific ways. The breeder may not know how many genes he is dealing with, but, because he is able to measure the trait, he can make selective decisions.

Most polygenic traits follow a normal curve. In other words, there are few individuals at the extremes of a range. Most cluster around the middle. If we look at something like litter size in the German Shepherd, it will vary from 1 through to 16, with the majority of litters averaging around 8 pups.

Although we do not know how many genes are involved in influencing litter size, it is possible to calculate the variance (variability) of the trait and to determine the proportion of that variance that is caused by genes. This is called the heritability of the trait, and it can vary from 0 to 1 or from 0 to 100 per cent. In scientific terms, heritability is represented by the symbol h^2 and, in a case like litter size, it would be low (0.10-0.20).

In selecting to increase or to improve a trait, the success of any programme will be determined by how heritable the trait is and how intensely it is selected. For example, if the average litter size of GSDs is 7.73 puppies and we were to breed only from bitches that averaged 10 puppies per litter, the superiority of the selected group (i.e. in comparison to the breed average) would be 10 minus 7.73, or 2.27. If heritability of the trait is assumed to be 0.15, the next generation should average 2.27 x 0.15, or 0.34. When this is added to the breed average of 7.73, the new average litter size should be 8.07. This slightly overestimates the advance because we have only selected females, but it can be seen that the increase is quite small because the heritability of litter size is small.

While a breed's litter size has a low heritability, a dog's height at the withers is approximately 65 per cent heritable (0.65). If Bernese Mountain Dog males average 26.4 inches (67 cms) in wither height and we breed from dogs that average 27.5 inches (70 cms), we are selecting from a population that is 1.1 inches (3 cms) larger than normal. Of this population, 65 per cent of the extra height is transmitted in the genes. This gives a heritability factor of 0.65 x 1.1. The resulting population should, therefore, be approximately 0.71 inches (1.95 cms) taller at the withers than the standard breed height. Again, only one sex has been considered in this example, but, in a highly heritable trait such as this, rapid progress can be made if breeders select rigorously. However, in many cases (and wither height is often a case in point), breeders are seeking to maintain the status quo and not to exaggerate the trait.

Progress in transmitting polygenic traits depends on two factors:
• The superiority of the breeding stock relative to the population they were drawn from.
• The heritability of the trait being transmitted.

Unfortunately, the heritability of various canine traits is not well studied, unlike farm livestock. However, some rough values are given in the following table. They will vary according to the breed being studied and the population of that breed; for this reason, ranges have been given in some instances.

HERITABILITY OF BREED CHARACTERISTICS

TRAIT	HERITABILITY %
Body weight	40
Body length	40
Hip dysplasia	25-55
Nervousness	50
Chest depth	40-50
Litter size	10-20

One of the most common defects transmitted polygenically is hip dysplasia. This is a faulty fitting of the ball and socket of the hip joint (see Chapter Four). First discovered in 1935, it received much publicity from the late 1950s onwards, and most developed nations organised schemes to identify the problem. Scandinavian countries led the field, followed by Britain and other European countries, as well as the US.

Most countries have adopted a grading system of five grades, into which animals are categorised following a hip X-ray at the age of 12 months. In Europe, grading has generally been A, B, C, D and E, with A being the best and E the worst. In Scandinavia, grades might be 0, I, II, III or IV, in ascending order of severity. Some kennel clubs then limit the use of specific animals depending upon their grade. This is usually agreed with the appropriate breed club. For example, in Norway,

Bernese Mountain Dogs have to be grade 0 to be used, while in another area of Europe, dogs of grade A-C can be used.

In 1965, Britain set up a grading scheme using only 3 grades, which is mathematically insufficient, and a new scoring scheme was established in 1978 for German Shepherds, and for all breeds in 1983. This looks at nine features of the hip and grades each feature on a scale of 0 (ideal) through to 6 (worst), with one feature using the scale 0-5. Given these nine features and these limits, a dog can score from 0 to 53 on a hip or from 0-106 on two hips combined. Breed averages can be calculated and the following table shows the top 25 breeds most likely to present with hip dysplasia based on at least 100 dogs scored (up to October 2000). To this date more than 141,000 animals have been scored from all breeds, with Labrador Retrievers having the most scored.

HIP DYSPLASIA HERITABILITY

The heritability of hip dysplasia varies with the breed and the system used to assess it, but, in broad terms, heritability ranges from 0.25 through to 0.55. Hip dysplasia is found among the human population as well as the canine one. Among humans, it is more common in girls than in boys, and it is present at birth, i.e. congenital. In man, it occurs only about once every 1,000 births, whereas in the dog it is much more frequent but is not congenital. Some cases can be seen as early as two months of age but evaluation needs a minimum age of 12 months to be certain. The condition is more severe in females in many breeds, and, while it is not a fatal condition and can be treated to a certain extent, hip dysplasia can lead to a proportion of animals being euthanased because of arthritic complications.

It is often argued that schemes to combat HD have not worked. This is not true. Where schemes have had some measure of breeding control, progress has been marked. In Sweden, where one of these schemes was undertaken, most breeds have shown a reduction in the incidence of HD. In Britain, Newfoundlands have advanced by about 0.63 points per year, which may not seem a lot but it has brought the breed mean down from around 35 in 1980 to 22 by 1999 (the figures opposite are a composite, covering the whole time period). In many breeds, although assessment of hips is undertaken conscientiously, many breeders then appear to do very little selection and can even concentrate on poor-producing or high-scoring animals, which makes progress unlikely.

WORST 25 BREEDS FOR HIP DYSPLASIA (BVA/KC SCHEME)

BREED	No. DOGS TESTED	BEST SCORE	WORST SCORE	MEAN SCORE
Airedale	902	0	91	16.8
Bernese Mountain Dog	3077	0	102	16.0
Bouvier des Flandres	132	4	76	18.0
Boxer	273	0	64	16.1
Briard	585	0	99	21.2
Brittany	239	0	74	18.2
Bullmastiff	690	0	104	28.2
Cavalier King Charles Spaniel	244	2	92	16.5
Clumber Spaniel	461	0	102	42.2
English Setter	1914	0	95	19.2
German Shepherd	30647	0	106	18.6
Golden Retriever	22503	0	106	19.1
Gordon Setter	1643	0	104	24.7
Hungarian Puli	352	1	102	17.6
Irish Water Spaniel	547	0	102	17.6
Labrador	34536	0	104	15.8
Mastiff	169	0	81	17.4
Newfoundland	2607	0	106	28.5
Old English Sheepdog	1212	0	100	20.5
Otterhound	115	4	102	43.1
Polish Lowland Sheepdog	277	5	59	16.9
Shetland Sheepdog	121	2	100	16.7
St. Bernard	229	0	73	23.0
Sussex Spaniel	104	7	101	37.4
Welsh Springer Spaniel	994	0	104	18.9

WORST 20 BREEDS FOR HIP DYSPLASIA IN THE US (OFA SCHEME)

BREED	No. DOGS TESTED	PER CENT DYSPLASTIC
Bernese Mountain Dog	2491	25.5
Bloodhound	1068	28.4
Boykin Spaniel	378	47.6
Bullmastiff	926	31.2
Chesapeake Bay Retriever	4180	24.4
Chow Chow	2447	22.8
Elkhound	1906	23.5
English Setter	3459	22.3
Field Spaniel	119	27.7
Giant Schnauzer	1945	22.6
Golden Retriever	44025	23.5
Gordon Setter	2645	23.1
Kuvasz	603	25.2
Mastiff	1291	23.4
Newfoundland	4795	30.5
Old English Sheepdog	6963	22.2
Rottweiler	374977	23.3
Staffordshire Bull Terrier	360	29.7
St. Bernard	1129	48.1
Welsh Springer Spaniel	401	24.1

PITUITARY DWARF GENE

Two 'carrier' parents for the pituitary dwarf gene (dw) would produce a litter where 25 per cent would be dwarfs. The breakdown of the puppies' genotypes is marked below.

25 per cent normal (DwDw)   *50 per cent carrier (Dwdw)*   *25 per cent dwarf (dwdw).*

BREEDING SYSTEMS

Having decided which dogs to breed from, breeders have to determine which dog is mated to which bitch.

INBREEDING

In early breeding programmes there was considerable inbreeding, and this is true of all species, not just the dog. Inbreeding is the mating of related animals, but, if you trace back any pedigree in any breed, you will find that, at some point, the same animals keep appearing and that all dogs within a breed are related to some degree. Inbreeding has to be defined as: the mating of animals more closely related than the average of the population from which they come.

In humans, the closest breeding that is permitted in law is that of first cousins. Such a mating would result in progeny that are 6.25 per cent inbred. In contrast, a mating of half siblings (i.e. by the same father but out of different mothers) would give an inbreeding coefficient of 12.5 per cent. Brother-sister or parent-offspring matings would be 25 per cent inbred.

In most breeds, the mean level of inbreeding based on a five-generation pedigree would be around four to six per cent, although it could be much higher in numerically small breeds. Inbreeding increases the chance that an individual could inherit the same gene from mother and father. Since many anomalies are recessive, the mating of close relatives could increase that chance that the progeny will inherit a deleterious recessive gene in duplicate. Therefore, one consequence of inbreeding is an increase in anomalies.

Inbreeding on a pituitary dwarf carrier in the German Shepherd would increase the risk of producing a dwarf puppy. The closer (higher) the inbreeding, the greater the risk. However, it is not inevitable that problems will result. A dog carrying a deleterious recessive trait on one chromosome will pass it to half his offspring but the other half will be free of the gene. Consequently, it is not inevitable that all descendants of a known carrier will be implicated in the problem.

More serious than the occurrence of anomalies is the phenomenon termed inbreeding depression. This arises when inbred animals show problems with certain features. Mostly, this involves reproduction and traits of low heritability. The more inbred an animal is, the greater the risk of infertility, reduced litter size, neonatal mortality and a general malaise in certain traits. Inbreeding on a specific constructional trait that is highly inherited may not be harmful, but high levels of inbreeding could lead to reproductive problems. The author has seen levels of inbreeding in excess of 60 per cent in Orlov Trotters (a Russian horse), but rarely values as high as 40 per cent in dog breeds. Most inbreeding is less than 20 per cent, and, while this does not mean that problems cannot ensue, the risk is less at lower levels.

Dog breeders are, by definition, pedigree breeders. Therefore, some level of inbreeding is inevitable – even if it is too far back in the pedigree for the breeder to know. However, breeders should not seek to undertake high levels of inbreeding unless they are prepared to face some problems.

LINEBREEDING

Many breeders undertake what is called like-to-like mating. In this, animals of similar construction and character are mated. Progeny tend to resemble their parents (having received 50 per cent of their genes from each parent), so the mating of parents that look alike will further increase the chance that the progeny resemble their parents. However, they may not be genetically alike and such matings are not free of error.

OUTCROSSING

From time to time, problems will ensue in which a breeder finds a problem seemingly 'fixed' in his kennel. In such cases, compensatory mating will be needed and the breeder will have to bring in an outside animal that possesses the virtue the kennel is lacking. Generally, it is easier to bring in a male, since one does not have to buy him but merely pay his stud fee. If, for example, the kennel stock shows a forward-placed shoulder assembly, one should select a sire with excellent shoulders descended from excellent-shouldered ancestors. Better still, a sire should be chosen that is known to be producing good shoulders in his offspring. The dog should be mated with several bitches in the home kennel, and the better-shouldered offspring selected to bring the stock back into line.

Any breeder must learn what is behind his stock in terms of defects, but also in terms of conformation and character. The breeder must then seek to breed to a policy rather than just use the latest Champion or the biggest winner. Big winners may be good producers but there is no guarantee of this. A successful breeder cannot work on a patchwork-quilt-type of pedigree, but must concentrate on producing a line that is consistent in terms of construction and character.

11 THE CANINE ATHLETE

The definition of an athlete is someone trained in exercises or contests requiring physical strengths, skill or speed. In humans, an athlete could be a sprinter, a marathon runner, or an archer. The definition is equally broad in dogs. There is a wide range of canine athletes, from the Greyhound, who will sprint short distances in a matter of seconds, to the sled dogs and herding dogs with stamina and endurance that can cover more than a hundred miles a day.

Some canine athletes are listed in the table opposite. The list is not exhaustive but it is meant to illustrate the range of breeds and types of activities they can be involved in (see chart opposite).

There are a number of opportunities for canine athletes of all breeds, including racing, gundog work, herding, search and rescue, and agility.

ACTIVITY	BREED
Racing	Greyhounds, Whippets
Coursing	Lurchers, Greyhounds
Gundog	Spaniels, Pointers, Retrievers
Cart pulling	Bernese Mountain Dogs, Newfoundlands
Sled pulling	Siberian Huskies, Alaskan Malamutes, Samoyeds
Search and rescue, Tracking	German Shepherd Dogs
Security and detection	German Shepherd Dogs, Spaniels, Labradors
Agility, Flyball	Border Collies (and many other breeds)
Herding	Border Collies, Australian Cattle Dogs, German Shepherd Dogs, etc.

EXERCISE REGIMES

A basic understanding of muscle structure and function will help you to design an appropriate exercise regime for your dog. Muscle is basically composed of two main types of fibre, one for fast activity (e.g. sprinting), and one for slower activity (e.g. jogging or walking). The fibres used for sprinting use up a lot of energy and so they tire very quickly – this is the reason why dogs or people cannot sprint for long distances. In comparison, fibres used for slower activities, or those requiring stamina, require much less energy – hence the reason why dogs can keep walking or jogging for hours. Training your dog to do fast work, such as sprinting, will increase the size and number of the 'fast fibres', whereas lots of walking and gentle exercise will build up and activate the 'slower fibres'. Therefore, a dog that needs to be very fast over short distances will benefit more from shorter bursts of intense training, while the endurance dog will benefit from being exercised less intensely but for longer periods.

A training programme must be developed to suit your dog and his sport. It is beyond the scope of this chapter to discuss training programmes for individual sports, but this section is intended as a basic guideline to training canine athletes.

The fundamental basis of training is this: if an increased workload is imposed on a muscle fibre, bone, ligament or enzyme chain, it will try to change itself to cope better with the load. In general, training should mimic the event being trained for. This produces the best results.

There are four important aspects to specific training:

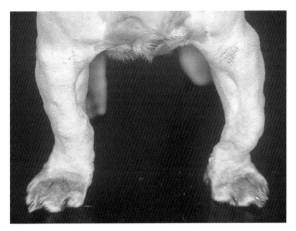

A puppy with contracture of tendons that flex the carpus or wrist joint. One cause of this condition is lack of exercise.

- **Rate**: The running speed during some of the training should be similar to that expected in competition.
- **Duration**: Some of the running, at or near race speed, should approach the race duration.
- **Function**: Some training should mimic the movements expected during competition. For example, training a Greyhound using a lure will help him to corner and to change direction swiftly, without stumbling or losing momentum.
- **Structural**: Training should develop the muscles to be used. Training a Greyhound to tug on a rope will develop his neck muscles, but it will not help him to run.

BEGINNING TRAINING

Underexercise can be as bad as overexercise in a young dog. Caging a puppy and restricting his exercise can result in tendon laxity or even, conversely, tendon contractures. The right amount of exercise is also important in the development of strong, yet supple ligaments. Getting the balance right is very important. The wolf puppy in the wild had periods of intense exercise and playing, followed by periods of deep sleep. Similarly, the domesticated dog should be given the opportunity to play, especially with other dogs of a similar age, as this will help his development and socialisation. The latter should not be neglected, especially in an animal intended for athletic use who is going to meet many strange dogs during his lifetime of events and competition.

A young dog should be introduced to aspects of his future life, such as lead-training, from the age of three to four months. Then, when he reaches the age where he can start more serious training, not everything is new. Dogs reach skeletal maturity between 10 and 14 months, with smaller dogs reaching maturity slightly earlier than giant breeds, and they should not be overexercised before this time.

Exercises such as short walks with periods on and off the lead should be started as soon as the puppy has completed his vaccination course. Building up to two or three short walks a day by the time your dog is a year of age is better than giving him just one long walk a day. However, taking a puppy jogging while you train for the marathon is not to be recommended – this would be too much exercise and would place significant stress on young tissues.

LARGE/GIANT BREEDS
There is a myth, particularly for large and giant breeds, that, if a puppy is not exercised until he is one year of age, joint problems such as hip dysplasia or osteochondrosis (Chapter Four) can be prevented. These conditions often have a hereditary component, so limiting the exercise a dog is given will not prevent the disease. A lack of exercise may mask or delay the onset of the disease but it may also impede your pet's development, socially as well as in the musculo-skeletal department. A moderate amount of exercise will allow for proper development of strong muscles, tendons, ligaments and bone, as well as encouraging socialisation skills in your dog at a young age.

FREQUENCY OF TRAINING
It takes variable periods of time for the different parts of the body to respond to training. Enzyme systems will adapt quickly, over a few weeks, but bones, joints, and tendons can take months to respond, with muscles lying somewhere in between. Therefore, many training programmes will start with walking, to initiate a response in the slow responders such as bone.

With training periods too far apart, adaptation is lost. Training periods too close together might not give the dog enough time to recover. Again, it is an area in which it is impossible to set fixed guidelines. The best trainer will assess the animal after his last run or event, and, depending on the dog's performance, a decision can then be made when to run him again – soon if he is running well, or after extended rest if he seems jaded.

STRESS FRACTURES
Starting off with too much intense exercise can lead to injury, as the body's organs have not had time to

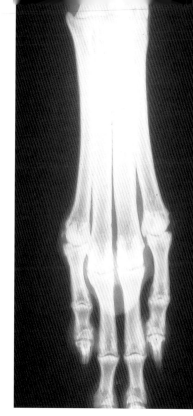

A stress fracture of the third metatarsal bone in a Greyhound. A small crack can be seen in the bone, surrounded by a whiter area of reactive bone.

adjust. One example of this is stress (fatigue) fractures. These stress fractures are seen in human athletes (particularly marathon runners), racehorses, and Greyhounds.

Stress fractures often occur in an intensely-exercised animal that has been brought into a training programme too quickly. The bone has not been allowed enough time to adjust, and, if the training periods are too close together, insufficient time has been allowed for the bone to recover. Stress fractures begin as a small crack in the bone, but they may progress to a complete catastrophic fracture if left untreated.

Affected dogs will vary from being mildly lame or stiff and sore after exercise, to having a non-weightbearing lameness. On examination, swelling, heat and pain may be palpable over the affected area. Stress fractures will only heal given the right conditions of rest and stabilisation. Surgery may be necessary to stimulate the blood supply to the bone to activate the healing process.

DIETARY REQUIREMENTS

NUTRITION FOR SPORTING DOGS
The performance of any sporting dog is only as good as genetics, training, and diet can support. Nutritional requirements will vary according to the dog's type and level of work, but an adequate and well-balanced diet is necessary for the health and optimum performance of the canine athlete. The decision of what and how much to feed should be based on some knowledge of the dog's requirements and the nutritional content of the food, and should

be balanced by the dog's condition, his level of work, and his likes and dislikes.

Dogs have varying metabolic rates, just like humans, so the recommended amount to feed – as determined by the feed manufacturer – may result in one dog becoming obese, while another dog may become thin and out of condition. Regular weighing – at least once weekly – is the best way to monitor the dog's condition and to adjust his diet if necessary.

Nutrition has been discussed in detail in Chapter Three; however, there are a few points, specific to sporting dogs, to emphasise.

BASIC RULES
A balanced diet for sporting dogs should:
• Be rich in nutrients
• Meet energy requirements
• Include optimal protein and fat levels
• Allow for replacement of muscle glycogen
• Contain enough fibre to promote a healthy gut
• Be palatable
• Be easy to prepare.

Ideally, energy expenditure should equal energy intake. This avoids large variations in body weight.

WATER
Water is the most important nutrient for survival in sporting dogs. Animals can survive after losing nearly all their fat and half their protein, but losing 10 per cent of body water can be fatal. Water is lost through three main routes – respiration, urine and faeces. Exercise can result in high respiration rates, which increases the water loss further, or it may cause stress-induced diarrhoea, common in performance dogs, which also contributes to excessive water loss. Extra water may be needed in either instance.

FAT
Fat provides a concentrated source of energy, as well as enhancing the palatability of food. A high-fat concentration is particularly important for athletes that need stamina to compete, such as sled dogs.

PROTEIN
Exercise probably increases the dietary protein requirement. One study has shown that dogs fed a low-protein diet were more prone to suffering injuries. From this research, a minimum protein requirement of 24 per cent has been suggested as the appropriate level for an adult canine athlete.

CARBOHYDRATE
Excessive amounts of carbohydrate have been associated with exertional rhabdomyolysis in dogs. This is caused by over-storage of glycogen, and lactic-acid production in the muscles. It can also be detrimental to feed simple carbohydrates (sweets) directly before a sporting event, as it can actually have the reverse effect and lead to low blood sugar (hypoglycaemia). Post-exercise carbohydrate supplementation, with more complex carbohydrates such as pasta or cereal, may be more beneficial.

FIBRE
Fibre is important in maintaining the body's hydration status and function of the gut. However, excessive fibre levels decrease diet digestibility, increasing the volume and frequency of defecation – all undesirable traits in the sporting dog.

TRAINING AND DIET
A dog out of training will become obese and lose condition if he is fed the same volume and type of food as he received while in training. However, it is better to feed a smaller volume of the same type of diet all year round, rather than to switch between different diets. Changing the diet to one lower in fat will effectively 'detrain' the dog and he will rapidly decline in fitness. Keeping to the same diet is also less likely to induce dietary diarrhoea.

If the diet is changed, it should be remembered that it takes four to six weeks for the body to adjust. Therefore, if the endurance dog is being given fat supplements or a change of diet, for maximum benefit this should be started at least a month before the start of the hunting season, at a similar time to when training is started.

NUTRITIONAL RECOMMENDATIONS FOR HEALTH AND PERFORMANCE	
Energy density	4000 kcal ME/kg or greater
Fat	50-65 per cent of calories
Fatty acid profile	Omega-6: omega-3; at a 5:1 to 10:1 ratio (animal-based sources)
Protein	30-35 per cent of calories (animal-based sources)
Carbohydrate	0-15 per cent of calories
Total dietary fibre	3-7 per cent of dry matter, moderately fermentable fibre

NUTRITION FOR SPRINTING ATHLETES

The most renowned sprinting canine athlete is the racing Greyhound. However, similar dietary principles can be followed for other canine athletes that perform strength or power events of short duration at maximal intensity. Traditional diets are home-made, consisting of a variety of fresh meat, offal, cereal products and vegetables. However, dry foods, specially formulated to meet the needs of racing and working dogs, have been developed recently.

The most important aspect is that the right amount of food is being fed. You can check this by monitoring body weight regularly – once a week, at least. This will be a useful way of ensuring energy intake balances energy expenditure.

Energy is one of the most important constituents of the Greyhound diet. Short bouts of intense exercise result in a high demand for muscle glycogen and blood sugar. A diet boosted by fat (30-60gm of vegetable oil) in the pre-race meal, fed six to eight hours before racing, will provide extra energy to cover that expended in pre-race anticipation. This may be particularly useful in hyperactive or nervous dogs.

Excitable dogs may have a higher metabolic rate because of panting, barking, or hyperactivity in the kennel, and such dogs may require a higher energy or fat level in the diet to help them maintain their body weight. A Greyhound housed in cold conditions will also require an increase in energy in order to maintain body warmth. At the other extreme, panting or exercise in hot weather will deplete glycogen stores more rapidly. It may also suppress appetite. An energy-dense diet, boosted with fat, may be useful in these conditions.

NUTRITION FOR ENDURANCE DOGS

Gundogs, sled dogs and herding dogs can be considered as endurance athletes. There are three basic factors to consider when feeding an endurance dog:
• The dog needs energy for running

ENERGY SOURCES IN THE DIET: IN ORDER OF IMPORTANCE FOR THE ACTIVITY		
SPRINTING	INTERMEDIATE	ENDURANCE
Carbohydrates	Carbohydrates	Fat
Protein	Fat	Carbohydrates
Fat	Protein	Protein

• Stress is induced by training and competition
• Dehydration can occur during prolonged competition.

Sled dogs trained for endurance can keep up a rate of 16 km/hr (10 mph), for 10 to 14 hours per day, for several days in succession. However, this is only possible when the diet consists predominantly of fat. As with any sporting dog, regular weighing can be a very useful means of monitoring the dog's optimal weight and adjusting the diet accordingly. Plenty of water should be provided to dogs, especially while competing.

CHECKING CONDITION

SOUNDNESS EXAMINATION

Lameness or limping is a variance from normal gait. Trainers and handlers should include a lameness examination in the training and conditioning programme, which should be done every week or two. Lameness can be caused by a variety of problems and a careful examination of the dog will be necessary to locate the cause of the problem. A lameness examination should consist of both an evaluation of gait (which will ascertain which leg is affected), and a physical examination (for gait evaluation, see Diagnosing Lameness, Chapter Four).

PHYSICAL EXAMINATION

Once it has been established which leg is affected, the dog can be examined. When your dog is a youngster, you should accustom him to having a full examination of his limbs. This will improve your knowledge of the normal, healthy dog and will help

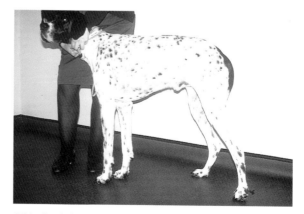

This dog is lame on a back leg. He can be seen 'pointing' or gently resting the leg on the ground, suggesting that it may be painful.

you recognise a problem. It will also make your dog more relaxed about being examined by a veterinarian, making the task of finding the problem easier.

Comparison is the key to a thorough examination. With the dog standing straight, run your hands up and down both front legs and then both back legs. Feel for swelling, enlargement, loss of muscle (atrophy), and areas of heat. Some dogs will have problems affecting the same joint in both legs – e.g. either stifles (knees) or hips. This makes comparison difficult, as one must know what is normal for the dog before abnormalities can be recognised.

The next step is a more detailed examination with the dog relaxed, involving the manipulation or movement of all the joints. This is best performed with the dog lying on his side – he should be more relaxed in this position. The best method is to start at the toes and work towards the top of the leg. Gently palpate all bones and joints, checking for heat, swelling, pain, and the range of motion in the joints. Pay particular attention to the feet – check all the pads for cuts or abrasions.

Checking the range of motion of the joints is particularly useful. If a dog has a painful joint, he will restrict the available movement in that joint to limit the pain, usually by tensing the muscles. Alternatively, the joint may be unable to flex to its full range because it is restricted by scar tissue or fibrosis around the joint. Again, comparison between the other hindleg or foreleg is important here. Gently move the joint – without forcing it – by fully straightening it out and then bending it. If the dog resists, stop. Checking joint range is easier in some dogs than in others. For example, a six-month-old Labrador puppy will think it is a great game, and he may tense up, ready for play.

If lameness is severe, particularly if it came on very suddenly or if your dog is not putting much weight on the leg, then veterinary attention should be sought. If a dog is mildly lame, often the most important initial treatment is rest. However, if the problem does not improve within a couple of days, a veterinary opinion should be sought.

CHECKING FOR STRESS
Stress is any stimulus, physical or emotional, that interferes with the normal physiological equilibrium of an animal. Stress can be fear, pain, exertion or injury. There are various stress-related clinical syndromes recognised in sporting dogs.

The major causes of stress can be separated into two categories:

- **Environmental**: e.g. inadequate housing, training regimes, poor-quality transport, temperature extremes, high humidity, overcrowding, poor hygiene, poor diet, and parasites.
- **Emotional**: e.g. fighting, the need to compete for food, and overwork.

Treatment depends on identifying the cause of the problem and addressing it.

MEDICAL PROBLEMS FACED BY DOGS IN SPORT

PADS
Cut pads are a common occurrence. Deep cuts need to be sutured by a veterinarian as soon as possible. Pads predisposed to becoming worn, which may be caused by exercising on gravel or hard surfaces, can be protected by boots.

A cut carpal pad in a dog.

WEB DISORDERS
The skin between the pads is called the web. This area may become sore and inflamed with splits or blisters. Prompt attention is needed when this happens. The area should be cleaned with a mild disinfectant, initially, with antibiotic tablets given for deep or infected lesions. Again, the use of boots may be recommended, particularly for sled dogs exercising in cold or snowy conditions.

NAILS AND TOES
Injuries include broken nails, nail-bed infections, or the loss of a nail. A broken or lost nail is obvious on examination. A lost nail will bleed profusely initially. Holding a clean towel over the affected foot will stem the flow, although bleeding should stop of its own accord within a few minutes. The 'quick' of the nail (the nerves and blood supply) will be exposed

A broken dewclaw in a Lurcher, which needs removal.

after a nail has come off, and this can be painful to your dog. After one or two days, it should not cause him any discomfort. Keep the area clean of mud and dirt until the exposed nail-bed has dried up.

A broken nail will need to be removed. If the nail is very loose, a quick pull, with someone restraining the patient, may quickly alleviate the problem. However, if the nail is only partially broken, most of it will still be firmly attached. In this case, the dog will need to be sedated by your veterinarian so that the nail can be removed.

Signs of a nail-bed infection include redness, swelling and discharge around the base of the nail. Cleaning the area with a mild, diluted antiseptic may resolve the problem, but antibiotic therapy may be necessary for deep-seated or chronic infections. Biopsy of the affected area, or removal of the nail, is occasionally necessary if the infection does not resolve. Keeping nails trimmed reduces the chance of such problems occurring.

RESPIRATORY PROBLEMS

Animals with respiratory disease will often display coughing, cyanosis, exercise intolerance or increased respiratory effort. Sudden-onset coughing may indicate inhalation of a foreign body. Coughing, particularly if it spreads between dogs, is most likely to be infectious. With dogs that mix (e.g. at sporting events), there is always a risk of spreading infections. Prevention, by ensuring your dog is regularly vaccinated, can go some way to minimise the risk, but, as with the flu injection for humans, there will always be new infections that are not protected by the most up-to-date vaccine. If you suspect your dog has kennel cough, it is important to rest him or her. Give moist or sloppy food, and isolate the dog while he is ill and for at least seven days after coughing has stopped. Antibiotics are recommended if signs are severe or if they last longer than a week. See also Chapter Six.

DIGESTIVE PROBLEMS

Bloat, or gastric dilation volvulus (GDV), is a dangerous and sometimes fatal condition seen most commonly in larger breeds. It is probably the most life-threatening condition seen in working dogs. Exercise after a large meal is one of the predisposing factors, and should be avoided.

See Chapter Three.

EXERTIONAL RHABDOMYOLYSIS

This condition is most common in the racing Greyhound, although it has been seen in other breeds following vigorous activity. Dogs are predisposed to the condition if they are unfit, hot or excited prior to racing, or if they have overexercised without a chance to recover. The signs include swollen, painful, tense back muscles, and dark yellow/brown urine. The disease can vary in severity, with some cases being fatal. Muscle breakdown products overload the kidneys and can cause acute renal failure. If the dog survives a serious bout of exertional rhabdomyolysis, muscle damage and scarring may prevent a return to work. Prompt veterinary therapy is essential – dogs need copious amounts of intravenous fluids, and anti-inflammatory drugs.

HEAT STRESS

Dogs do not sweat to cool off. Instead, excess body heat is removed by panting, submerging in water, and, after they get out of the water, losing heat by evaporation. The ability to generate heat is proportional to the animal's mass, and the ability to cool off is proportional to the dog's surface area. Therefore, large, bulky and hairy dogs are much more liable to overheat than thinner, smaller dogs.

Sporting dogs are often expected to work long hours in varying environmental temperatures. Travel to and from sporting events may involve long distances in cars, and waiting around between classes may involve long periods in hot cars. It is very important to be aware of the dangers of allowing your dog to overheat. Dogs can die if left in a hot car with insufficient shade and ventilation. Access to plenty of fresh, cool water is essential, and some dogs will need to be encouraged to stop and drink.

Have a thermometer handy and know your dog's normal temperature. The normal, resting, rectal temperature of a dog is 37.8 degrees Celsius (101.5 degrees Fahrenheit). It is not unusual for the temperature of an excited dog, or one that has just finished a race, to rise by one or two degrees. However, if the temperature approaches, or is greater than 41 degrees Celsius (105 degrees Fahrenheit), and it stays at this level, heat stroke should be suspected. Your dog may seem distressed and agitated, and he may pant excessively and produce large quantities of thick, ropey saliva. Seizures or fits may follow.

Immediate first aid should consist of cooling your dog down with wet towels or water from a hosepipe. In severe cases, intravenous fluid therapy, administered by a veterinarian, will be needed. It is often insufficient to spray a large hairy dog with a fine mist of water – submerging or hosing will be necessary to cool him off. Remember that dogs are more sensitive to heat and high humidity than humans – a situation that is merely uncomfortable to us may kill a dog.

Prevention of heat stroke is easier than cure:
- Do not leave your dog in a hot car. Leaving the windows open is not enough on a hot day. Shade must be sought or the windows covered with reflective sheets.
- Do not leave a hot dog in a muzzle – he must be able to pant.
- Provide plenty of fresh cool water and encourage drinking.
- Cool down a hot dog by wrapping him in wet towels, immersing him in water, or spraying him with water from a hosepipe.

WOUNDS

Any active dog can sustain small cuts, but they are especially likely in dogs that work in the undergrowth or on rough ground (e.g. gundogs and coursers). Small or superficial cuts, which are not gaping and where there are no skin flaps, normally heal well with some simple first aid. Clean the wound with a little dilute antiseptic solution and ensure it stays clean. Deeper or larger cuts, or those with flaps of skin, will heal more satisfactorily and cosmetically if they are sutured.

Some cuts, such as those on the ears, tail, tongue and pads, will bleed. Generally, bleeding should stop within two to three minutes, but assistance may be given by applying pressure to the area with a clean pad of material. If an artery has been nicked, and blood is spurting out, then firm pressure should be applied to the bleeding area until veterinary attention is available. The artery may need to be 'tied off' or ligated with suture material to stop bleeding.

SEVERED TENDONS

The tendons to the toes are the most commonly damaged. Tendons can be severed if the dog cuts himself, or they may rupture during violent or unco-ordinated activity. A severed or ruptured tendon will result in loss of function of the affected limb.

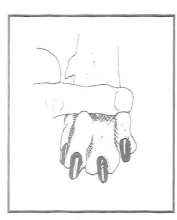

A dropped toe indicates rupture of a digital flexor tendon.

Severed tendons to the toes may result in a 'knocked-up', 'dropped' or 'flat toe' appearance. Rupture of the tendons of the Achilles tendon complex (gastrocnemius and superficial digital flexor) will result in an inability of the animal to extend the hock joint – the joint may appear to collapse or bend on weightbearing.

Damaged tendons need rapid surgical attention. The tendon needs to be carefully sutured back together, and the repair must be protected for at least three to six weeks. Tendons have a poor blood supply so they heal slowly – this is why casts or splints are needed to prevent your dog from using the leg for a period of time after surgery.

HIP DYSPLASIA

Hip dysplasia is characterised by laxity or looseness of the hip joints. Some dogs will show lameness at a young age, but often the condition is not recognised until the animal is older. As a consequence of hip dysplasia, dogs will develop arthritis. Signs of hip arthritis can present in a dog of any age. The signs of dysplasia or arthritis will consist of hindlimb stiffness, lameness, reluctance to jump and a swaying

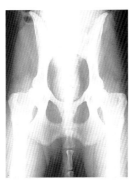

A radiograph of a dog with normal hips.

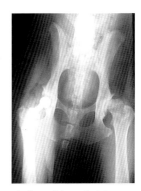

A dog with arthritis secondary to hip dysplasia. A total hip replacement has been performed on the right hip.

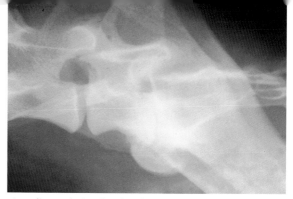

A radiograph showing lumbosacral disease.

gait. Some dogs will 'bunny hop' where both hindlimbs are used together, especially if the dog is moving at a fast gait. A variety of treatment options are available.

See Chapter Four.

OSTEOCHONDROSIS

Osteochondrosis or OCD is a bone and cartilage disease most commonly seen in large and giant breed dogs. The cartilage of various joints fragments or begins to form flaps. Most commonly affected is the elbow, followed by the shoulder, hock and stifle.

Dogs usually develop lameness between five and ten months of age, or mature dogs may present with lameness secondary to the arthritis that the condition causes. In immature dogs without arthritis, surgery may sometimes be recommended to remove the loose pieces of bone and cartilage. The prognosis is variable. Dogs with shoulder osteochondrosis generally have a good prognosis and can return to work. The prognosis for the elbow, hock and stifle is less favourable, although some dogs will return to soundness and work.

In an adult dog suffering with lameness due to arthritis as a secondary side effect to OCD, it will be worth resting the dog, placing him on a diet if necessary, and using prescription anti-inflammatory drugs. Whether the dog will still be able to work depends on both the severity of the lameness and the type and amount of work he is expected to do.

Osteochondrosis has been proved to be hereditary in certain breeds, so it is not recommended that affected dogs, their siblings or their parents, should be bred from.

See also Chapter Four.

LUMBOSACRAL DISEASE

The area between the dog's lumbar spine (lower back) and his sacral bone is prone to problems. The nerves to the back legs travel through the spinal canal in this part of the spine and it is an area of high motion. Exercises that cause extension of the lower back, such as jumping during Agility events or police work, are likely to exacerbate lower back problems. German Shepherd Dogs are particularly prone to this condition. The signs your dog may show include hindlimb stiffness, reluctance to wag his tail, a change in the carriage of his tail, and a reluctance to jump, for example over a fence or into the back of a car.

In severe cases, the hindlimbs may become weak and dogs may even show faecal or urinary incontinence. In some cases, the problem may affect the nerves to one back leg only, so that the dog suffers from lameness in a single hindlimb.

Dogs will generally have pain when the lower back is examined. If your veterinary surgeon suspects that your dog has this problem, he or she will need to perform a radiograph to investigate the condition further. In most cases, there will be some evidence of bone formation around the lumbosacral joint. However, if one of the discs in the vertebrae is the cause of the problem, radiographs may not show any abnormalities. An alternative imaging technique for looking at the disc is Magnetic Resonance Imaging. MRI produces images by a combination of magnetism and radiowaves. With conventional radiography, only the bones are visualised. The advantage of MRI is that images can be obtained of the soft tissues, including the spinal cord nerves and discs.

The initial treatment for lumbosacral disease is medical. This involves altering the dog's exercise regime, avoiding any activities that will exacerbate the problem, and giving anti-inflammatory drugs, as prescribed by your veterinarian. In unresponsive or severe cases, surgery may be recommended.

HYGROMAS

Swelling and thickening of the skin can occur over bony prominences, especially the elbow, sternum and hock. These are most commonly seen in large and giant breeds. Prevention is better than cure and should consist of providing plenty of soft bedding, although it can sometimes be hard to persuade your dog not to lie where he wants, often on the cold concrete or tiled floor! Fluid can sometimes collect underneath the thickened skin. In severe cases, the area can ulcerate.

Treatment is difficult. Surgical removal can be attempted, but it is not recommended unless there is no other option. Getting the area to heal after surgery can be very troublesome.

LIGAMENT INJURIES

Ligament injuries can vary from a mild sprain to a complete rupture. Sprains, where the damage does not cause loss of function, will generally cause a mild limp with localised swelling over the affected area. Initial treatment should consist of ice-packing the

This Border Collie has suffered complete ruptures of the ligaments supporting the carpal (wrist) joints. This injury occurs most commonly after a fall or a jump from a great height.

area, rest, bandaging, and anti-inflammatory drugs. If the ligament is stretched or completely torn, then surgery is often required. The most commonly damaged ligament is the cranial cruciate ligament.

See Chapter Four.

KNEE DISORDERS

PATELLAR LUXATION

The patella is the dog's kneecap, which runs in a groove on the femur and directs the pull of the quadriceps muscle over the stifle joint. The patella can dislocate and affect the dog's ability to straighten his back leg. The problem may be a mild, intermittent one, where he occasionally lifts the leg off the ground, hops for a few steps and then puts it back down again. Alternatively, the problem may be more serious if the patella becomes permanently dislocated or luxated. In this situation, the dog may have a permanent limp or he may be reluctant to put any weight on the leg at all.

See also Chapter Four.

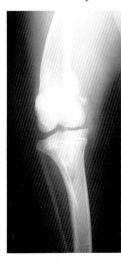

A radiograph showing a luxated patella (kneecap), which should 'sit' in the middle of the bone in a normal dog.

CRUCIATE LIGAMENT INJURY

The cranial cruciate ligament is one of the most important supporting structures in the canine knee joint. If the ligament is damaged, the dog loses the ability to support the knee joint. The ligament can rupture acutely after severe trauma (such as catching the foot in a rabbit hole or on a fence). Other ligaments, such as the collateral ligaments, can be damaged as well after this magnitude of trauma. More commonly, the ligament undergoes premature degeneration and it can rupture or partially rupture after very little trauma. It will cause chronic hindlimb lameness. The dog may improve initially but the lameness will often persist or even worsen with time. Other stifle joint structures, such as the meniscal cartilages, can be damaged after the cranial cruciate ligament ruptures.

Generally, the treatment of choice for a ruptured cranial cruciate ligament is surgery. The ruptured ends of ligament should be removed, and the joint supported by alternative means. The prognosis is variable. A new surgical technique has been recently introduced, which may help to improve the prognosis – tibial plateau levelling procedure, which may be successful in getting a dog back to work. The theory behind the procedure is that by altering the slope of the tibia, abnormal movement is prevented in the joint.

See also Chapter Four.

SPECIFIC INJURIES SEEN IN CERTAIN SPORTING DOGS

COURSING

Coursing injuries occur as the result of two main
Causes:
• The high speeds
• The unevenness of the terrain.

Foot injuries are common, including torn ligaments and fractures.

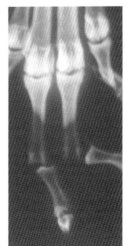

Radiograph of a Lurcher's foot. There is one broken bone and two dislocated digits after a fall that occurred while running.

AGILITY AND FLYBALL

Falling off an obstacle, or contacting an obstacle when jumping over it, are the main causes of injuries in these sports. Falls and knocks can cause bruises or soft-tissue injuries. Rarely will a bad fall result in a more serious injury, such as a fracture or dislocation.

HERDING DOGS

The most common sheep-herding dog is the Border Collie. This breed works very hard and can cover tens of miles daily.

Monitoring the weight of the Collie is important, as this breed is predisposed to losing weight if insufficient nutrition is provided, particularly at busy periods during the year. If lack of weight or weight loss is a problem, gradually switching to a diet with a higher percentage of fat may be advantageous.

Orthopaedic conditions are seen in the Border Collie, with hip dysplasia and shoulder osteochondrosis being two of note in this breed. They are also prone to certain unusual fractures and dislocations.

SLED DOGS

Foot, web, nail injuries and lameness are common injuries seen in sled dogs. Highly-trained, fit sled dogs will have bigger hearts than normal. Heart murmurs are present in up to 50 per cent of human athletes and this murmur is normal or physiological rather than being pathological or abnormal. A similar situation exists in sled dogs, and recognition of this can prevent expensive investigations (see Chapter Five).

Hypothyroidism (Chapter Seven) has been recognised in Huskies and Malamutes. The signs include a decrease in pulling power, lethargy, and hair loss. Diagnosis involves blood tests performed by your veterinarian. Treatment with thyroid supplements is usually successful.

RACING DOGS

The racing Greyhound tends to suffer from a variety of specific injuries. A detailed discussion is beyond the scope of this chapter and more detailed information should be sought from specialised texts.

Injury to the hock (tarsus), metatarsal bones and toes account for more than 50 per cent of racing Greyhound injuries. Muscle problems account for a further 10 per cent of all injuries. Stress fractures can develop in young dogs if they are overexercised because the bones cannot adapt or remodel quickly enough to cope with the stress of racing (see page 184).

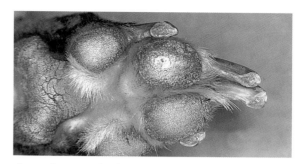

A corn is present in the pad of this Greyhound. It appears as a small, circumscribed pale area, distinct from the rest of the pad.

Dogs injured during a race should be examined by the track veterinarian. He or she will perform first-aid measures, such as bandaging and giving analgesia. More definitive investigations and treatment should be done by your own veterinarian. It is important not to delay seeking veterinary advice, as some injuries need to be treated promptly. The prognosis for a return to racing can often decrease if treatment is markedly delayed.

Corns are cone-shaped, hard, fibrous or keratinous masses. They are seen in the pads of racing Greyhounds and they may arise as a result of repetitive trauma, a puncture wound, or a virus. The corn should be obvious on careful examination of the pad and palpation of the area will be painful to the dog if the corn is the cause of lameness. The dog will often prefer to walk on soft surfaces, such as grass, rather than on a hard or rough surface such as tarmac. Corns can be surgically removed, but they can recur.

Nasal bone fractures will occasionally result from the dog striking his muzzle against the front of the trap before it is released at the start of the race. Blood or swelling will be evident on the nose. Ice-packing and cage rest will often be sufficient to control the bleeding.

GUNDOGS

LABRADOR MYOPATHY

A form of muscular dystrophy has been recognised in Labradors, often occurring in dogs from a working strain. The disease has previously been called by many names, but it is now known as autosomal recessive muscular dystrophy (ARMD) or Labrador myopathy. The disease is inherited as an autosomal recessive trait (see Chapter Ten), therefore both parents are carriers and should not be bred from again.

Ice-packing constricts blood vessels, reduces swelling, and gives pain relief, so can be used for nosebleeds, sprains, and strains.

- Put some ice in a bag, or wrap in a cloth.
- In the case of a nosebleed, apply directly to the muzzle, making sure you do not obstruct the nostrils. Hold in place for 10 to 15 minutes.
- For sprains or strains, apply directly to the affected area for 10 to 15 minutes, three times daily.

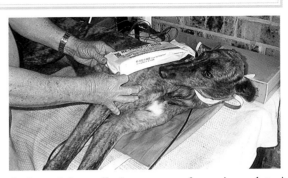

An ice pack is an effective treatment for sprains and strains.

ARMD is normally recognised when a dog reaches three to six months of age. Affected animals are weak and do not have the stamina to exercise for long periods of time. They are generally long-legged, poorly muscled, and of a narrow conformation. They may have a low head carriage. A definitive diagnosis can be difficult but a thorough examination, both orthopaedic and neurological, together with muscle biopsies can help to make a diagnosis. Affected animals can make good pets but will not be able to perform satisfactorily as working dogs.

FOREIGN BODIES

Foreign bodies, particularly of plant origin (e.g. sticks or grass awns) can find their way into some amazing places. Sporting dogs working in the undergrowth are particularly prone to such problems. The most common sites of entry are the interdigital area between the toes, the ears, and the nose, or the trachea and lungs. Checking between the toes of dogs after working, particularly in dogs with a lot of interdigital hair, is very important. Grass awns in particular can be removed before they penetrate the skin and start migrating. Keeping the hair between the toes trimmed short will also make it less likely that the grass awns will penetrate.

Sudden-onset snorting, head-shaking and sneezing is often a sign that the dog has taken a foreign body into the nose, particularly if the sneezing does not stop quickly. Foreign material that is left in place will decompose, become infected and give the dog a foul-smelling nasal discharge.

Sporting dogs are particularly prone to the inhalation of foreign bodies at the end of summer, when the grass is high. Sudden-onset coughing is often the most predominant sign. Prompt removal is the best course of action. If left in situ, foreign material can cause abscesses and severe lung disease. Removal of material is more difficult the further into the lung it gets. Foreign bodies in the trachea or windpipe may be fairly easily removed, with the dog anaesthetised, using a bronchoscope and forceps, whereas material in the lung or bronchi may need to be removed via chest (thoracic) surgery.

SECURITY AND DETECTOR DOGS

Working dogs need a good set of teeth. Broken teeth, especially canine teeth, should not be removed but should be preserved. Specialist veterinarians who perform dentistry work should be sought out to perform root canal work, although caps or crowns are generally ineffective. Regular dental descaling to remove calculus is necessary (although prevention with regular, daily tooth brushing is better), but care must be taken with a dog trained to bite.

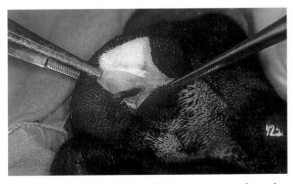

A piece of thorn in a dog's pad. Surgery was performed under tourniquet as pads bleed profusely and can therefore make the search for the foreign body difficult.

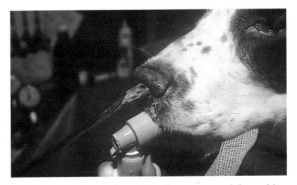

A six-inch (15-cm) piece of wood was removed from this Springer Spaniel's nose. It had been in place for seven months.

12 ALTERNATIVE APPROACHES

Many people are interested in 'alternative' or complementary treatments for their pets. The information contained in this chapter presents several 'alternative' schools of thought which readers may find helpful.

ACUPUNCTURE AND ACUPRESSURE

The ancient practice of acupuncture dates from 3000 BC, with the first documented use carried out on elephants in India. Acupuncture needles made of stone and bone have been found in Korea, dating to the same period, and the first records of acupuncture in China date to 1000 BC.

Combined with Chinese herbal medicine, acupuncture now forms the basis of Traditional Chinese Medicine (TCM). While few animals are treated with Chinese herbal medicine, the use of acupuncture is steadily growing.

THEORY
Acupuncture involves placing needles at specific points on the body, which lie on channels known as meridians. It is possible to stimulate these points by other means, such as by laser or by simple pressure (acupressure). This stimulation initiates a complex cascade of responses and the release of hormones and other chemicals (including neurotransmitters and endorphins) to bring about changes within the body.

The viewpoint offered by TCM does not see acupuncture as a stand-alone therapy; it considers diet, exercise, environment and the use of herbal remedies to be of equal importance in maintaining health. It sees the body as a series of integrated systems, which are closely linked and exist in a state of harmony.

The familiar yin-yang symbol encapsulates the balanced harmony of opposites.

YIN AND YANG
The most familiar concept of TCM is that of 'yin and yang', which represent a state of dynamic balance between opposites, although neither can exist without the other. Within each is a little of the other. We see examples in everyday life: day and night, male and female, and positive and negative. We also see examples in health, such as chill and fever, and constipation and diarrhoea. Ill health or disease arises when there is an imbalance between the forces of yin and yang, meaning energy is unable to flow along the meridian pathways.

FUNDAMENTAL SUBSTANCES
In TCM there are five important substances, vital to the mental and physical balance of the body. These substances are interrelated and subject to imbalances, giving rise to symptoms of ill health. All can be corrected using acupuncture.

QI
This is the vital force of the body, arising from the interactions of yin and yang. However, Qi is more than just energy. Chinese medicine considers that

there are different forms of Qi, which fulfil a variety of functions. The basic functions of Qi irrespective of the type include:
- Transforming food and water into substances that can be used by the body
- Transportation or movement of Qi and fluids to parts of the body
- Warming the body
- Defence of the body against infection
- Holding the body's organs in place and keeping blood in circulation.

JIN-YE

This represents the body's fluids, encompassing the clear fluids circulating near to the exterior of the body (e.g. saliva and tears) and the thicker fluids deeper within the body (e.g. mucus and joint fluid).

BLOOD

Blood is a form of Qi and circulates in the body through the meridians and the blood vessels, moistening and maintaining the body.

JING (LIFE ESSENCE)

This fluid-like substance helps to sustain life, supporting growth, reproduction and development. Jing comes in three forms. The first is acquired from the parents and forms the basis of the animal's constitutional strength and vitality. It is similar to the principle behind modern genetics. Another form comes from food (and leads to the production of Qi). The third, kidney jing, is derived from, and stored in, the kidneys, and is responsible for conception and pregnancy. Kidney jing also produces marrow, which not only includes the familiar bone marrow that fills the long bones, but also the substance that fills the spinal cord and the brain.

SHEN (SPIRIT)

This relates to the mind, affording it the ability to think rationally and to make decisions. Shen controls mental activity, emotions, consciousness, memory, and sleep, and resides mainly in the heart.

MERIDIAN SYSTEMS

Qi, in its different forms, circulates through the meridian system in a self-regulating way. There are 12 major paired meridians relating to the organs of Chinese medicine (sometimes called the 'zang fu organs'), together with what are known as the eight extraordinary vessels, of which two are of major importance. Qi travels through the 12 main meridians in a set order, residing in each for two

hours before moving on to the next.

Qi flows from the lung to the large intestine, then on to the stomach, spleen, heart, small intestine, bladder, kidney, pericardium, triple heater (pages 196-197), gall bladder and liver in sequence, and then back to the lung again, over a 24-hour period. This is known as the Chinese circadian clock. Imbalance in an organ can block or slow the passage of Qi through the related meridian, and similarly, damage to a meridian can cause problems with the related organ. When this happens, one of the ways of restoring balance is to use acupuncture.

The meridians are paired into yin and yang couples known as sister meridians. The yin organs are the solid organs of the body and are by far the most important, having specific functions unique to Chinese medicine. They also relate to the senses and emotions, and govern specific areas of the body. The yang or hollow organs have less important functions that are broadly similar to those of western medicine.

PAIRED YIN AND YANG MERIDIANS	
YIN	YANG
Lung	Large intestine
Spleen	Stomach
Heart	Small intestine
Kidney	Bladder
Pericardium	Triple heater
Liver	Gall bladder

LUNG MERIDIAN (LU)

The lungs govern Qi, respiration, and the passage of water. They govern the skin and hair, and are linked with the emotion of grief. They open into the nose, linking with the sense of smell. The meridian has 11 points and runs from the axilla (armpit), down the front leg to end on the dewclaw (if present) or on the end of the first toe.
Uses: Skin and respiratory problems, grief and pining, arthritic conditions of the elbow and carpus.

LARGE INTESTINE MERIDIAN (LI)

This meridian has 20 points and originates from the second toe on the front leg and runs up the arm to the outside of the elbow, then up to the shoulder joint before passing over the lower neck to end near the nostrils.
Uses: Respiratory conditions, constipation or diarrhoea, neck problems, skin conditions, arthritis of the elbow and shoulder joints, and the immune system.

over the knee joint, and then curves forward to finish near the ninth rib. The liver stores blood and ensures that Qi flows smoothly. It governs the ligaments and tendons, and opens into the eyes. It also has influence over the nails and is associated with the emotion of anger.

Uses: Ligament, tendon and joint problems, digestion, eye problems, behavioural problems, such as anger or aggression.

GOVERNING VESSEL MERIDIAN (GV)

This is a single meridian that runs over the top of the body, starting at a point between the tail and the anus. It then runs up over the spine, towards the head, ending at a point between the upper lip and the gum. It is one of the eight extraordinary meridians and has 26 points along its course. It has influence over the yang meridians.

Uses: Back pain, stimulation of the immune system, fever, and resuscitation.

CONCEPTION VESSEL MERIDIAN (CV)

This is a single meridian that runs along the underside of the body from just below the rectum, through the hindlegs, genitals, chest and neck, to end on the lower lip. It is also one of the eight extraordinary meridians. It has 24 points and can influence the yin meridians.

Uses: Neck pain, and problems with the throat, the reproductive system, and the chest.

ACUPUNCTURE POINTS

There are about 350 acupuncture points that lie on the meridians. Of these, approximately 50 are in regular use. Some of the points are classified into specific groups. Some of the most important are:

- **Alarm or mu points**: These lie on the underside of the body. There is one for each of the zang fu organs. They will often be painful when the related organ has a problem, and can be used diagnostically.
- **Association or back shu points**: All lie on the bladder meridian. Again, there is one for each organ. Their function is to transport Qi to the associated organ.
- **Connecting or luo points**: These connect the sister yin and yang organs so that Qi can pass from one to the other.
- **Accumulation points**: These are points where Qi and blood accumulate within a given meridian.
- **Influential points**: These have effects on particular areas of the body. Lung 9 influences the arteries, Bladder 11 the bones, and Gallbladder 34 the tendons and ligaments.
- **Master points**: These relate to a specific area of

the body. Bladder 40 relates to the hips and the lower back, Large intestine 4 to the face and mouth, and Stomach 36 to the digestive system and abdomen.

ACUPUNCTURE APPLICATIONS

Acupuncture has a wide number of applications, but it is particularly useful in the treatment of pain, including conditions such as arthritis, spondylosis and disc prolapse. Other uses include nerve damage, immune system support, diarrhoea and vomiting, epilepsy, kidney and liver disease, heart disease, and respiratory problems.

ACUPRESSURE

Traditional needle acupuncture is considered an act of veterinary surgery, and can only be carried out by a qualified veterinarian. However, it is possible to stimulate acupuncture points manually, using acupressure. The technique and location of points is beyond the scope of this book, so readers are urged to seek extra information if they wish to pursue this technique.

HOMOEOPATHY

ORIGINS

The fundamental basis of homoeopathy is that an illness can be treated using a substance that produces symptoms similar to those suffered by the patient. It is the principle that like can cure like.

Modern-day homoeopathy owes much to the German scientist and physician Samuel Hahnemann, who discovered the underlying principles of this form of healing in 1796. However, the concept was by no means new, even then. Hahnemann attributed the original theory to Hippocrates, the fifth-century Greek physician, who noted that *"by similar things disease is produced, and by similar things administered to the sick they are healed of their disease"*. The word homoeopathy is derived from two Greek words: *Homoios*, meaning 'like', and *Pathos*, meaning 'suffering'.

DILUTION FACTOR

Many of the medicines Hahnemann used were toxic. To minimise the unpleasant side effects, he diluted them. Strangely, the symptoms of some of his patients seemed to get worse before improving. He termed this effect an 'aggravation', and, to prevent it, he changed the way in which he diluted his remedies. His revised method involved diluting a remedy and shaking it vigorously, banging it down on a hard surface at each stage of the dilution, a method known as succussion. The diluted medicines seemed to provoke less aggravation, and appeared to work faster and more effectively. These new dilutions Hahnemann termed 'potentisations'. The word potency is still used to describe the strength or dilution of a remedy.

One of the main stumbling blocks to the acceptance of homoeopathy has been the dilution factor. Past a specific point, there are no molecules of the original substance left. This suggests that homoeopathic remedies must work beyond chemical interaction, the principle on which most modern drugs work. It seems that they use the energy inherent within the original medicine, which then is able to interact with the body.

Hahnemann proposed that the body must contain some form of energy, which responded to the small energetic prompts from the remedies to encourage healing. Termed the 'vital force', Hahnemann believed this to be responsible for maintaining health and harmony within the body. A great many factors can influence the vital force, including diet, environment, stress, genetic factors, and conventional drugs.

A homoeopathic remedy acts on the underlying imbalance that caused the patient's initial problem, as opposed to attempting to treat the current symptoms. For this reason, homoeopaths take detailed histories, to find the correct remedy.

HOMOEOPATHY TODAY

Homoeopathy aims to balance mind, body and spirit. It is a truly holistic therapy, which can tackle a wide range of diseases, both acute and chronic, but it excels in treating chronic conditions, such as allergic skin problems, colitis, back pain, asthma and arthritis. It can also be of benefit in resolving grief and anxiety, and in supporting some of the body's major organs.

REMEDIES

Almost any substance can be made into a homoeopathic remedy. Most are made from plant, animal and mineral extracts, but sunlight, radiation and magnetism have all been potentised into remedies.

To produce homoeopathic potencies, the original material is serially diluted, starting with a special preparation of the substance, known as the mother tincture. Two dilution ranges are commonly used by homoeopaths:
- **Decimal potencies**: Denoted by the suffix 'x', produced by a 1 in 10 dilution.
- **Centesimal range**: Denoted by 'c', using dilution steps of 1 in 100. For example, to produce the 6c

potency of a remedy, one drop of the mother tincture would be added to 99 drops of an alcohol/water mixture. One drop of the resulting solution (the 1c potency) would then be added to 99 drops of alcohol/ water mixture and shaken to produce the 2c potency. The process would be repeated a further four times to produce the 6c potency. A few drops of this solution would then be added to blank lactose tablets, powders, pillules or granules, to activate them with the remedy.

SIDE EFFECTS AND PRECAUTIONS

Homoeopathy has few side effects. However, you may observe some changes in your dog: the symptoms may seem to worsen before improving, or old illnesses may reappear. The former is termed an aggravation, the latter recapitulation. The symptoms are caused by the body healing itself, and should be viewed in a favourable light.

COMPATABILITY

Where possible, avoid mixing homoeopathy with conventional drugs, particularly steroids and non-steroidal anti-inflammatories (NSAIDS), some of which can adversely affect the way in which the remedies work.

Homoeopathic treatments can be used alongside other forms of complementary medicine, but only with professional guidance. Acupuncture and herbal remedies can work well, but the oils used in aromatherapy may prevent homoeopathic remedies from working effectively.

OVER-THE-COUNTER REMEDIES

Most health-food stores and pharmacies stock a limited range of low-potency homoeopathic remedies for everyday problems. For more complex problems, always seek professional help from a homoeopathic veterinarian.

USEFUL REMEDIES

Here is a summary of commonly-used remedies and the conditions for which they are used. Please note, however, that remedies should only be used when prescribed by a veterinarian. Self-dosage can be inappropriate and dangerous.
- **Aconite**: Fever, fear, anxiety, conjunctivitis (with watery discharge).
- **Apis mel**: Pulmonary oedema, allergic swellings, hot, swollen, painful joints.
- **Arnica**: Injury, sprains, strains, over-exertion, bruising. Often used post-operatively and after dental extractions.

- **Arsenicum album**: Restlessness, anxiety (especially at night), dry, scaly, itchy skin, violent vomiting, diarrhoea (particularly associated with food poisoning), allergic asthma.
- **Belladonna**: High fever (with bounding pulse and dilated pupils), anger and aggression, acute ear infections, abscesses, epilepsy.
- **Bryonia**: Dry, hacking cough, arthritis, joint pain.
- **Calc fluor**: Hard masses and lumps (particularly arthritic joints and glandular swellings). Reduces risk of adhesions after abdominal surgery.
- **Calendula**: Skin abrasions, surgical incisions. Used both internally and externally.
- **Cantharis**: Cystitis, burns, skin rash.
- **Carbo veg** ('The great reviver'): Collapse, fading puppy syndrome, dysenteric diarrhoea, flatulence, and poor oxygenation.
- **Cocculus**: Travel sickness, disorientation, loss of balance.
- **Colocynthis**: Spasmodic colic, abdominal pain, hip pain.
- **Euphrasia**: Conjunctivitis (with sticky discharge), allergic eye problems. Used internally and externally.
- **Gelsemium**: Anticipatory anxiety, trembling, ear of thunder, hind limb weakness, urinary incontinence, fever.
- **Hepar sulph**: Infections, suppuration (especially where affected areas are touch-sensitive), reabsorption of pus.
- **Hypericum**: Nerve injuries, spinal injuries, lacerated wounds, post-operative pain.
- **Ledum palustre**: Puncture wounds, arthritis, traumatic eye injuries.
- **Nux vomica**: Digestive upsets, constipation, vomiting, hind limb weakness, liver disease, back pain, irritability.
- **Phosphorus**: Noise sensitivity (e.g. fear of thunder), bone degeneration, vomiting, haemorrhage, liver disease (hepatitis, jaundice), kidney disease, pancreatic problems, dry coughs.
- **Pulsatilla**: Catarrh, false pregnancy, conjunctivitis (with yellow, ocular discharge), digestive upsets.
- **Rhus tox**: Arthritis, sprains and strains, skin rashes and itching, cellulits (inflammation of superficial tissues), severe corneal ulceration.
- **Ruta grav**: Sprains, bone, ligament and tendon injuries, hind leg weakness.
- **Sepia**: Female urinary incontinence, false pregnancy, abnormal oestrus cycles, seborrhoea, ringworm.

Herbal medicine is a popular treatment for many dog owners. Pictured: comfrey, used to relieve coughs and respiratory-tract problems.

- **Silica**: Chronic infections, scarring, discharging abscesses, fistulae and wounds, foreign bodies (e.g. grass awns), eye ulcers, sinusitis, bone diseases.
- **Sulphur**: Skin problems (mange, dermatitis and eczema), general body cleanser.

HERBAL MEDICINE

Phytotherapy (herbal medicine) uses the inherent healing properties of plants to treat illness and disease. The earliest recorded use of the healing properties of plants was in Mesopotamia, around 4000 BC. The Egyptians also practised phytotherapy, and the Greeks are known to have used plant-based medication in 300 BC. Healing was based on the concept of four humours: blood, phlegm, yellow bile and black bile, which needed to balance. Plants were ascribed qualities that helped to redress any imbalance between these four humours.

In the 17th century, the concept of the doctrine of signatures emerged, which maintained that every plant had a medicinal use suggested by its appearance. For example, the contortions within a cut nutmeg resemble the brain, so nutmeg could be used to treat brain disorders.

Today, there is a growing recognition that herbal remedies have a place in medicine. Research, accessible information, and an ever-increasing interest from doctors, veterinarians and patients, have led to a revival in this traditional form of healthcare.

HERBAL HEALING PROPERTIES

CLASS	ACTION	EXAMPLES
Alteratives (blood cleansers)	Help to restore function	Nettles, burdock
Anodynes/analgesics	Reduce pain	Jamaican dogwood, skullcap
Anthelmintics	Help to expel worms (not often used today)	Garlic
Anti-catarrhals	Remove excess mucus or catarrh, treat nasal and sinus problems	Plantain, peppermint, elderberry
Anti-emetics	Relieve nausea (vomiting)	Meadowsweet
Anti-inflammatories	Reduce inflammation and pain, treat musculo-skeletal problems	Willow bark, meadowsweet, devil's claw
Anti-lithics	Prevent formation of bladder stones	Corn silk, parsley piert
Anti-microbials	Help to fight infection, support immune system	Echinacea, garlic, thyme
Anti-spasmodics	Ease cramp-like pain or spasms	Valerian, camomile
Aromatics	Stimulate digestion	Aniseed
Astringents	Reduce inflammation and provide protection to allow healing.	Agrimony, yarrow, couchgrass, witch hazel
Bitters	Stimulate digestion	Gentian, hops
Cardiac tonics	Support the heart	Hawthorn, motherwort
Carminatives	Stimulate digestion, reduce risk of colic	Aniseed, dill
Cholagogues	Stimulate production of bile, act as a laxative	Dandelion root, barberry
Demulcents and emollients	Protect inflamed/damaged mucous membranes. Can be used internally and externally depending on the herb	Marshmallow root, slippery elm, comfrey
Diuretics	Increase urine output	Dandelion root, dandelion leaf, buchu
Expectorants	Remove mucus from respiratory tract, ease coughs	Elecampane, comfrey, garlic
Galactogogues	Increase milk production in lactating animals	Milk thistle, goat's rue
Hepatics	Provide liver support, treat liver conditions (e.g. jaundice)	Dandelion, milk thistle, yellow dock
Hypnotics	Induce sleep, promote calm	Camomile, skullcap, valerian
Laxatives	Relieve constipation	Aloe, senna
Nervines	Tonics acting either to stimulate or relax the nervous system	Vervain, Valerian (relaxants), kola (stimulant)
Sedatives	Reduce stress, anxiety and fear	Valerian, skullcap, passion flower
Stimulants	Support various physiological functions	Cayenne, rosemary, ginger, ginseng, juniper
Tonics	Strengthen particular organs	Hawthorn (circulation), garlic (lungs), buchu (urinary system), calendula (skin)
Vulneraries	Encourage healing, internally and externally	Calendula, marshmallow, burdock

From a scientific angle, it is interesting to examine the chemical constituents that herbal remedies contain and to determine how and why they work. However, herbalists tend to classify remedies by their actions in comparison to the more scientific approach, as this is far more practical in terms of putting together a prescription.

By doing this, it is possible to see what kinds of conditions the remedies can be used to treat and which herbs can be combined together to deal with a specific problem for an individual patient. Many herbs fall into more than one category, demonstrating just how versatile individual herbal remedies can be.

COMMONLY USED HERBS		
HERB	**MEDICINAL PROPERTIES**	**USES**
Agrimony (*Agrimonia eupatoria*)	Astringent, diuretic, vulnery, arrests bleeding, cholagogue, tonic	Diarrhoea, colitis, indigestion, cystitis, urinary incontinence, bronchitis
Barberry (*Berberis vulgaris*)	Hepatic, cholagogue, mild laxative, regulates digestion	Liver disease (including jaundice), constipation, weak digestion
Buchu (*Barosama betulina*)	Diuretic, urinary antiseptic, bladder tonic	Kidney failure, cystitis, bladder stones, gravel
Bearberry (*Arctostaphylos uva-ursi*)	Diuretic, urinary antiseptic, demulcent, astringent	Cystitis, bladder stones, urinary incontinence, renal failure
Cleavers (*Galium aparine*)	Diuretic, mild astringent, lymphatic tonic, alterative, blood cleanser	Swollen lymph nodes, lymphatic problems, tonsillitis, cystitis, skin conditions, cancer support
Dandelion (*Taraxacum officinale*)	Diuretic (containing potassium), tonic, improves appetite, liver stimulant, cholagogue, mild laxative, blood cleanser	Liver disease, constipation, toxin removal, mild diuretic
Purple cone flower *Echinacea augustifolia*	Antibiotic, anti-bacterial, anti-viral, anti-fungal, immune stimulant, anti-allergy, lymphatic tonic	Fevers, bacteria, viral and fungal infections, chronic respiratory infections, cystitis, gingivitis
Garlic (*Allium sativum*)	Diuretic, expectorant, anti-septic, anti-bacterial, anti-viral, anti-fungal, cholagogue, anti-spasmodic, promotes growth of healthy gut bacteria, helps regulate blood glucose levels	Respiratory conditions, skin conditions, diarrhoea, supports immune system
Liquorice (*Glycyrrhiza glabra*)	Demulcent, expectorant, antiinflammatory, stimulates adrenal function, anti-spasmodic, mild laxative, cholagogue, lowers stomach pH, anti-bacterial	Gastritis, vomiting, colic, colitis, coughs
Marigold (*Calendula officinalis*)	Astringent, antiseptic, anti-fungal, anti-inflammatory, vulnerary	Skin conditions, indigestion, inflammation of digestive tract, digestive ulcers, burns, wounds
Marshmallow (*Althaea officinalis*)	Root: Demulcent, vulnerary, diuretic Leaf: Demulcent, expectorant, anti-catarrhal	Respiratory problems, diarrhoea, colitis, cystitis
Milk thistle (*Silybum marianum*)	Cholagogue, galatogogue, demulcent	Liver support, liver disease, poisoning, milk production in nursing bitches
Nettles Greater Nettle (*Urtica dioica*) Lesser Nettle (*Urtica urens*)	Alterative, antiseptic, expectorant, astringent, arrests bleeding, weak diuretic, tonic, lowers blood glucose	Eczema, dermatitis, arthritis, rheumatism, bladder stones, detoxification, renal failure, anaemia
Peppermint (*Mentha piperita*)	Carminative, anti-spasmodic, anti-emetic, antiseptic, analgesic	Vomiting, travel sickness, colitis, diarrhoea, flatulence
Raspberry (*Rubus idaeus*)	Reproductive tract tonic, astringent, assists whelping	Strengthens and tones reproductive tract, assists whelping (regulates contractions), limits post-parturient haemorrhage
Seaweed (kelp, bladderwrack, *Fucus vesiculosus*)	Anti-rheumatic, anti-inflammatory, metabolic stimulant, thyroid stimulant	Rheumatism, hypothyroidism, obesity, lack of skin pigmentation, improves coat condition and growth, anaemia
Skullcap (*Scutellaria laterfolia*)	Sedative, nerve tonic, anti-spasmodic	Hysteria and excitability, anxiety, restlessness, insomnia, travel sickness, epilepsy
Valerian (*Valeriana officinalis*)	Calming, carminative, anti-spasmodic, expectorant, diuretic, pain relief	Anxiety, nervousness, hysteria and excitability, fear, pain control, epilepsy

Bach flower remedies are so popular they are now available in many pharmacies and health-food shops.

BACH FLOWER REMEDIES

Dr Edward Bach (pronounced 'Batch') was born in 1886, near Birmingham, England. He trained as a doctor, working in London, and was appointed to The Royal London Homoeopathic Hospital in Great Ormond Street as a pathologist and bacteriologist.

His interest in using flowers to deal with emotional states and illness was born during a dinner party. There, he observed his fellow guests, watching their facial expressions and body language, and listening to their different tones of voice. He classified the guests into one of seven distinct types, and claimed that each person's personality and emotional state was as important as any physical symptoms they had.

Bach studied a selection of plants from every aspect – how and where they grew, shape, size and colour. Looking at dew-covered blossoms one morning, he thought that the action of strong sunlight on the flowers would energise the dew with the healing energy of the plant. Tasting the dew from a plant, he realised immediately that he was right. Collecting the dew into bottles, he began the very first step in creating his world-famous flower remedies.

He painstakingly searched for remedies that would change negative states of mind to positive, and produced 38 remedies that could treat emotional upsets and any associated physical symptoms by acting at a deep, psychological level.

PRINCIPLES

Using the remedies requires perception of mental disharmony, rather than of physical illness. In many cases, several remedies may be combined together, to cover the totality of symptoms. It is equally as important to look at diet, environment, interaction with other animals and humans, as well as sources of stress. Always seek advice from a trained behaviourist where necessary.

It is not clear how Bach flower remedies work, but it is thought they work on similar principles to homoeopathy. Each flower has a unique energy of a particular vibrational wavelength. Each of these is 'in tune' with the frequency that surrounds each and every living being. With illness, stress or psychological disturbance, this field falls out of harmony, having a negative effect on the whole animal, and possibly leading to physical illness. By carefully selecting the correct flower remedies, it is possible to correct the frequency distortion and to return the animal to a state of health.

PREPARING REMEDIES

The flowers are gathered from unspoilt areas, where they can be found growing wild. The main reason for this is that cultivated varieties lose their powers of healing rapidly. The plant is neither destroyed nor damaged when the flowers are picked.

The flowers must be picked at full maturity, when the essential energies are concentrated, and must be done when there is a cloudless, sunny sky. The time between picking the flowers and preparing the remedies must be kept to a minimum, so that vital energy is not lost.

Having gathered the flowers, they are allowed to float on water, transferring their energy to the liquid. The resulting energised water is then used to produce stock solutions for medication, by adding a few drops of brandy, which acts as a preservative. The normal dilution is 1 part water to 240 parts grape alcohol or brandy. The resulting stock keeps indefinitely.

REMEDY GROUPS

There are 38 Bach flower remedies, each classified into 1 of 7 main groups, and one combination remedy, Bach's famous Rescue Remedy. Each group has a defined set of negative emotional states, and the positive effects to be gained from using the remedy. The following are the most important.

exercise, and, when performed correctly, it may be used post-operatively or following injury. Any stretch should be held for a minimum of 15 seconds to be effective and held in a static position – not bounced. It is imperative that a stretching programme is incorporated with an exercise regime.

RANGE OF MOTION

Non-use of a joint can easily lead to contracture (a shortening of surrounding tissues, resulting in a tight and contracted restriction of joint or muscle) and adhesions, and the technique of range of motion aims to prevent this. It is the technique of moving a joint through its entire available range. It is important after surgery, when a patient avoids use of a limb or joint due to pain or fear of pain. Post-traumatic injuries can also benefit from this technique. The technique must be performed in a gentle and comfortable manner.

ULTRASOUND

Sound waves are pressure waves travelling through a medium. They have specific wavelength, frequency and velocity. Physiotherapists use these waves by attaching a vibrating crystal to a transducer and bombarding it with a high-frequency current to produce an ultrasound wave. This can increase blood flow, increase the elasticity of scar tissue, decrease the conductivity of nerve fibres, and increase cellular metabolism and permeability to remove traumatic exudates (secretions) and to encourage tissue repair.

Indications: Muscle spasm, pain modulation, trigger points, adhesions, contractures, scars, wound healing, contusions, haematomas, bursitis (an arthritic disorder), tendonitis, fracture healing, calcified tendons, joint swelling, chronic synovitis (longstanding inflammation of the joint lining), warts, muscle lesions, tendon and ligament lesions, periosteal-tendonous lesions (injuries occuring where a tendon inserts into the bone).

Contraindications: Burnt tissues, cellular cavitation (an implosion of a cell caused by an explosive reaction within the cell that bursts the cell inwards), static blood flow, endothelial damage (damage to the lining of the heart and blood/lymph vessels), platelet aggregation (where the platelets stick together), acute infection, sepsis, tumours.

LASER TREATMENT

LASER stands for 'Light Amplification by Stimulated Emission of Radiation'.
Therapeutic lasers are 'cold', low-powered lasers.

They can influence the lymph, circulatory, and nervous system, as well as promoting wound healing and post-operative healing. They may also be used to stimulate acupuncture or trigger points.

Indications: Arthritic disorders, wounds, tendon or ligament injuries, gross swelling, pain, contractures or scar tissue, muscle spasm, increased circulation, haematomas, acupuncture benefits (when used on acupuncture points).

Contraindications: Lasering in the eye, on a pregnant abdomen, on a cancerous lesion, over photosensitive (light sensitive) washes and scrubs or after recent cortisone injections.

ELECTRICAL MUSCLE STIMULATION

This is the use of an electrical current to stimulate tissues. It is imperative that appropriate muscle function and contraction occurs, or adjacent muscle groups will take over the work of the dysfunctional muscle, creating secondary problems (e.g. ligament and joint strain, back pain, and over-use injuries in the over-working muscle).

Indications: Improper muscle firing sequences, pain, joint effusion (swelling), protective muscle spasm, muscle disuse atrophy, neurological atrophy, to facilitate normal contraction of a muscle, circulatory disorders, dermal ulcers, tendon healing and fracture healing.

Contraindications: Infection, active inflammation, skin lesions, dermatological conditions.

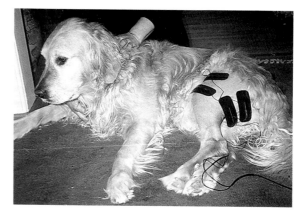

Electrical muscle stimulation to help build muscle strength following knee surgery.

ACUPUNCTURE

For a less invasive approach, acupuncture can be performed using laser or electrical stimulation instead of needles. The effects are very similar. See pages 194 to 198.

COLD APPLICATION

Cryotherapy is the application of cold (ice packs, ice massage, cold water, etc.) to affected areas.

Indications: Pain relief, fever, inflammation, muscle-guarding spasm, swelling, control bleeding.

Contraindications: Hypertension, cold sensitivity, over open wounds in the initial two- to three-week period (or it may stunt the repair of the tissue).

Hydrotherapy has a number of benefits, including relieving joint stiffness and strengthening weak muscles.

HYDROTHERAPY

Hydrotherapy (i.e. pool therapy) can prevent musculoskeletal disability, decrease healing time, and help to restore normal functions to damaged tissues.

Indications: Muscle spasm, increased circulation, pain, swelling, joint stiffness, surgical scar/wound healing, gait retraining, muscle strengthening.

HEAT APPLICATION

The application of heat to affected areas.

Indications: Pain relief, muscle spasm, increased circulation, tissue healing, preparation of a stiff/tight joint or muscle for exercise, chronic swelling, tissue adhesions.

Contraindications: Circulatory impairment, cancerous lesions, areas prone to haemorrhaging, areas of abnormal pain sensation.

SENSORY INTEGRATION

Sensory integration is the ability to take in, sort out, and connect information from the world around us. A very important sense is proprioception (from the Latin word 'one's own'). Receptors are triggered by sensation from muscle and joints, which tell the brain when and how muscles are contracting or stretching, and when and how the joints are bending, extending, or being pulled and compressed. This information enables the brain to know where each part of the body is and how it is moving in space.

DISASSOCIATION

Following an injury or surgery, dogs tend to under-utilise, or cease to use completely, their affected limb. If the dog does not use the limb for a prolonged period of time, he may develop a form of sensory dysfunction known as 'disassociation', i.e. he stops using his limb, forgets he has it, and compensates for its 'not being there'.

TREATMENT

The treatment of sensory dysfunction uses the following methods:

- Deep pressure
- Joint approximation (pressing the joint ends together)
- Heavy weights and blankets
- Rubbing with heat (hot packs)
- Deep pressure brushing, followed by deep proprioceptive exercise
- Low jumps.

Treatment should be tailored to the individual dog, with treatment options including:

- Physio-ball (used to lay the dog on and roll it in different directions to initiate postural reflexes, see below)

A physio-ball can be used to encourage weightbearing on one or both hind legs.

F

G

H

I

J

K

L

M

N

O

T

U